AMERICA
BEYOND
2001

OPPOSING VIEWPOINTS®

Other Books of Related Interest in the Opposing
Viewpoints Series:

AMERICA BEYOND 2001

OPPOSING VIEWPOINTS®

David Bender & Bruno Leone, *Series Editors*

Oliver W. Markley and Walter R. McCuan, *Editors*
Graduate Program in Studies of the Future,
Institute for Futures Research, University of
Houston—Clear Lake

Research and editorial assistance were provided
by Susan Jette, Thomas Nicodemus, and
Thomas Conger

Charles P. Cozic, *Opposing Viewpoints® Editor*

OPPOSING
VIEWPOINTS®
SERIES

Greenhaven Press, Inc., San Diego, CA

Cover photo: Digital Stock

Greenhaven Press, Inc.
PO Box 289009
San Diego, CA 92198-9009

Library of Congress Cataloging-in-Publication Data

America beyond 2001: opposing viewpoints / Oliver W. Markley & Walter R. McCuan, book editors.
    p.   cm. — (Opposing viewpoints series)
  Includes bibliographical references and index.
  ISBN 1-56510-292-4 (pbk.) — ISBN 1-56510-293-2 (lib. bdg.)
  1. United States—Social conditions—Forecasting. 2. United States—Economic conditions—Forecasting. 3. United States—Politics and government—Forecasting. 4. Twenty-first century—Forecasts. I. Markley, O. W. II. McCuan, Walter R., 1947-   . III. Series: Opposing viewpoints series (Unnumbered)
HN59.2.A445   1996
306'.0973—dc20   94-46738
                                                           CIP

955135

"Congress shall make no law . . .
abridging the freedom of speech,
or of the press."

First Amendment to the U.S. Constitution

The basic foundation of our democracy is the First Amendment
guarantee of freedom of expression. The Opposing Viewpoints
Series is dedicated to the concept of this basic freedom and the
idea that it is more important to practice it than to enshrine it.

Contents

Why Consider Opposing Viewpoints?

"The only way in which a human being can make some approach to knowing the whole of a subject is by hearing what can be said about it by persons of every variety of opinion and studying all modes in which it can be looked at by every character of mind. No wise man ever acquired his wisdom in any mode but this."

John Stuart Mill

In our media-intensive culture it is not difficult to find differing opinions. Thousands of newspapers and magazines and dozens of radio and television talk shows resound with differing points of view. The difficulty lies in deciding which opinion to agree with and which "experts" seem the most credible. The more inundated we become with differing opinions and claims, the more essential it is to hone critical reading and thinking skills to evaluate these ideas. Opposing Viewpoints books address this problem directly by presenting stimulating debates that can be used to enhance and teach these skills. The varied opinions contained in each book examine many different aspects of a single issue. While examining these conveniently edited opposing views, readers can develop critical thinking skills such as the ability to compare and contrast authors' credibility, facts, argumentation styles, use of persuasive techniques, and other stylistic tools. In short, the Opposing Viewpoints Series is an ideal way to attain the higher-level thinking and reading skills so essential in a culture of diverse and contradictory opinions.

In addition to providing a tool for critical thinking, Opposing Viewpoints books challenge readers to question their own strongly held opinions and assumptions. Most people form their opinions on the basis of upbringing, peer pressure, and personal, cultural, or professional bias. By reading carefully balanced opposing views, readers must directly confront new ideas as well as the opinions of those with whom they disagree. This is not to simplistically argue that everyone who reads opposing views will—or should—change his or her opinion. Instead, the series enhances readers' depth of understanding of their own views by encouraging confrontation with opposing ideas. Careful examination of others' views can lead to the readers' understanding of the logical inconsistencies in their own opinions, perspective on why they hold an opinion, and the consideration of the possibility that their opinion requires further evaluation.

Evaluating Other Opinions

To ensure that this type of examination occurs, Opposing Viewpoints books present all types of opinions. Prominent spokespeople on different sides of each issue as well as well-known professionals from many disciplines challenge the reader. An additional goal of the series is to provide a forum for other, less known, or even unpopular viewpoints. The opinion of an ordinary person who has had to make the decision to cut off life support from a terminally ill relative, for example, may be just as valuable and provide just as much insight as a medical ethicist's professional opinion. The editors have two additional purposes in including these less known views. One, the editors encourage readers to respect others' opinions—even when not enhanced by professional credibility. It is only by reading or listening to and objectively evaluating others' ideas that one can determine whether they are worthy of consideration. Two, the inclusion of such viewpoints encourages the important critical thinking skill of objectively evaluating an author's credentials and bias. This evaluation will illuminate an author's reasons for taking a particular stance on an issue and will aid in readers' evaluation of the author's ideas.

As series editors of the Opposing Viewpoints Series, it is our hope that these books will give readers a deeper understanding of the issues debated and an appreciation of the complexity of even seemingly simple issues when good and honest people disagree. This awareness is particularly important in a democratic society such as ours in which people enter into public debate to determine the common good. Those with whom one disagrees should not be regarded as enemies but rather as people whose views deserve careful examination and may shed light on one's own.

Thomas Jefferson once said that "difference of opinion leads to inquiry, and inquiry to truth." Jefferson, a broadly educated man, argued that "if a nation expects to be ignorant and free . . . it expects what never was and never will be." As individuals and as a nation, it is imperative that we consider the opinions of others and examine them with skill and discernment. The Opposing Viewpoints Series is intended to help readers achieve this goal.

David L. Bender & Bruno Leone,
Series Editors

Introduction

> *"The fundamental uncertainties of our time will shape the context for many of our business and personal decisions. Will there be war or peace? Prosperity or depression? An atmosphere of freedom or one of restraint?"*
>
> *Peter Schwartz,* The Art of the Long View, *1991*

As the year 2000 approaches, there is a natural surge of interest among Americans about the future. Many are asking the following questions: Where is the nation headed? Where *should* it be headed? *Will we like it when we get there?*

Although not widely recognized, the purpose of futures research is not to predict the future, but to use foresight about possible, probable, preferable, and feared futures in order to make better decisions in the present. Claims of being able to predict the future with precision should be viewed with great skepticism. The approach of considering opposing viewpoints, then, is an appropriate one to follow when contemplating alternative futures.

There is no consensus about either the likely or the desirable future. To a great extent, what one anticipates depends on personal opinion, which may vary according to one's ideology, profession, region, religion, and culture. Through their opinions, many people concerned with the future hope to influence exactly what type of future unfolds.

There are four fairly distinct schools of thought about the future: Positive Extrapolist/Technological Enthusiast, Negative Extrapolist/Technological Alarmist, Visionary/Technocultural Transformationist, and Client-Oriented. Each school answers the following questions in a distinct way:

- What types of future are most likely?
- Which are most desirable?
- Which are most threatening?
- What are the best ways to ensure the desired—and prevent the feared—future?

1. Positive Extrapolist/Technological Enthusiast. Proponents of this viewpoint see no major roadblocks to progress in America's future. They believe that technology will provide solutions to natural resource limits and population pressures and spur economic growth. Futurists who embrace this viewpoint include Gerald K. O'Neill, author of *2081: A Hopeful View of the Human Future*, who writes, "The human race stands now on the threshold of a new frontier whose richness is a thousand times greater than that of the new western world of five hundred years ago." Positive Extrapolists anticipate unlimited human potential.

2. Negative Extrapolist/Technological Alarmist. Those who espouse this view believe that the economic growth and technological advancement that marked America's past will prove unsustainable in the future. They conclude that the exponential growth in "ecological load" (essentially population multiplied by per capita consumption) and the impact of technology are causing systemic problems faster than solutions can be found. Negative Extrapolists thus see decreasing potential for long-term economic and technological progress. According to Dennis Meadows and Donella Meadows, coauthors of *Limits to Growth* and *Beyond the Limits*, "If the present growth trends in world population, industrialization, pollution, food production, and resource depletion continue unchanged, the limits to growth on this planet will be reached within the next one hundred years."

3. Visionary/Technocultural Transformationist. Holders of this viewpoint believe that American society is more or less "stuck" in a limited set of attitudes, premises, policies, and behaviors (that is, the prevailing "paradigm" of society). By revisioning these, they think, it should be possible to see how to evolve into a new paradigm that would be both sustainable and humane. Different members of this group emphasize environmental, social, or spiritual factors as the place to start—each having his or her own views regarding "appropriate" technology for cultural transformation. In *Global Mind Change*, author Willis Harman describes this transition: "Society will, only a few generations from now, be as different from modern industrial society as that is from society of the middle ages."

4. Client-Oriented. These futurists, unlike the others, avoid taking an ideological position regarding America's future. Instead, they serve the demands of clients—primarily corporations and small companies—by satisfying their questions and interests. In *What Futurists Believe*, Joseph Coates and Jennifer Jarrett explain how practicing futurists often blend their views with those of clients. The futurist is valuable to the client, according to Coates and Jarrett, because in contrast to the perspective of the client, "the generally longer-range view of the futurist may be particularly rich and helpful on scientific and technological developments."

Of course, these four schools overlap; many futurists can place themselves in more than just one category. Whether the future will be better or worse, these experts agree that it will be extensively different from the present or recent past. Opinions from the four schools are reflected in *America Beyond 2001: Opposing Viewpoints* in the following chapters: The Social Fabric of America: What Is Its Future? Technological Change: How Fast and to What End? What Will Become of America's Economy? The Ecological Environment: Sustainable or Not? and America's Political Status: What Does the Future Hold? This anthology examines the myriad forces and opinions shaping the future of America.

The Social Fabric of America: What Is Its Future?

**AMERICA
BEYOND
2001**

Chapter Preface

Americans have witnessed significant social change in the last few decades, including an increase in single-parent families, an expansion of minorities' rights, a reevaluation of male/female roles, and growing conflict over social and sexual norms. While such change continues, and perhaps accelerates, many commentators disagree about its effect on the social "fabric" and whether change will usher in a brighter or darker future.

Alan Wolfe, a dean at the New School for Social Research in New York City, describing "the disappearing center of American society," catalogs what he views as some of the larger forces changing American life: an increasingly elderly and immigrant population, influential ideological/political movements, neglect of social problems, and disregard for rules and laws. Daniel Burstein, editor of the book *Critical Intelligence: Global Political Economy and the American Future*, argues that various social problems will escalate into social upheaval: "We are struggling upstream against rising social dysfunction, confused purpose, shattered communities, declining living standards, and the destruction of the American dream."

On the other hand, some experts anticipate a more glowing future. Futurist Marvin Cetron, well known for his optimistic outlook, predicts that "by the dawn of the twenty-first century, America will have passed the crisis." Social changes Cetron foresees include a decline in poverty, slight growth of the middle class, growing acceptance of cultural diversity, renewed emphasis on marriage, the creation of a new family ethic, and rising prosperity.

Social change, for good or ill, will continue to affect American society into the twenty-first century. Several possible changes in American society are discussed by the authors in this chapter.

"*Families . . . can master information technology
and use it as a means to strengthen family life.*"

Technology Will Strengthen the Traditional Family

Christopher J. Check

The nuclear family in America can be restored to its previous
prominence, Christopher J. Check argues in the following viewpoint. Check contends that information technology can benefit
those families that harness its power. Check asserts that such
technology could encourage families to stay home to telecommute, run a family business, or home school their children. He
believes that a family that travels on the "information highway"
can recapture and strengthen its autonomy and home life.
Check, a former Marine Corps captain, is the associate director
of the Rockford Institute Center on the Family in America, a
Rockford, Illinois, research organization that affirms traditional
families as the foundation of society.

As you read, consider the following questions:

1. According to Check, how has the information-based economy
   grown?
2. How could telecommuting and home schooling benefit
   families, in the author's opinion?
3. What are the four main sources of resistance to the
   "information technology family," according to Check?

Abridged from Christopher J. Check, "Rediscovering Family in the Information Age, Part 2,"
The Family in America, July 1994. Reprinted with permission.

As the second millennium draws to a close, two things are happening at a more rapid rate than ever in history: the development of technology and the decline of the family. Although some might argue that the former is driving the latter, for most of us the Benedictine cave is an impractical solution. Rather than shying from it, many families equipped with sufficient self-discipline can master information technology and use it as a means to strengthen family life.

The Ideal Commute

I recall waiting as a child for my father to return from work in the late afternoon. His routes were two, and I would sit on the front step of our Maryland home looking from one end of the street to the other trying to guess around which corner he would come striding. Although I had little understanding of my father's work, I came to believe that walking to work was the hallmark of a civilized life. Two years of enduring a daily hour-long commute on the crowded freeways of southern California confirmed what I had learned as a little boy. The ideal commute was made shank's mare [by one's own legs].

Of late, however, I have come to realize that the ideal commute is no commute at all—and not because the trip from bedroom to study is so short, but rather because when work is performed at home, work and home life are no longer so divided.

Popular estimates suggest that many Americans agree with me. [As reported by Ameritech, a Midwest telephone company,] the number of Americans "who do some type of income-producing or job-related work at home is now approaching 40 million." Further, the number of at-home workers is growing at five times the rate of the total labor force. This figure is sure to grow as an increasing number of Americans ask themselves if they could be doing their jobs, at least part of the time, under their own roofs. The rapid development of information technology is making the answer to that question a solid yes.

The arrival of inexpensive computers and modems, however, is only half of the story. The type of work Americans do has dramatically changed. In 1950, information jobs accounted for roughly 17 percent of the work force. By the early 1980's that number exceeded 60 percent. Simultaneously, the number of manufacturing jobs decreased such that by the mid-80's they composed only 13 percent of the labor force.

This shift from a manufacturing-based to an information-based economy, dubbed "the third wave" by Alvin Toffler, may not be an improvement. Indeed, Toffler's view of the coming information age extols a "rich diversity of family forms" that "might or might not be heterosexual" and will include such practices as "share[d] sex across marriage lines." Further, as we will explore later, a manufacturing-based economy need not be a "factory-based" economy. Whatever the case, waiting for the information age to pass seems counterproductive. An information-based economy, combined with readily available information machines, has created a variety of opportunities for families to reclaim at least part of their erstwhile autonomy.

Some mothers, for example, telecommute. Unwilling to sacrifice their careers entirely, they perform some work at home in order to devote more time to their children. At the very least, such an arrangement is preferable to full-time day care. Others have quit the workplace, but continue to work from home part-time as consultants or contract workers, shaping their work schedule around the needs of their families. On the other hand, some families have abandoned the corporate work place altogether and have started their own home-run business. Families in this latter group, like their pre-industrial ancestors, enjoy the inestimable bonds strengthened through pursuit of common enterprise.

Information technology has created opportunities not just for family-run businesses, but for family-run schools as well. The rapidly growing home-school population can now not only access a wealth of academic information without ever leaving the home, but also consult via electronic bulletin boards with one another for advice, ideas, and mutual support.

The Telecommuters

The term *telecommuter* suggests an image of anyone who works at home from behind his computer terminal. Experts, however, distinguish telecommuters from other home-based workers such as the self-employed. Strictly speaking, telecommuters are individuals who work for a larger company, are carried on its rolls as full-time employees, yet work, at least part-time, out of their homes. According to Link Resources, full-time telecommuting is rare: only 16 percent of telecommuters work more than 35 hours a week at home. The vast majority spend two or three days a week at the office. Most telecommuters consider the split between office and home to be [, according to Francis W. Horvath,] "the ideal work arrangement."

Some parents, however, might think it ideal if they never had to commute. Although at this point, full-time telecommuting is uncommon, parents considering it as a means to spend more time with their children should not be discouraged. They may already have the leverage they need to negotiate more time at home. Ameritech telecommuting expert Jim Livers praises telecommuting as "a bottom up phenomenon." He explains that self-reliant employees across America are approaching their supervisors bargaining for time at home. Employees with solid reputations bring their skills to the bargaining tables, and if companies want them, they will accommodate their demands.

In addition, parents should avoid thinking that the sort of work they do is incompatible with working at home. Workers in a wide variety of occupations constitute the telecommuter population: workers in fields ranging from education to health care, from graphic design to sales, from clerical to art and music— even some government and public-sector workers telecommute. While supervisors and managers may find that they must spend more time at the office, more independent workers such as salesmen, engineers, computer programmers, and writers are good candidates for more time at home.

Parents in the Information Age

In *The Third Wave*, Alvin Toffler popularized the concept of the "electronic cottage," the use of modern telecommunications technology to bring work back into the home. Toffler foresaw the possibility of building the strong family bonds of pre-industrial times by creating home-based, electronic mom-and-pop businesses. Once again, he wrote, home could become "the center of society"; once again, whole families could work together on a common economic enterprise.

Nancy R. Pearcey, *The Family in America*, March 1994.

Although telecommuting parents are not necessarily home full-time, their increased presence in the home can strengthen family life. Parents confident in their authority need not always be within arm's reach to encourage the good behavior of their children. For example, children whose parents forbid daytime television are unlikely to vegetate in front of MTV or cable television after school if mom is in the study down the hall. Several studies have shown that children whose mothers are home in the afternoon are less likely to engage in after school delinquency and promiscuity than children whose mothers work away from the home.

The benefits of telecommuting, however, do not end with mom's or dad's increased presence around the house. Spared the distractions of the corporate office, and more focused on results than punching a clock, telecommuters often prove to be more efficient workers. Management consultant Gil Gordon claims that their efficiency increases as much as 30 percent. Others put the increase higher. A telecommuting pilot program conducted by Ameritech in 1993, involving a dozen customer-service representatives, measured productivity increases of 40 percent. Whatever the figure, parents with the self-discipline and motivation to accomplish their work quickly will find more time to spend with their families.

Results-oriented work can also generate more flexible hours, which in turn can spell more family time. A telecommuting father, for example, who can tailor his work schedule around the school schedules of his children may find time in the afternoon to attend his son's baseball game or his daughter's bassoon recital. He may even find time to devote summer afternoons to weekly outings with his children. Increased work efficiency and more flexible hours, properly applied, can add up to more family recreation. . . .

Who Owns the Machines?

Of course, many who taste of freedom will decide to go it alone. Once a consultant, for example, realizes he can ply his trade from his home office what is to keep him tied to his employer?

What keeps the employee tied to the company now is access to information. As a result, he must spend part of the week at the office. Even the full-time telecommuter remains an agent of a larger corporation. As such, he will never achieve true family autonomy. In the first place, he will forever be discovering conflict between his job and his home life, as in the example of the father uncertain whether to spend his evenings with his children or earning more money at the word processor. Further, even if he were free to work every day from his home, the home-based worker would remain what the great Roman Catholic thinker Hillaire Belloc called "servile." Not owning the means of production himself, he performs "compulsory labor . . . for the advantage of those who do."

While Belloc spoke of an economy based on manufacturing, his wisdom applies easily to one based on information. Many large corporations are today's equivalent of yesterday's large factories, seeking out of fear and ignorance to maintain a stranglehold on the "means of production." Owning the means of production today means controlling access to information. The telecommuter who deals in information and ideas is limited in his access to other information and ideas, and his ability to market his own, by the corporation for which he works. Thus he remains servile. Until he can access information himself, he will never be his own master. Developing technology, however, now makes that possible. As George Gilder argues in his essay "Life After Television," fiber-optics technology may soon render centralized data bases obsolete, granting millions of Americans equal access to today's means of production. One might liken corporations standing athwart this change to the buggy-whip manufacturers conspiring against the automobile makers in 1905. . . .

Some parents, whose trades are sufficiently focused such that they can already access all the information they need, have already severed the corporate umbilical cord and started their own businesses. Although they may pursue a wide variety of trades, home-based workers share a common sentiment, the joy of being one's own boss. As a latter-day Belloc [Roxane Farmanfarmaian], writing in *Psychology Today*, puts it, "with such freedom there is also a greater sense of intimacy with one's work and its relationship to the rest of one's life. You are no longer working on someone else's time for someone else's profit." George Delany, who runs his own Delany Design Group, explains how his home-based business has enriched his life as father. "I'd like my two young sons to one day know who their dad was through my work, not through what I bought or earned."

Neither self-employment nor its joys and strengthened family bonds are new, yet information technology has given birth to a new breed of the self-employed called [by Sandra D. Atchison in *Business Week*] "lone eagles," professionals "who, aided by modern communications technology [are] able to work just about anywhere [they] want." In fact, small towns in Colorado and Wyoming are actively courting such businesses by "upgrading" their "communications systems." The advantages for families are many—everything from escaping the violent crime of large cities to living in the midst of abundant fishing and hunting. If children are too young to contribute to the family business, a remote environment would provide them with ample room to run around without fear.

The Home School

Not only businesses, but also schools can be family run. The popularity of the home school has increased in direct response to the decay of education in America. While advocates of homosexuality, paganism, feminism, environmentalism, and assorted other -isms discover new ways to displace all that is great in Western Christian culture in the public schools, it is little wonder home-schooling rolls are growing. The Home School Legal Defense Fund estimates that today roughly one million children are being schooled at home.

Although most are as qualified as the average public school-teacher, many parents feel they lack the means to properly educate their children at home. Given that the children raised on Bibles and McGuffey Readers were substantially better educated than their peers of today, such concern on the part of parents is generally unfounded. Nevertheless, parents who equate good education with state-of-the-art technology have at their disposal a wide variety of resource materials with which to teach. Compact Disc-Read Only Memory (CD-ROM) technology, for example, has made possible the storage of many volumes on a single compact disc, thereby lending themselves not only to immediate access, but often to rapid cross-reference. Encyclopedias, atlases, versions of the Bible, great works of history and fiction, even a tour of the San Diego Zoo, complete with stereo sound and moving pictures, are all available on compact disc.

The currently available technology, however, pales in comparison with what is possible once information becomes widely accessible. Gilder believes that parents of the future using an interactive "telecomputer" will be able to "create a school in [their] home that offers the nation's best teachers imparting the moral, cultural, and religious values [they] cherish." Now that many of our nation's universities have devolved into little more than ideological communes, students seeking genuine education may soon be able to take classes "on line" from the professors of their choice. Gilder dreams that one day students "could take a fully interactive course in physics or computer science with the world's most exciting professors, who respond to your questions and move at your own speed."

Like home-based work, however, the home school, no matter how graced with technology, functions properly when its students are sufficiently disciplined. As Scott McNealy of Sun Microsystems said in 1994, "Every child I know has an Encyclopedia Britannica within reach as they watch MTV. Why is wiring them up to the Library of Congress going to change things? Get a grip!"

Resistance

The principal source of resistance to the rapidly growing telecommuting, work-at-home, and home-school industries is not technological. Many local merchants, for example, oppose home-based businesses because they are not subject to the same business taxes and pay far less overhead. The real resistance, however, comes from the long-time enemies of family and the free market: feminists, organized labor, teachers' unions, and big government. . . .

Government, with its history of laws either forbidding or discouraging home enterprise, now finds itself in something of a quandary. Eager to support their traditional constituents, the labor and teachers' unions and the feminists, some politicians resist home-based work. In 1989, Congressman Austin Murphy, D-PA, referred to an effort to lift an outdated ban on home-based work imposed by the Fair Labor Standards Act as an "attempt to convert the basements and garages of America into sweatshops." Other politicians, however, enthusiastically embrace telecommuting, citing its advantages for the environment and the handicapped. Our Vice President Al Gore clamors for the connection of "all of our classrooms, libraries, hospitals and clinics by the year 2000" as a first step toward "universal" access to the "National Information Infrastructure."

While the thought of a direct link to the Vice President may be as appealing to some as it is unpleasant to others, the debates in the coming years—as technology advances and regulations increase—are sure to affect families directly. Asserting their autonomy will require that families are more than just conversant in information technology. If not, they may find themselves simply part of the pavement in the information superhighway, rather than its travelers.

Many argue that technology has made our lives easier. Perhaps it has. It certainly has not made any easier the pursuit of virtue. As such, reluctance to embrace every new technology that appears is wise. Nevertheless, if technology can help some families recapture their roles as the origins of education and industry, shying away from it would be foolish.

"As the nuclear family dissolves, what is likely to evolve is a sort of make-your-own-family approach."

The Traditional Family Will Be Less Prevalent

Claudia Wallis

In the following viewpoint, Claudia Wallis argues that "loosely knit clans" will become the norm for future families. According to Wallis, traditional families will diminish, evolving into more fractured, tribal affinities of divorced parents, stepparents, grandparents, and their children. Demographic changes will result in the elderly outnumbering children. Wallis maintains that these social changes will leave family members increasingly confused over their individual roles and require new institutions and policies to assist families. Wallis is a senior editor for *Time*, a weekly newsmagazine.

As you read, consider the following questions:

1. According to Wallis, what are the trends affecting traditional family values?
2. How could a demographically aging America affect the typical family, according to Wallis?
3. How will male/female roles change in the future, in the author's opinion?

Claudia Wallis, "The Nuclear Family Goes Boom!" *Time* (special issue), Fall 1992. Copyright ©1992 Time Inc. Reprinted by permission.

When cartoon-show creators William Hanna and Joseph Barbera strained their imaginations (ever so slightly) to picture the family of the future, it was a pretty simple exercise. Take your basic nuclear family: the modern, shop-happy housewife, the corporate-drone dad, two rambunctious kids and a dog; house them in a spacy-looking split-level; power their car with atomic energy; equip their home with a robot maid; and, whammo, you had it—a space-age Cleaver family named *The Jetsons.*

In an age of working mothers, single parents and gay matrimony, George Jetson and his clan already seem quaint even to the baby boomers who grew up with them. The very term nuclear family gives off a musty smell. The family of the 21st century may have a robot maid, but the chances are good that it will also be interracial or bisexual, divided by divorce, multiplied by remarriage, expanded by new birth technologies—or perhaps all of the above. Single parents and working moms will become increasingly the norm, as will out-of-wedlock babies, though there will surely be a more modern term for them. "The concept of the illegitimate child will vanish because the concept of the patriarchal nuclear family will vanish," says Leslie Wolfe, executive director of the Center for Women Policy Studies.

The clock cannot be turned back, despite the current political exploitation of old-fashioned family values. "The isolated nuclear family of the 1950s was a small blip on the radar," says Wolfe. "We've been looking at it as normal, but in fact it was a fascinating anomaly." While a strict reinforcement of traditional family roles is already under way in parts of the Muslim world and a backlash against feminism has occurred in the West, such counterrevolutions are likely to fail. "The fact of change is the one constant throughout the history of the family," says Maris Vinovskis, a professor at the University of Michigan. "The family is the most flexible, adaptive institution. It is constantly evolving."

The rise of divorce in the late 20th century will be a primary influence on the family in the century to come. Divorce rates have recently stabilized, but they have done so at such a high level—50% of marriages will end in court—that splitting up will be considered a natural thing. One reason the rate of divorce will remain high is that people will live longer. At the last turn of the century, at least one partner in a couple usually died before age 50, so husbands and wives were preoccupied with child rearing for nearly the entire length of their union. Now and in the future, "you may find yourself empty nesting at age 45, with 40 years of life to go," observes Ken Dychtwald, a San Francisco consultant specializing in the impact of longevity. As a result, he says, "it will become more normal to have several marriages. Divorce will not be seen as a failure but as a normal occurrence at various stages of life." Marriage contracts might be revised to include sunset clauses that would enable aging couples to escape an until-death-do-us-part commitment.

Dychtwald cites the late anthropologist Margaret Mead as a pioneer of the kind of serial monogamy that may become popular in the next century. Mead liked to say that she was married three times, all successfully. Mead's husbands suited her needs at different points in her long and varied life. Her first partner, whom she called her "student-husband," provided a conventional and comfortable marriage. As her career progressed, however, she sought a traveling partner who was interested in her fieldwork. Finally, she found a romantic and intellectual soul mate.

Reprinted with special permission of King Features Syndicate.

It will still be possible for a husband and wife to endure together the vicissitudes of many decades, but Dychtwald believes such couples will be rare. Once society has lost most of its taboos against divorce, it will take unusual commitment, flexibility and loyalty (perhaps fortified by a religious vow) to stick it out. Couples who endure to celebrate their golden anniversaries "will have mastered marriage," says Dychtwald. "It will be like mastering the violin or the cello."

The nonvirtuosos will spend significant stretches of their adulthood rediscovering the single life. Current trends suggest that this will be particularly true of women, both because they live longer than men and because they are less likely to remarry. Women will adapt by developing new types of relationships: dating younger men, seeing more males in platonic friendships and living together in groups with other women, not unlike the *Golden Girls* model. Computer and videophone dating services will help with matchmaking far more than they do today.

Serial monogamy will make family structures a great deal more complicated. The accretion of step-relatives and former in-laws will be legally messy and increasingly bewildering to children, who will have to divide their loyalties and love among step-mothers, birth mothers, biological fathers and ex-stepparents. An entire new body of case law will unfold as courts try to settle complex custody disputes and determine where a child's best interest may lie in a forest of hyphenated relatives.

The growth of the extended family does not mean that huge clans will gather under one roof. "They'll want intimacy at a distance," says Andrew Cherlin, a sociology professor at Johns Hopkins University. The extended family will be more of a network of crisscrossing loyalties and obligations. As life-spans lengthen and marriages multiply, middle-aged couples could find themselves crushed by the responsibilities of caring all at once for aging parents, frail grandparents, children still completing their education and perhaps even a stepgrandchild or two. In short, the "sandwich generation," already feeling so much pressure in the 1990s, could give way to a multilayered club sandwich.

As family relationships grow more complex, role confusion is bound to become epidemic. More battles will be fought over household turf, inheritance and rivalries for affection. Even incest, long considered an absolute taboo, will become a more complicated issue because the fracturing of families will make it harder to define. If nonrelatives within a family have sex, is that incest or something else?

Many of the biggest changes in the next century, at least in the developed world, will be driven by the demographic tilt away from children and toward the elderly. A snapshot of a family gathering in 2050 will show lots of gray hair and not too many diapers. Even now, for the first time in history, the average American has more parents living than children. People age 65 and older, who constitute 11.3% of the U.S. population in 1980, will make up 22% of the country by 2050. Moreover, in the next three decades the number of Americans age 85 and older is expected to increase fivefold, to 15 million.

That growth will spur a boom in the development of retirement communities. Those catering to the affluent will be highly sought after by regional civic boosters. "I can envision countries competing for these luxury communities in the same way they used to compete for auto plants, because they are such wealth engines," says William Johnston, a fellow at the Hudson Institute. A new, economical form of elderly residence called "assisted housing" is likely to be popular as well. In these complexes, the elderly are supervised but allowed to live alone. "It's not like a nursing home," says Karen Wilson, whose company, Concepts Community Living, operates two such residences in Oregon. "These are places where older people can live independently and where their family can come and do their laundry, bathe them and even stay with them."

Some people in America will be unable, either emotionally or financially, to meet their family obligations. "We cannot be hopeful about their ability to preserve or create any kind of family structure, unless we step in to change their circumstances," says Margaret Mark, director of the Young & Rubicam Education Group. The worst victims may be children. "You may see kids trying to survive on the street," says Edward Cornish, president of the World Future Society in Bethesda, Maryland. "Think of Dickens' London. Worse, think of Brazil, where there are armies of children with no place to go."

New technology and social institutions will have to emerge to help the fractured families of the future. Some forecasters, like Mark, predict that in poorer neighborhoods, schools will become 24-hour family-support systems offering child care, quiet study places, a sanctuary for abused or neglected youngsters, even a place to sleep for those who need one. At the same time, government computers will be far more efficient about tracking the legal obligations of citizens. Parents who fail to meet child-support payments will find it hard to hide.

As corporations become more dependent on women workers and staffed by female executives at high levels, policies will become more accommodating toward families. Video-conferencing and other improvements in communications technology will make it easier for work to be done remotely from home, though it remains to be seen whether this would be truly a boon for family life. While work will be less tied to the office, it will also be more international and therefore more round-the-clock. Making a clear separation between work life and home life may actually become more difficult.

With women constituting nearly half the work force, the remaining vestiges of gender inequality will gradually disappear, according to most forecasters. Slowly but inexorably, as women continue to move into fields once dominated by men, the gap between male and female wages will close. As it does, power balances will shift not only at the office but also in the kitchen. When both sexes have equivalent jobs and equivalent paychecks, it won't always be the woman who works "the second shift" of housework after hours or who stays home when a child is sick. Nor, for that matter, will it generally be the woman who receives child custody in a divorce.

To help families cope with ever more intricate obligations, the government should allow large, extended families to incorporate themselves as businesses, suggests David Pearce Snyder, a consulting futurist. This would make families more productive and independent by giving them huge tax advantages that corporations enjoy: generous write-offs for helping each other with new business ventures, tuition funds and the ability to transfer wealth among members without being taxed. Such families would then be much better equipped to look after all their members, relieving the government and other institutions of that burden.

On the other hand, an even more radical approach may evolve. It is reasonable to ask whether there will be a family at all. Given the propensity for divorce, the growing number of adults who choose to remain single, the declining popularity of having children and the evaporation of the time families spend together, another way may eventually evolve. It may be quicker and more efficient to dispense with family-based reproduction. Society could then produce its future generations in institutions that might resemble the state-sponsored baby hatcheries in Aldous Huxley's *Brave New World*. People of any age or marital status could submit their genetic material, pay a fee, perhaps apply for a permit and then produce offspring. "Embryos could be brought to fetal and infant stage all in the laboratory, outside the womb," says Cornish. "Once ready, the children could be fed by nurses or even automated machinery."

In any event, as the nuclear family dissolves, what is likely to evolve is a sort of make-your-own-family approach, which Dychtwald calls "the family of choice." Institutions, employers, neighbors and friends will take on roles once dominated by relatives. "The need and craving for family has not diminished," he says. "It's just that people are forming their own little tribes based on choice and affinity and not on blood." These new pseudo-relatives could overcome the one immutable truth about families: you can't pick your parents. Someday, maybe, you will be able to.

"The 'Plug-In School' is a possible first step toward the flexible learning environments of the twenty-first century."

A Vision of Revitalized Education

David Pesanelli

In the following viewpoint, David Pesanelli argues that new technologies will revolutionize learning in the future. Students of the twenty-first century, Pesanelli maintains, will use both state-of-the-art and less sophisticated learning modules designed to meet students' changing needs. Two scenarios of the future are narrated by Pesanelli on the classroom of the future to give readers a sense of his concept of twenty-first-century learning. Pesanelli believes that the electronic school of the future will allow learning at home, in education centers, or at work. Pesanelli is an advanced planner who heads his own conceptual design company in Rockville, Maryland.

As you read, consider the following questions:

1. How will new technologies change the learning experience in twenty-first-century America, in Pesanelli's opinion?
2. What does the author mean by the term "Plug-In School"?

David Pesanelli, "The Plug-In School," *The Futurist*, September/October 1993. Reproduced with permission from *The Futurist*, published by the World Future Society, 7910 Woodmont Ave., Suite 450, Bethesda, MD 20814.

In the future, technologies will allow learning to take place virtually everywhere. School buildings as they now exist could even be eliminated, replaced with a ubiquitous array of stimulating, interactive, and flexible learning technologies embedded in all human habitats.

While eliminating the school is a revolutionary change in the distribution of education services that deserves serious consideration, it is also fruitful to examine ways in which the educational physical plant might shed its "factory school" format and emerge in new forms. We can then begin to see how the classroom could become a precursor of true twenty-first-century environments, a prototype for the evolving workplace and home.

New, integrated technologies enrich the learning experience by giving students access to encyclopedic amounts of information and data in any of their subject areas, integrated with rich images and animation. Curriculums enhanced by these exciting technologies could help teachers expose students to history and its meanings: Names and dates of historical events and actors come alive in full costumes of the times, embellished by period music.

The advanced physical learning environment would also teach students about life in the twenty-first century—at work, at home, and in places yet to be imagined.

The school, the workplace, and the home are clearly integrating. Responsibilities, functions, activities, and tasks that once occurred exclusively within each domain are crossing over into the other environments. Corporate workers have home offices, students and older learners take cable-access university courses, and parents bring their toddlers to day-care learning centers at work sites. It may no longer be sensible to think about the school, the office, and the home as separate from one another. These three once-distinct entities are breaking apart, combining, and overlapping in new and unexpected ways. The next-generation school can lead this process of blending aspects of learning, living, and working.

The School as Change Agent

Dramatic and pervasive changes are occurring in the workplace, to which the advanced school environment can help orient students. Organization charts are flattening, team assignments are becoming prevalent, off-site work is increasing, and teleconferencing is expanding. Just beneath the surface of these visible transformations are powerful change-themes such as "fluidity," "mobility," "flexibility," and "adaptability." These underlying qualities can guide the planning and design of advanced schools.

For example, children could easily rearrange colorful and mobile work stations in the classroom as they switch from teacher-led programs to individual assignments to team projects to distance-learning via satellite or cable broadcasts. These flexible learning situations have parallels in the ways that office and factory work are evolving.

The Plug-In School

The "Plug-In School" is a possible first step toward the flexible learning environments of the twenty-first century. As now envisioned, this facility serves as a hub for receiving learning modules "injected" into its classrooms. The school has a physical structure that opens its walls to become part of the library, museum, science center, planetarium, laboratory, and corporation that is plugged in to it. Yet, the school never loses its own identity as the students' and teachers' environment.

The Plug-In School is conceived as a facility that, in addition to its traditional roles, functions at the center of a delivery and distribution system for education "packages." A key goal is to strengthen the school's relationships with informal learning centers and with employers to create both academic and career-oriented instructional programs.

Transporters deliver containerized modules to school facilities. These "packages" are planned, designed, and manufactured at science centers and museums. They might contain interactive exhibits or materials that will be used for pursuing creative problem-solving exercises. Corporations could create stimulating, career-oriented modules. An architectural firm might send models of buildings accompanied by optical discs showing computer-aided design. An industrial laboratory could provide a module that demonstrates state-of-the-art laser applications.

These education and career packages need not be exclusively high tech. A crafts company might send an entire section of a woodworking shop, complete with work benches and tools for the students to use in creating artistic and personal objects. Some containerized modules might literally plug in to openings in the school walls, and the craft shop or robotics lab or architectural studio would become a walk-in extension of the classroom.

, At the center of the Plug-In School is a storage and staging core, where the school's own mobile learning modules are prepared for classroom use. Teachers request combinations of models, mockups, specimens, interactive devices, and media to enhance course experiences.

What might it be like to spend some time in this dynamic facility?

Scenario One: The Morning Surprise

The young children have been waiting impatiently for this morning's "surprises" to appear. And now their wait is over.

Two sleek transporters have arrived, and their drivers unload containerized "packages" at one of the school's loading bays. One module is from Chicago's Adler Planetarium. Tina, Beverly, and Tom—a student teaching assistant—eagerly assemble the traveling planetarium. The projection instrument is a compact model designed to be transported easily. The inflatable dome will soon be in place and swept with galaxies, quasars, and galactic black holes.

Classrooms at the Mall

The classrooms look traditional enough, with teachers at their desks and students reading. But step outside: Instead of a football field and parking lot, there's a department store and a kitchen store. Instead of a basketball court, there's a food court.

This is the mall school of Fairfax County, Va., an alternative public high school inside the Landmark Shopping Center. The school, along with five others like it around the country, is part of a national experiment to address the needs of both educators and retailers.

For educators, these schools, partially funded by businesses, bring the classroom to the youths—offering students an attractive place to study in a setting they enjoy. Most of these new schools are for teenagers who are less interested in college than in spending part of the high school day learning job skills by working in stores.

Mary Jordan, *The Washington Post National Weekly Edition*, September 5-11, 1994.

The second vehicle brings a robotics lab from the National Institute of Science and Technology. Jimmy and Quan insert a program card into the instructor robot, which launches into a comedy routine while instructing the boys on assembling a mini-manufacturing plant to be used in the classroom this morning. A second section of the robotics lab, including microbots and videos depicting careers in the field, is loaded onto a mobile learning module and delivered to the school's storage core. Later, it will be sent to a physics class for a career-oriented program.

Scenario Two: Afternoon Career Class

The sun-drenched classroom is filled with bright, gregarious 15- to 17-year-old students, who chatter excitedly as they rearrange the room for the afternoon's career class. They reposition soft partitions and program the track lighting, then decide how to arrange their work stations for the two-hour session's rigorous agenda. The "stations" hold the snap-in computers that they will carry home in backpacks and use for their homework assignments.

As the session on robotics careers begins, a section of the classroom wall slides aside, and the students grow quiet. The teacher and a robotics expert enter the environment just ahead of a self-guided mobile unit. The "package" that it carries arrived earlier that day after being picked up at another school complex in the next county.

A teaching assistant slides back the cover of the mobile learning module. Inside are a laboratory's products—microbots. The module's video camera scans the array of electronic and mechanical marvels, and enlarged images appear on a suspended video screen. The lab expert explains how microbots are developed and manufactured, as well as what they can do.

After taking turns manipulating the microbots, the students watch a video on careers in the rapidly expanding robotics field and related disciplines. Interested students press a module section and receive a printout that identifies robotics labs and corporations in the region where interns are employed during vacation breaks.

The career-oriented session ends, and some of the class members eagerly rearrange their work stations for a team project. Others reconfigure the classroom area for a distance-learning course taught by a robotics engineer broadcasting via satellite from an upstate New York laboratory.

Everywhere Learning

Learning environments of the future should provide a context for technologies as well as a counterpoint to them. The "little red schoolhouse" of yore will disappear, replaced with a more futuristic design in which brilliant technologies seem natural and not overwhelming or intimidating. But at the same time, this high-tech environment should embrace its natural surroundings. The classrooms, for instance, might have large windows to give students a view of trees, meadows, and lakes, providing a serene visual respite for kids spending many hours with computer screens and electronic devices of one type or another.

The Plug-In School is but one potential concept for a twenty-first-century school. Students—and adult learners as well—will likely use several facilities of different sizes and complexity, including study environments in the home and workplace. In the twenty-first century, it will be possible for all of us to plug in to "schools"—wherever we may be.

"To put matters bluntly, the United States potentially is to education what the Soviet Union was to economics."

A Vision of Declining Education

George H. Jacobson

In the following viewpoint, George H. Jacobson presents a bleak picture of American education, with U.S. students lagging far behind those of other industrialized countries. Jacobson argues that such decline does not bode well for the future information-age workforce, which will require more skills than the current educational system provides. Underachievement, Jacobson maintains, means a weakened America domestically and globally. To improve education, Jacobson proposes high but reasonable standards of educational performance and testing. He also supports voucher programs—enabling parents to choose among public and private schools—to reform education. Jacobson believes these strategies will improve learning and help meet the demands of business in the future. Jacobson is an associate professor of information systems at California State University in Los Angeles.

As you read, consider the following questions:

1. According to Jacobson, what are the three main problems posed by the decline in American education?
2. Why does Jacobson doubt that the goals of the U.S. Department of Education are achievable?

From George H. Jacobson, "Are We Producing a Future Work Force of Bart Simpsons?" *Business Forum*, Winter 1992. Reprinted with permission.

News items: a 50 percent dropout rate plagues many high schools, one out of every five high school students carries a firearm, knife, or club; only 10 percent of students who finish grammar school in one urban city can read and write, and 40 percent cannot even read their graduation certificate of attendance; major ethnic population shifts in some districts have caused massive communication problems between students and teachers; and a poll finds 56 percent of the residents of Los Angeles and Orange counties in California believe the overall state of their school system is poor, and 40 percent of the respondents with school-age children believe the quality of local education is so poor as to warrant moving out of Southern California altogether.

These are not encouraging developments for prospective employers to ponder, and their concern was very much reflected in the 1991 *Business Forum* survey of 780 chief executive officers. For example, in a question on infrastructure, education was by far the most important category singled out (over environment, telecommunications, transportation, energy, and health services). In a question on technology, the most important area of concern was "personnel supply." Also highly ranked was "intellectual property." In a question on human resources, the biggest area of concern by a significant margin was "skilled worker shortages."

In an overall rating of the areas of concern, "infrastructure," which included an important educational component tied for second place [rated at 4.5]. When you consider that the executives gave an average score of 3.5 on the scale of 1 to 5 to all areas of concern in the survey, the overwhelming importance that business leaders place on education is obvious.

Underachievement Means Trouble Ahead

While business leaders and all other segments of society recognize the importance of education, measures of educational performance in the United States have suffered both an absolute and relative decline. For example, 1992 results of the Scholastic Aptitude Test (SAT) serve to confirm this trend of academic descent. The average verbal score of 422 was the lowest on record. The average mathematics score was 474, a decline of 2 points. In 1969, the average mathematics score was 493, and in 1967 the average verbal score was 463. According to Albert Shanker, president of the American Federation of Teachers, the "federal test scores indicate that only 4 percent of high school graduates 'really know algebra,' although 96 percent of those who took the SAT reported taking an algebra class. Ninety-three percent took geometry. Yet on the math section of the SAT, which is largely a test of algebra and geometry, students got an average of only 26 of 60 questions correct." Verbal scores were even more disastrous than those in mathematics.

Steve Brown, president and CEO of the John Hancock Mutual Life Insurance Company, told attendees at a national conference, "In a 1989 study funded in part by the U.S. Department of Education, America's 13-year-olds came in dead last in math and science skills when compared with their peers in other countries. South Korean children came in first, followed by Spanish, British, Irish and Canadian 13-year-olds." Other studies show similar results. For example, Paul Gray reported in *The Chronicle of Higher Education*, a "survey by the International Association for the Evaluation of Educational Achievement, which compared students of various ages with their peers in 17 countries, [revealed] American 14-year-olds ranked 14 in science and mathematics. Among 17-year-olds, the Americans placed in the bottom quartile in biology, chemistry and physics, behind students in such countries as Australia, England, Hungary, Japan, Norway, and Poland."

Educational Credibility

Today, public education is in much the same position our automakers faced in the seventies. They simply fell behind their worldwide competitors—in quality, fuel economy, safety, reliability, and so on. It has taken them nearly 20 years to begin to reestablish their credibility with the American car-buyer, and the jury is still out as to whether they can fully succeed.

We must re-establish our educational system's credibility, as well. Working together, it can be done faster than the automakers have been at it—perhaps even by the year 2000.

Steve Brown, *Vital Speeches of the Day*, June 15, 1991.

The absolute and relative decline in American education poses three main problems. The first is the mismatch between technology and education. In the information age greater educational achievement is constantly required. For example, in the fields of computers and telecommunications, the amount of knowledge is doubling every three years. A match of technology and education would require American educational achievement to be reaching new highs yearly, not new lows. The job market in the information age increasingly focuses on verbal and technical skills and understanding. According to Brown, "An estimated three-quarters of new workers through the year 2000 will be qualified to fill just 40 percent of the available jobs. That mismatch of skills to jobs will damage competitiveness and lives."

The second problem posed by the decline in American education is the increased threat of foreign competition. According to at least one expert, Paul Gray, the consequences of our scientific illiteracy will be "a work force that cannot meet, let alone understand, the technological standards of their competition abroad. We tolerate this situation at our national peril."

A third major problem posed by inadequate education levels is the threat to the democratic process itself. Citizens will not be able to understand issues, many of which are technological, sufficiently to make intelligent choices.

To put matters bluntly, the United States potentially is to education what the Soviet Union was to economics. The U.S. may face a disaster of similar proportions.

Employers Eye Foreign Work Sites

The difficulty of American schools to produce a competent future work force may foster the growth of companies hiring workers at remote job sites—even outside the United States. This could be especially the case in the field of telecommuting, which is a process that has made the office a function rather than a place. Telecommuting involves office workers' and executives' working part time or full time out of their homes or at distant locations communicating through computers using a telecommunications network. Some experts even insist telecommuting will become a predominant work style in the 21st century.

A recent extension of this concept involves hiring workers in foreign lands who transmit their work product to U.S. companies by satellite. A *Star Trek* idea? Not at all. The continual reduction in the cost of computers and telecommunications is serving to make the idea of having office work done overseas an increasingly attractive option. This is an ominous development facing the American work force, which is increasingly at a disadvantage in the world marketplace because of high wages and low educational levels. A *Wall Street Journal* staffer in 1991 wrote, "The 1990s may reveal the darker side of the information age: If you work at a computer, your job could be moved halfway around the world." He also noted, "In the late 1970s and 80s, many blue-collar jobs migrated overseas. Today there is a movement of data-processing and other 'back office' jobs offshore to places where wages are cheaper, people speak English, and state-of-the-art telecommunications facilities allow instantaneous links to the American company's host computers. Barbados, Jamaica, the Philippines, Singapore and Ireland have emerged as among the most popular 'back office' locations. The jobs range from simple data entry to accounting, medical transcription, telemarketing, and technical support for high-technology products." These developments prompted researchers Robert Metzger and Mary Ann Von Glinow to ask, "What will the organization of the future be if most or all data entry and back office administration is so fragmented that it resides amidst the lowest bidder anywhere in the world? And what is the implication for the employer if he has the opportunity to move the back office offshore with a flick of a switch?"

Perhaps an even more important question is what is the implication for the American employee? Will the decline in blue-collar employment opportunities seen in the last few decades be duplicated in the office of the future?

Mediocre Scores

According to the 1994 SAT (Scholastic Assessment Test, formerly known as the Scholastic Aptitude Test) scores released by The College Board, not much progress in academics has been made by America's college-bound students. The national verbal score of 423 is just one point above the lowest score of 422 achieved in 1991 and 30 points below the 1972 score of 453, while in mathematics the 1994 national score of 479 is only one point above that of 1993 but five points below the 1972 score of 484.

Samuel L. Blumenfeld, *The Blumenfeld Education Letter*, October 1994.

There is general agreement with the concept [according to Susan Fry, Judy Gordon, and Adam Shell] that "education or lack thereof will play a key role in the quality of life for individuals in the year 2000 [or that] better education of more Americans, especially youth, will be the key to remaining competitive in the worldwide marketplace."

Unless the marginal productivity on extra dollars spent on education is negative, some positive results can be expected. But greater investment in the current education system will not provide the answer. A 1990 U.S. Department of Education report said, "Total spending for elementary and secondary schools more than doubled since 1980—while the number of students remained about the same. In real terms, education spending increased approximately 33 percent more per public school student." Columnist Thomas Sowell points out that "the United States spends more per child than most of the countries whose students consistently outperform ours on the same tests. Moreover, spending on education increased, both in money terms and real terms, throughout the long period from the early 1960s to the early 1980s, while test scores went steadily downward."

Besides the issue of inefficiency in educational spending, there is a question of limited financial resources. The federal government is currently running a deficit of nearly a billion dollars a day. In addition, many state and local governments are facing budget crises.

There is growing involvement of the business sector in the public schools. This is good but it is not the ultimate answer to our needs. A 1991 *Fortune* survey of service and industrial firms revealed companies are giving more money and more of their employees' time than ever before. *Fortune* reported in 1991, "Top management in 83 percent of the companies surveyed say they participate actively in educational reform, vs. 70 percent a year ago. In some cases it's the employees, not their bosses, who best illustrate a company's involvement. [For example] Eastman Kodak expects more than 3000 employees in Rochester, New York, to be tutors or mentors in local schools this year."

Goals for the Year 2000

The U.S. Department of Education in 1990 proposed a solution to the educational morass. The stated goals for American education by the year 2000 are

1. All children in America will start school ready to learn.
2. The high school graduation rate will increase to at least 90 percent.
3. American students will leave grades four, eight, and twelve having demonstrated competency in challenging subject matters.
4. U.S. students will be first in the world in science and mathematics achievement.
5. Every adult American will be literate and will possess knowledge and skills necessary to compete in a global economy and exercise the rights and responsibilities of citizenship.
6. Every school in America will be free of drugs and violence and will offer a disciplined environment conducive to learning.

While these goals are desirable, they cannot be achieved in the proposed timetable. Further, the means by which these six goals would be reached are unclear. For example, the U.S. Department of Education report states that "achieving the goals requires a renaissance of sound American values—proven values such as strength of family, parental responsibility, neighborly commitment, the community-wide caring of churches, civil organizations, business, labor and the media." Again, the achievement of objectives in education is laudable, but it assumes that rapid and positive changes will occur in values and behavior.

Another method to increase educational achievement focuses on improvement of self-esteem. An example of this approach is the "Curriculum of Inclusion" in the state of New York. I agree with the opinion of author Diane Ravitch, who said, "Behind the 'Curriculum of Inclusion' lies a pedagogical theory, a conviction that changes in the curriculum will raise the self-esteem of children from racial and ethnic minorities and will lead to improved academic performance. . . . But it is dubious to assert that programs to bolster racial pride will raise children's self-esteem or their academic performance. For one thing, there is no evidence to support this claim; for another, international assessments have shown that American students have higher self-esteem than their counterparts in other countries but do worse on academic tests. Genuine self-esteem means self-respect and confidence in one's ability; self-confidence is the product of experience, the reward that comes as a result of working hard to achieve one's goals." Two groups that have traditionally done well in American education are Jews and Asians. Neither of these owe their academic success to campaigns by school boards to raise their self-esteem.

The education problems in the United States are immense and multifaceted. There are no easy answers. However, I believe that three measures would serve to improve the situation.

The first step is to establish high, but reasonable, standards. Albert Shanker writes that "we should realize that the overwhelming majority of American children—perhaps 90 percent—are not learning much. Middle-class parents are happy with the education their children get because the kids go on to college. They don't realize that most of these youngsters would not be admitted to a university in any other industrialized country. Their kids are getting their junior high and high school educations in college." Higher standards would provide students with an incentive to work harder.

The increased standards should be national in scope and publicized so Americans know what the targets are. Testing should be conducted. The results of the testing would, among other things, provide students, schools, cities, states, and the nation with data on how successfully education goals are being met. In contrast, the U.S. Department of Education wants to establish a voluntary test based on five core subjects.

The next step is the establishment of a voucher system. Students and parents supplied with information as to the students' areas of abilities and interests could select schools that have the potential to provide these new educational consumers with a quality product. Schools would now have a greater incentive to be competitive with other educational institutions or risk losing students. . . .

Monopolies in economics have a tendency to produce low-quality products with high cost and are often not responsible to consumer demands. Competition serves to reverse these tendencies. Why not add competition to the American educational system and provide real choice to all segments of society, not just to those who can currently afford to attend private schools?

"If we increase the flow of immigrants to the United States, our future economy could benefit."

Immigrants Will Strengthen America's Future

Peter Francese

Peter Francese is the publisher of *American Demographics* magazine. In Part I of the following viewpoint, he argues that due to the rapid increase in the number of elderly, combined with possibly the lowest population growth rate in American history, America faces a labor shortage as well as higher taxes to cover the income security and medical costs of the nation's aging population. Francese argues that the solution to these developments is increased immigration. He argues that higher levels of immigration would provide the workers and tax revenues the country will need in the future. In Part II, Francese extends his argument, concluding that immigration is the key to keeping America's Social Security system solvent.

As you read, consider the following questions:

1. What three problems do regional declines in population present, according to Francese?
2. In Francese's opinion, how much could health care costs for the elderly increase in the future?
3. Why does the author believe that immigration should take higher priority than trade?

Peter Francese, "Aging America Needs Foreign Blood," *The Wall Street Journal*, March 27, 1990. Reprinted with permission of *The Wall Street Journal*, ©1990 Dow Jones & Company, Inc. All rights reserved. "Social Security Solution," *American Demographics* magazine, February 1993, ©1993. Reprinted with permission.

I

There are powerful demographic forces at work in the U.S. that virtually mandate federal policy be changed to permit more immigration than we have now. The rapid increase in the number of very elderly people, combined with declining numbers of young adults and a record low population growth rate, will put this nation in a demographic vise.

Paying for the income security and medical needs of the elderly while at the same time improving the educational opportunities and well-being of children (not to mention paying interest on the federal deficit and rebuilding infrastructure) will squeeze future U.S. workers in the grip of higher federal payroll taxes, state taxes and local property taxes. This is not just some distant problem beginning when the huge baby boom starts retiring in 20 years. The vise is closing now, particularly in the slow-growing Northeast and Midwest regions.

Low Growth

Overall U.S. population growth for the 1990s is projected to be only about 7%, a record low. The previous low was 7.2% growth during the Depression years of the 1930s. But almost all states in the Northeast and Midwest are expected to have growth rates below even that meager average. Regional population projections done by the Census Bureau using interstate migration trends show a continuing outflow of people from the Northeast and Midwest resulting in growth rates for the 1990s of less than 2.1%. According to one scenario, four states in those regions could lose a combined total of nearly half a million people in the 1990s.

A state or region without any population growth loses on three fronts.

First, it loses political representation and therefore, political power: The Northeast, for example, which lost nine congressional representatives after the 1980 census, is projected to lose an additional six following the 1990 census. [The region lost seven seats.] This is on top of nine lost after the 1980 census. Loss of population can also result in less federal aid because population size is frequently included in grant formulas.

Second, in the U.S. no-growth areas age more rapidly than those that are growing, thus driving up health-care expenditures. Pennsylvania, for example, which could lose more than 100,000 residents in the 1990s, is the second-oldest state in the nation, with half its population over age 35 vs. the national median age of 33. Within 15 years half of Pennsylvania residents are expected to be more than 40 years old. As a result, it will be one of the first states to experience more deaths than births, perpetuating its population decline.

Third, areas in the U.S. with no growth or a decline in population will experience more severe labor shortages in the years ahead, which tends to discourage new business investments. Labor shortages will be exacerbated by the shrinking population of young adults. Nationally, the number of people age 20 to 29 is projected by the Census Bureau to drop 12% in the 1990s. But in the Northeast and Midwest regions, the number is projected to shrink even more.

Employers or governments in regions with little or no growth could relieve labor shortages if they could recruit freely from abroad. Or they could reverse their population decline and offset the aging effect if they could encourage young adults to emigrate from other countries. But they can't because while money and goods flow quite freely across our borders, workers do not. People from other countries can buy all the U.S. property or corporations they can afford, but they can't come to work here except in very small numbers.

Our Elderly and Children

Lack of population growth is a phenomenon specific to certain regions or states, but rapid growth of the very elderly and the need to improve educational opportunities for our children are national in scope. During the 1990s, for example, the number of people age 85 and older is projected by the Census Bureau to grow 42%, six times the rate of overall population growth. This is on top of a 44% increase during the 1980s, when the overall population grew only 10%.

The medical needs of this population are enormous. A majority suffer from one or more chronic conditions and one-fifth are in long-term-care facilities. The nursing-home requirement alone means creating 75 to 100 nursing-home beds every day for at least the next 20 years. If the cost of a stay in a nursing home averages only $100 per day during the 1990s, providing such care for the additional people age 85 and older will add at least a billion dollars a year to our national health-care bill. But every two to three nursing-home beds requires an additional health-care worker. The worsening shortage of health-care workers will make this problem even more complex and expensive.

At the other end of the age scale, the school-age population is projected to grow 7% during the 1990s, the same rate as the overall population. This would seem to be a manageable growth rate in ordinary circumstances. But these are not ordinary times. U.S. schools need to be brought up to the standards of our overseas competitors, whose students spend more hours a day in school and attend more days per year. At the same time we need to compensate for the serious problem that one-fifth of U.S. schoolchildren live in poverty. Learning under those circumstances is more difficult and requires more support staffers.

Caring for our elderly and creating a brighter future for our children will certainly require a lot more money, but it will also require more people to teach and to care. Neither of those functions lend themselves to automation.

Future Immigrants

By continuing to tightly restrict immigration we shoot ourselves in both feet. In the short run, our productive capacity is crippled by worker shortages, and in the long run, we will be hobbled by high dependency ratios—too many elderly dependents for too few workers.

Restrictive U.S. immigration laws are not just our problem, either. The weak economies of Latin America cannot possibly create jobs rapidly enough to absorb the additional 14 million young adults (age 20 to 29) expected there between 1990 and 2000. Many of those unable to find enough work to sustain themselves and their families will either come here illegally or worsen the already serious problem of political instability in Latin America. Increased illegal immigration breeds disrespect for a law that cannot be enforced. Stopping the flow of illegal immigration from Latin America may become a law-enforcement quagmire like trying to stop the flow of illegal drugs.

Tens of millions of legal immigrants and their descendants have contributed their imagination and vitality to the building of this nation. Future immigrants can contribute greatly to its rebuilding, because most immigrants are young and pay much more in taxes than they use in public services. Thus they can ease the squeeze future U.S. workers will feel as our slow-growing population ages.

We cannot wait 20 years to see what will happen when the baby-boomers retire and ask what happened to their Social Security trust fund. The U.S. needs to admit more immigrants now to get us out of the demographic bind we put ourselves in by restricting immigration in the first place.

II

Whenever the economy is bad, people make proposals to restrict immigration. If there aren't enough jobs for Americans, they ask, why should we let more people in? Some add that immigrants should be kept out because they increase environmental degradation, or use government services without paying taxes. But I pay attention to the people who say that our Social Security system is approaching insolvency. And when I look at immigrants, I see solutions.

If present population trends continue, Social Security and Medicare could take half of the average American's paycheck by 2040. The reason is our aging population, which produces retirees faster than it produces workers. One way to ease this problem is to admit enough young immigrants to keep the worker/retiree ratio where it is today. If we increase the flow of immigrants to the United States, our future economy could benefit.

Our leaders are now making enormous efforts to negotiate trade agreements with other countries. They are forging agreements on such arcane subjects as the proper subsidy for cooking oil seeds from France. They should also negotiate the acceptable demographics of immigrants to ensure that the newest Americans will be young enough or skilled enough to make a meaningful contribution to our society. Foreign nationals are already allowed to buy property and businesses in America. Why can't the same people become U.S. citizens?

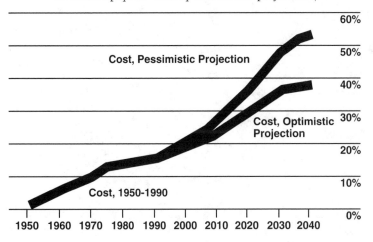

Security Spending

(total Social Security and Medicare benefits as a percent of taxable payroll—history and official projections)

Source: Social Security Administration, 1992.

Canada is already following this path. After years of liberal policies, they recently tightened their immigration laws. Their new laws may not decrease immigration. But they will give an edge to people who have youth, resources, and skills. "Applying to Canada will be like applying to law school," says Howard Greenberg of the Canadian Bar Association.

If the United States admitted the same proportion of immigrants as Canada does, we would open our borders to 2 million people a year instead of the 1 million who have arrived every year since 1985. The additional people and their offspring, if chosen carefully, would surely pay a lot of Social Security taxes. Perhaps they could even keep our system solvent.

Previous generations of immigrants to this country have been hard-working, risk-taking, entrepreneurial people who create jobs and wealth. Will future immigrants be as good for America? I think it's a risk worth taking. Perhaps I'm biased: my father came to this country with no education and virtually no knowledge of English, started a business, and put five children through college.

I believe that similar American dreams can still be realized. Even if you don't, we ought to debate this issue with as much effort and hard data as we do trade agreements. After all, America's future depends more on people than it does on products.

> *"A shift in American values and new respect for cultural diversity have weakened the pressures on immigrants to learn the language, go to school, and prepare for work."*

Immigrants Will Weaken America's Future

Joseph F. Coates

Historically, many immigrant groups successfully assimilated into American culture, embracing its traditions and values. In the following viewpoint, futurist Joseph F. Coates argues that this phenomenon of assimilation no longer holds true. As a prime example, Coates cites what he views as the lack of assimilation of Mexican immigrants in America's Southwest. Coates contends that Mexico's proximity to the Southwest and the ease with which Mexicans in the United States can return to their native country help maintain their cultural and linguistic ties to Mexico. Coates is president of Coates & Jarratt Inc., a Washington, D.C., policy research organization specializing in the study of the future.

As you read, consider the following questions:

1. How does Coates describe the "old American model" of immigration?
2. What does Coates believe could occur when Mexican-Americans gain more political power in the Southwest?
3. Which ethnic groups are and are not assimilating, in the author's opinion?

Joseph F. Coates, "America: 2001," *Across the Board*, April 1992. Reprinted by permission of The Conference Board, New York.

In a book entitled *The Future in America*, published in 1906, H.G. Wells wrote that America had "a vast and increasing proportion of unassimilable aliens in her substance" leading to "an ever-intensifying complication." Among these "aliens," he listed "South European peasants, Russian Jews, and the like." He then proceeded with intensely anti-Semitic sentiments, focusing on what he perceived as the self-isolation of the Jews.

Clearly, Wells, one of the greatest visionaries of the late-19th and early-20th centuries, stumbled badly in his assessment of the American immigration situation. In my opinion, there is no large population in the United States that more effectively embodies the aspirations of America—social, political, economic, educational, cultural, philanthropic, or otherwise—than Russian and other Eastern European Jews. Theirs is an incredible story of integration, assimilation, and ascendancy to success in every field of endeavor.

Similarly, the "South European peasants," by which Wells most likely meant Italians, represent another of the great immigration successes of America. One can scarcely pick up an annual report, a government agency profile, a Congressional agenda, or a program for arts and entertainment without seeing evidence of Italian-Americans' entrenchment in America's most esteemed institutions.

Among other things, Wells seems to have missed the essence of the American immigration success story. In contrast to the European model of permanent ghettoization and hundreds of years of hostility toward immigrants, or Britain's selective but standoffish assimilation, the American accomplishment has been to help its immigrants to Americanize.

The Old Model

America's social process has forced immigrants to go to school, learn the language, and seek education for jobs. In return, it has opened up to them opportunities in government and business. Yet this assimilation, unique in modern history, has also allowed these diverse masses to hold on to their individual cultural heritage—including food, entertainment, recreation, religious practices, annual celebrations, and so on—in any way they have chosen. In my judgment, the great American achievement has been homogenization in values, expectations, and performance at the public level, with reserve of and respect for cultural, social, and religious differences at the private level.

Today, however, we are fast approaching the limits of the old American model. This model worked fine for the waves of European immigrants arriving in our country up until the middle of this century. But it fails to apply to a more recent immigrant group, Mexicans, who are now entering the United States in large numbers. As of 1990, Mexican immigrants and their descendants comprised about 5.8 percent of the U.S. population and are among the fastest-growing minority groups. By early next century they surely will comprise at least 8 percent of the population.

The current Mexican immigration differs from previous immigration in two critical ways. First, Mexicans settle primarily along our Southern border, which means adjacent to their homeland. In comparison, immigrants who got off the boat at Ellis Island were thousands of miles away from their native countries. However much they may have wished to return to the homeland in 5 or 10 years, most found it economically impossible. Retiring in the homeland also proved to be unrealistic and undesirable for most immigrants; living in America for the bulk of one's lifetime changes one's views. In the case of Mexicans, however, an inexpensive airplane flight, bus ride, or a simple walk on foot will carry them back to the bosom of their family and cultural heritage. Thus, there is little of the psychological, economic, and linguistic rending apart of ties to the homeland that is so essential to the assimilation process.

Another difference in the Mexican immigration situation is that it is in large part illegal. In 1991 more than one million people were apprehended illegally entering the United States, most of them through the Mexican border. Unlike the open, legal entry that marked most European arrivals, much of the Mexican migration is characterized by fear and hiding, which further hinders assimilation.

Flexing Political Muscle

Given these conditions, my prediction is that, by the end of the century, Mexican-American political muscle will be exercised in our Southern states in unprecedented ways. Why the turn of the century? History shows that since the Civil War and the subsequent urbanization of America, almost all immigrant groups have lagged one to one-and-a-half generations behind their numbers in the exercise of political power. The reasons: unfamiliarity with American politics, uncertainty, fear of government, indifference, and attention to a personal agenda. By the turn of the century, Mexicans will have been immigrating into this country in large numbers for roughly 50 years, and will be poised to burst forth on the political scene.

Yet their political agenda will most likely not be in line with prevailing American values and aspirations; rather, it will be the hardscrabble agenda of a disaffected, alienated, poorly educated, occupationally underprepared group, with close cultural and linguistic affiliations to its home country and an incomplete assimilation into the American culture.

A shift in American values and new respect for cultural diversity have weakened the pressures on immigrants to learn the language, go to school, and prepare for work. The bizarre shape that bilingual education has taken in the United States guarantees that the bulk of the "beneficiaries" of bilingual education will speak no language well and be prepared for nothing in particular. Although the research is unequivocal that bilingual children perform better in school, the data distort the situation. Those data are based on children who are brought up in middle-class households, who speak two languages well, and who are therefore likely to live in an environment that promotes occupational achievement through education. The harsh, irreducible reality of bilingualism in the United States is that it is a sop to a particularly strident subgroup of minorities. In fact, bilingualism works to the disinterest of the putative beneficiaries. Bilingual education, as practiced in recent decades, is a divisive, not a unifying, force.

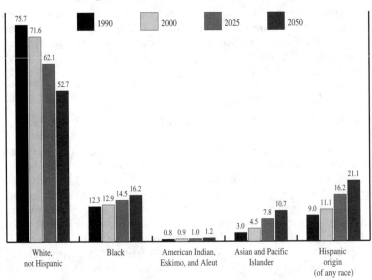

Percent of the Population, by Race and Hispanic Origin: 1990, 2000, 2025, and 2050

Source: U.S. Bureau of the Census, 1993.

By the turn of the century or shortly thereafter, politically active Mexican-Americans will call for greater recognition of their culture and their language, and for attention to the economic well-being of their people. Political concern for the Mexican homeland, burdened by its swelling population, underdeveloped industry, and stifling poverty, will increase to the point of being a full-fledged foreign-policy issue in the United States.

When Mexican-Americans finally begin to exercise their political power, there could well be a backlash as other groups struggle to adjust to the tipping political scales. At an extreme, all or portions of Canada could be courted to join the Union and provide a rebalance to favor the non-Hispanic population. In turn, this could encourage an irredentist movement in the South.

Indians and Chinese

Mexicans, of course, aren't the only immigrant group that will affect U.S. society. Indian and Chinese immigrants are entering the United States in large numbers. By the turn of the century, they will together make up more than 3 percent of the U.S. population. The Indians, unlike any other post–Civil War immigrant group, do not ghettoize, but arrive ready to merge into urban and suburban life. On the whole, Indian immigrants to this country are relatively well educated; they speak English, seek professional employment in business, science, and engineering, and have comparatively few problems assimilating. Chinese immigrants, however, have not only ghettoized but seem to be remaining so in large numbers even in the third and fourth generations. More research is in order to better understand the assimilation of both these groups, culturally and socially different than the European immigrants of years past.

In the future, the pace of assimilation by the Indian and Chinese immigrants will be slower than it has been because of decreasing transportation costs, which, as previously noted, allow immigrants to continually renew old ties to their homelands, thereby reducing the pace, pressure, and extent of assimilation. Nevertheless, because of their strong belief in education as the route to upward mobility and their commitment to professional occupations, these two groups will be a key to revitalizing the tired American economic machine.

Other Immigrants

In the next decade, we can also expect waves of well-educated and professional workers from central Europe and what was formerly the Soviet Union, as expectations of healthy economic growth in that region are disappointed. Western Europe will be the preferred first stop, with Canada and the United States the strong second choices.

Also on the move into the European and American communities are people of Muslim cultures. In Germany, and to an even greater extent in Sweden, extensive and consistent efforts to assimilate Turkish "guest workers"—laborers, many of them Muslim, who were originally brought into the countries on temporary work visas—have largely failed. Meanwhile, France is currently in turmoil over its relatively large numbers of unassimilated North Africans, primarily of Muslim background. A policy that allows the homelands of the immigrants to appoint clergymen to the Islamic churches in France is thought to be one factor that is hindering their assimilation into French society. This has slowed down the evolution of a French version of Islam that's more compatible with the cultural patterns of the larger society. The 1991 fundamentalist victory in national elections in Algeria [later nullified by the ruling government] has also raised fears of an aggressive religious fundamentalist movement in France.

The question remains of what will happen in the United States, which has recently seen an influx of Muslims from the Middle East and Pakistan. A growing Muslim fundamentalist movement in this country might be able to push its own agenda—particularly in regards to American policy toward countries in the Muslim world. This would be akin to the American Jewish population's general political support of Israel. By and large, however, religious fundamentalists in the United States, whether Christian, Jewish, post-Christian, or other, have tended to isolate themselves rather than seek radical political change.

Another sidelight on the changing patterns of immigration is the new migration of blacks from Haiti, West Africa, and the English-speaking islands of the Caribbean. Ambitious black immigrants may move ahead economically at a more rapid pace than much of the native-born black population, dividing the black community and stirring up ethnic crosscurrents in that racial bloc. To date, there has been virtually no exploration of the implications of new black immigration for native-born blacks.

Policy Changes

A foreseeable change in immigration policy over the next decade or so is the creation of a new transborder status of guest worker. Most transboundary migration is under the auspices of immigration for naturalization, refugee status, student status, or some other narrow or specific base of entry. The guest worker, however, has become such a phenomenon around the world that international legislation is likely. Such legislation will specifically preclude naturalization by marriage and automatic naturalization of the guest workers' children.

With the United States on course toward an increasingly polyethnic and polycultural society in the third millennium, it seems appropriate and timely that the United States reexamine its policies toward immigrants. A national commission should be created, under public or private auspices, to look at the implications of America's immigration policies for the next century. [The Immigration Enforcement Review Commission was created in 1990 and made various recommendations in 1994.] U.S. business involvement in such a commission would force the business community to address its long-term strategic interest in migration, investigate methods of increasing the economic well-being of immigrants to make them more effective producers and consumers of American goods, and evaluate the costs and benefits of restricted immigration. We should become what we want to be; but first we must know where our present circumstances are leading us.

"Aging is among the more powerful and ubiquitous structural trends occurring in the United States."

The Aging of America: Alternative Visions

Walter A. Hahn

In the following alternative visions of America's future, Walter A. Hahn presents four "future history" scenarios. Each scenario is from the viewpoint of the elder generation from one of four future time periods: Toward 1999, 2001+, 2020, and 2040. The demographic parameters of America are shifting to those of an aging population, and Hahn creates these scenarios to describe what he believes will be the viewpoint of elders at different times in the future. The story lines Hahn creates include potentially serious problems involving generational equity, health care, and other issues. His purpose is to urge policymakers to think in terms of the possible impacts that an increasingly aged population will have on America. Hahn (1921-1993), a futurist, was a senior fellow of the National Academy of Public Administration in Washington, D.C.

As you read, consider the following questions:

1. How will aging impact Social Security, according to Hahn?
2. What paradoxes does Hahn describe at the end of his first scenario?
3. What domestic conditions are forecast in Hahn's fourth scenario?

Excerpted from Walter A. Hahn, "Aging America," *The Annals of the American Academy of Political and Social Science*, vol. 522, July 1992, pp. 116-29. Copyright ©1992 by The American Academy of Political and Social Science. Reprinted by permission of Sage Publications, Inc.

Aging is among the more powerful and ubiquitous structural trends occurring in the United States. Present public policymakers and private institutional managers often behave as if they are unaware of the existence, size, or potential consequences of the aging trend. Most likely, they are postponing dealing with it, leaving it for their successors. The economic, social, political, and environmental impacts of this irreversible trend will continue to affect all of us well into the next century. What follows is a look at this trend from the viewpoint of a participant-observer futurist and elder—the term "senior citizen" can have negative connotations—who is both part of the problem and desires to be part of the solution.

This viewpoint opens with the parameters of the aging trend. . . . Then the focus narrows to elders, with specific examples of their thinking which may in part shape their and younger persons' futures. To give policymakers a substantive view of the aging trend over the next several decades, next are examples of the use of one of the futurist's more powerful tools, scenarios. Four time periods are covered: Toward 1999, 2001+, 2020, and 2040. These dates coincide with the time when, starting with the present, each succeeding generation of elders is active on the national scene. Note that it will be the elders of the time stated who are speaking.

The Trend(s)

Just what is this structural trend on aging in America that is receiving increased attention? . . . What "Aging America" is specifically about is that increasingly large proportion of us in the U.S. who are middle-aged, young old, or old old. The median age of 33 in 1990 will advance to 36.5 in 2000. Life expectancy is increasing, especially for women. Also, the aged are aging as we all live longer. In 1990, 12.4 percent of the population was over 65. By 2040 it will be over 20 percent. The number of those aged 85 to 94 will grow from 2.9 to 4 million between 1990 and the year 2000. But it is not only those numbers, ratios, and rates that make the difference for the future. We need to be aware of the impacts these changes are having on us at present and may have in the future. We also need to know what choices we have for affecting changes: positively, negatively, and for avoidance.

The qualitative view of "Aging America" is as dramatic as the quantitative. Past policies and institutional arrangements now present us with some very difficult situations. Although made with the best of intentions, most past decisions were based on the pervasive youth model of our society and without clear views of their future consequences. Take Social Security. We now have a large cadre of aging seniors, increasing in size. Due to the way we chose to fund Social Security, this group must now, and in the future, be supported by a much smaller group of current wage earners. Increases in both benefits and eligibility have exacerbated this situation. We are in a similar bind with health care benefits. Increasing costs for longer living by less well persons, the skyrocketing costs of new technology defensively applied, and a crushing load of paperwork combine to overload both the public and private capacities to pay for it all. . . .

Selected Scenarios

Scenarios help us to explore alternative futures for the enlightenment of policymaking and other decision makers. Scenarios are internally consistent stories, creative verbal snapshots in future time. They are not predictions or forecasts, but they help us to deal with both complexity and uncertainty. They usually respond to the question "What if . . . ?" and focus on a few consistent assumptions and variables of specific interest. Mostly, they are used in groups of three to seven and are from one to tens of pages long. The set of four to be presented here is typical in that one scenario is a view of more of the same, one is optimistic, another pessimistic, and one is a wild card. Often, all of the scenarios in one set are for the same time period, say, 15 years in the future.

The sample "future history" scenarios to follow, however, are each for a different time period: Toward 1999, 2001+, 2020, and 2040. The constant and unique factor will be that each scenario is told from the viewpoint of the generation of elders in the time period selected. The "we" in the text refers to each elder generation speaking as Americans of their time. These very brief scenarios only signal the story line and leave out much more than they include. *Omni* magazine would call them "thought bites."

Some assumptions pertain to all of the scenarios presented: no global wars or nuclear holocaust; no major natural or human-caused catastrophes; global interdependence (acknowledged or not); global population growth and environmental deterioration; surprises; and change, change, change.

Scenario 1: **Toward 1999**

Born between 1901 and 1924, we depression kids are better known as the GI generation. After all, we've seen five big wars and more little ones than we wanted to, but it was Pearl Harbor that defined us. We've also been through depressions, recessions, and some of the best times our country has known. We both shaped and were shaped by the twentieth century, and neither process is yet over for us. We are still 30 million strong. Some of us have imprinted lasting impressions on subsequent generations: Bob Hope, Billy Graham, Joe DiMaggio, Walt Disney, Ann

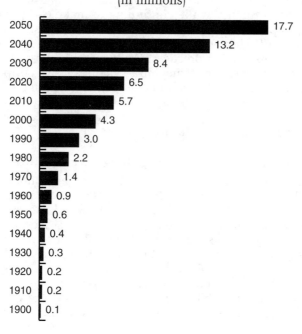

Population 85 Years and Older: 1900 to 2050
(in millions)

Year	Population
2050	17.7
2040	13.2
2030	8.4
2020	6.5
2010	5.7
2000	4.3
1990	3.0
1980	2.2
1970	1.4
1960	0.9
1950	0.6
1940	0.4
1930	0.3
1920	0.2
1910	0.2
1900	0.1

Source: U.S. Bureau of the Census, 1993.

Landers, John Wayne, and Tip O'Neill. We have supplied the last seven presidents and [elected] the first non-GI president in decades. Business as usual, more of the same, muddling through, and continuing to exercise our traditional values characterize our mood. Our world technological, economic, and political leadership positions are weakening but remain strong enough to be envied by most of the world's citizens. We watched passively while Germany and the European Community got together and the Soviet Union and Yugoslavia disintegrated. We are simultaneously a manufacturing, service, and agricultural nation with these sectors, respectively, declining, expanding, and hovering in precarious balance. We are weakened by structural employment, a ghetto underclass, growing illiteracy, huge debt, and massive apathy. Enough of us are personally well enough off, unthreatened, and hopeful of a better future to postpone dramatic reform. We support research in the billions for a Supercollider [a program for a massive tunnel of superconducting magnets] and in the low millions for dealing with the common cold. All this as drugs and rampant crime threaten our way of life. We have difficulty learning to live with our cultural diversity and to tolerate a widening range of life-styles and values. We want improved environmental quality while continuing to make exceptions and grant postponements in meeting standards. We desire more energy self-sufficiency as we expand imports and ease but not abandon conservation practices. We view with alarm the crumbling of urban and connecting infrastructures as we postpone the inevitable to the next guy's watch, forgetting—ignoring?—that it's our children who have the next watch. We push harder for our rights than we do in meeting our responsibilities, and we have yet to exercise foresight effectively.

Scenario 2: 2001 + : Launching a New Century

Sandwiched between the GI and Boomer generations, we radio kids were born between 1925 and 1942. The 40 million of us are now known as the Silent generation, which is a misnomer when noting some of our members: Gore Vidal, Ted Koppel, Pat Schroeder, Jesse Jackson, and T. Boone Pickens. We have lost John and Robert Kennedy, Martin Luther King, Marilyn Monroe, and (we think) Elvis Presley. We have early memories of V-E [Victory in Europe] and V-J [Victory in Japan] days and the A-bomb detonations, and later ones of Watergate and the Jimmy Carter "malaise." As elders, we get to help launch both a new century and a new millennium. But our predecessors have left us some mega-messes for our point of departure. Domestically, we continue to face crushing debts, ubiquitous crime and drug assaults, dependence on fossil fuels, growing tribalism and reemergent racism, decayed and obsolete infrastructures, consumption without saving, and more. We are still fighting learning to live *with* nature—a late-'90s northeaster this time wiped out ex-President George Bush's retirement home in Kennebunkport. Our Congress and the other 80,000-plus units of government are obsolete, overstaffed, underfunded, and increasingly incapable of both governance and service. Compensating for this is the increase of the vigor of the voluntary third sector in providing a wide variety of services. The one-term presidency and 12-year limit on legislators is helping to restore ethics in government. We still struggle under the staggering costs of the savings and loan crimes, cleaning up decades of toxic wastes, and dealing with acquired immune deficiency syndrome (AIDS). We are beginning to see the awesome bill for long-term elder care. Means-tested Medicare and taxing high-income-earner Social Security benefits have given us a modest start in vitalizing and extending those support mechanisms, but much remains. Lengthening the school year and other small changes have helped to educate the populace and the emerging knowledge-worker work force, but in the meantime we must suffer the pangs and losses due to illiteracy and an apathetic underclass. The 1998-99 tax increases have yet to generate sufficient income for reform. Globally, we have not reversed the decline in our technological and marketing leadership positions, not joined with other nations in pollution control and global management of critical resources like water and farmland, and not dealt with AIDS; we do not even have any assurance that peaceful coexistence with others will continue. Some launching!

Scenario 3: 2020: Boomers as Elders

We Boomers, born from 1943 to 1960, have always been the pig in the demographic python and still number about 25 million. Though variously called TV Babies, Hippies, Yuppies, or New Agers, we differ even more than a sample of our members would suggest: Oliver North, Donald Trump, Janis Joplin, Oprah Winfrey, Dan Quayle, John McEnroe, Al Gore, and Steve Jobs. Phrases like *"Brown* v. *Board of Ed,"* "Kent State," "Woodstock," "Apollo landing," "Cold War," "Nam," "Earth Day," and "Watergate" recall vivid memories. The new United Nations Peace Force helps stabilize the still-turbulent global scene. Domestically, the Social Security system is stressed to its limits and senior discounts have disappeared under the weight of numbers. The GI generation ran things so long that the Silents before us never learned how to do it. Their pitiful attempts to revitalize America at the turn of the century have only delayed reform. But at last things have gotten so bad that Americans of all stripes are being typically American and are acting together to "fix it." We banned guns in 2015 but it will take decades to get them off the streets. Elder Boomers lead in restructuring the education system and in repairing and modernizing our infrastructures. This is dramatically evidenced in our new integrated national compunications (computers plus communications) networks and in developing an effective multimode transportation system increasingly independent of fossil fuels. Ethical standards and efficiency are evidenced in the new streamlined participatory democracy forms of government at all levels. Privatization helps, while government sets the standards and rules. We all enjoy more leisure, much of which is spent in the now continuous learning we all pursue. Knowledge work dominates this "post-business" society, as Peter Drucker called it three decades ago. Quality and civility now dominate quantity and me-ism in economic and political affairs. Maybe some of this is due not only to the hands-on experience women have gained over the last thirty years as managers and leaders but also to the fact that they now significantly outnumber males at the polls and in the power centers. We seem to be beginning to realize that our mutual interest

61

is also our self-interest. There is a sense of positiveness and movement toward a more vibrant America—just in time!

Scenario 4: 2040: The Good Old Days Are Here Again

In the nineties we computer, latchkey kids had no catchy name as a group. We were just labeled "13ers" as the thirteenth American generation. We who were born from 1961 to 1981 now think of ourselves as the "Survivors." Recognizable names include Michael J. Fox, Mary Lou Retton, Tom Cruise, Brooke Shields, and Mike Tyson, but many new famous have evolved in the ensuing years. Our early memories are of *Roe v. Wade*, the *Challenger* disaster, Desert Storm and Panama, *A Nation At Risk*, Iran hostages, and the collapse of the USSR and the Cold War. Not all of the mega-messes of the turn of the century have been cleaned up, but we have survived the doomsday predictions of generations preceding us. We have inherited the new dynamics and style set by our immediate predecessors, which we feel bound to continue and to expand upon in building a revitalized America. AIDS was licked in the twenties and advanced knowledge of the human genome helps prevent similar scourges. National health care is improving and is now extended to all citizens. We elders are economically less well off than those before us, but culturally we have turned America's ethnic diversity to advantage. "Mosaic America" is a positive label these days. The economy is sound if not robust. The Canadian-Quebec-Mexican-U.S. North American Economic Community is at last functioning well. Also, we now focus more on the Pacific Rim and see a united, quasi-democratic China as a huge market. We now recycle more and pollute less, but we have decades of toxic wastes to deal with. Education is now seen as both a personal and national resource and is pursued on a life-long in-and-out basis in the now integrated public-private National Learning System. Globally, peace—as the absence of war—obtains but the Middle East continues to fester. The larger nations of the world threaten to splinter and many of the smaller ones constantly explore various forms of federation. Another step toward world governance was taken with the formation of the United Nations Green Force to set and enforce standards for global pollution and its cleanup. In the United States, we try to exercise our dual roles as American and Global citizens. We now recognize as a functioning generation the centurians, those within ten years (either way) of their hundredth birthday. The majority are women, of course.

So What?

America is aging. No one needs a futurist to see the numbers, but futurists can enhance policymakers' ability to see the scope and range of the impacts of the trend. The present and future aged are already born and there are lots of them. Some of you are reading this viewpoint. The large numbers of active, thinking elders will have consequences throughout society, the economy, and politics. Serious problems of housing, health care and delivery (who pays?), generational equity, social harmony (who decides?), and political action head a long list of yet-to-be-squarely-faced issues—and opportunities? More serious than being unaware of some of the consequences of America's aging is that many of the known issues are being ignored or postponed for successors to deal with. Whether the cause is current political or economic survival, or deeper feelings of being overwhelmed in the face of the insoluble, is not clear. It is no comfort to note that the aging issue must be handled in parallel with other issues.

Ten Major Trends

1. There are more elderly than ever before in history.
2. The elderly are an increasing proportion of our population.
3. Growth of the elderly will be steady but undramatic until 2011 when the Baby Boom begins to reach age 65.
4. Elderly women outnumber elderly men.
5. More persons will survive to the oldest ages.
6. As more survive, more also face chronic illness and disabilities.
7. Issues surrounding the care of the frail elderly will become more prevalent. At the same time, the young old have become pacesetters in new ways to spend the retirement years.
8. The elderly population will be more diverse in terms of racial composition and Hispanic origin in the coming decades.
9. The educational attainment of the elderly population will increase significantly in the coming years because younger cohorts were more likely to have completed high school and attended college than is true for the elderly of today.
10. Some elderly are economically secure. Others, especially many of the oldest old, those living alone, Blacks, American Indians, some Asian groups, and Hispanics have relatively high rates of poverty.

Source: U.S. Bureau of the Census, 1993.

Up to now, only one or two examples of the consequences of a trend or event have been offered, almost as if both the trends and the consequences were independent of each other. But, of course, we all know that everything is related to everything else. What might be the impacts of a number of such issues if they were acting in concert? For example, consider the breakup of families, immigration, population mobility, more self-selected TV than directed reading. Also look at the breakdown in education, with almost no geography, with little mathematics or civics, and with attractive electives outcompeting the hard stuff. All the generations born after the GIs and the boomers suffer from almost all of the foregoing divisive, rather than integrating, common knowledge and life-style experiences. Additionally, ethnic, racial, and religious rivalries have splintered our former common base of shared knowledge and customs. We have all but lost our historical melting-pot drives and our base of shared knowledge and experience. Therefore, we must now turn to a weakened and directionless education system to restore our ability to live together, function economically, and to govern ourselves.

The Three "Cs"

In the future, it will be necessary to think of formal education and literacy beyond the three Rs. The proposition is that for us in America to work, play, and live in peace in the twenty-first century, everyone needs to be literate in both the *same* three Rs and the *same* three Cs. The three Cs are culture, civics, and 'cience. Culture includes awareness and understanding of our heritage and values and the exercise of our intellectual and social creativity. Civics deals with how our public sector democracy works—its strategy, structure, and style. Lastly, 'cience concerns how nature, our artifacts, and our bodies and minds function. Additionally, of overriding importance is for every citizen to learn how to continue to learn.

Maybe the current generation of elders can help in the transition from a society that mostly grew up and grew older together to the more mosaic, individualized one of the present and future. . . .

The foregoing material has attempted to outline the present and future of aging in America in its global and national contexts. It has focused on the aged as part of the solution along with the usual approach of seeing the elders as the problem. As with other subjects, one of our critical needs is to not view the current and future situation only through the images and assumptions of the past. To deal with current and future problems and opportunities will require rethinking the conventional wisdom that constrains us from constructive innovation, action, and change. It is hoped that these dual views of aging from the inside and as generations moving through time will assist.

"We will not survive the twenty-first century with the twentieth century's ethics. The dangers are simply too great."

Ethics for the Twenty-First Century

Rushworth M. Kidder

Rushworth M. Kidder is president of the Institute for Global Ethics, a research and educational organization in Camden, Maine, and author of *Reinventing the Future: Global Goals for the Twenty-First Century*. In the following viewpoint, Kidder argues that society is developing new technologies without consideration of their moral and ethical consequences. Kidder criticizes the educational system for teaching about technology without discussing these consequences. Ethics and values, though, can change for the better in the future, the author contends. Kidder concludes that since important changes in society are preceded by changes in values, shifts in ethics and values must be studied now.

As you read, consider the following questions:

1. What was the real reason for the Chernobyl disaster, according to Kidder?
2. Why does Kidder believe the Human Genome Project will create serious privacy concerns in the next century?
3. According to the Harris poll cited by the author, where do American students look for authority in matters of truth?

Rushworth M. Kidder, "Ethics: A Matter of Survival," *The Futurist*, March/April 1992. Reproduced with permission from *The Futurist*, published by the World Future Society, 7910 Woodmont Ave., Suite 450, Bethesda, MD 20814.

Several years ago, I was—as far as I can tell—the first Western journalist to visit the Chernobyl nuclear power plant. I was taken there on a tour in the company of several engineers called in after the April 1986 explosion to clean it up. I learned that, on the night of the accident, two electrical engineers were "playing around" with reactor #4 in what the Soviets later described as an unauthorized experiment. The two engineers wanted to see how long a turbine would freewheel if they took the power off it. That meant shutting down reactor #4.

To do so, they had to override six separate computer-driven alarm systems. The first system came on and said, "Stop, go no further, terribly dangerous." And they shut off the alarm rather than the experiment, and went on to the next level. They even padlocked valves in the open position so that they would not shut automatically and stop the experiment.

Think for a minute about who these people were. In the context of the Soviet Union, jobs like those at Chernobyl were plum jobs. They went to the 4.0 averages, the 800 SATs, the Phi Beta Kappas of the Soviet Union. These men were not *dumb*. Then what was missing? What they lacked, apparently, was the sense of responsibility, the moral understanding, the sense of conscience, the understanding of ethics—however you want to put it—that somehow would have prevented them from going forward.

Before you can override a computer-alarm system, you have first got to engage some kind of an ethical override in your own consciousness. You've first got to block out that little voice that says, "Don't do this, it's dangerous!" Somehow, the two engineers at Chernobyl were capable of turning aside and shutting down that voice. And that shutdown is not a question of technology. It's a matter of ethics.

Technology and Ethics

Think back to the nineteenth century. What do you suppose we could have put two people in front of, saying "Do whatever you want, in as unethical a way as you wish," that could have produced the damage caused by Chernobyl? Suppose we loaded up the biggest ship of the nineteenth century and put a drunken captain in charge, so he could run it aground in Prince William Sound; could it possibly do the kind of damage the Exxon *Valdez* did? Where do you find in the nineteenth century a financial structure as big and as complicated and as powerful as today's savings-and-loan business in the United States that would have allowed a group of unethical bankers to produce the damage the S&L crisis has produced?

And we're still only in the twentieth century. Shift your thinking forward into the early years of the twenty-first century and ask yourself about the kinds of ethical questions that will arise there. Perhaps the biggest and most complex arise from the Human Genome Project—not because it will be a big *medical* issue, but because it will be a big *employment* issue.

Reprinted by permission of *The Futurist*.

Suppose your genetic "book" can be read. It tells me, your potential employer, that at such-and-such an age you are liable to develop this-or-that problem, and I am going to have to foot the bill for the problem. So what is my interest in hiring you as compared with somebody whose book is a bit cleaner? How does society cope with such an issue? We have no record at all as a society of willingly choosing not to know what is knowable. So it is inconceivable that we will choose *not* to know our employees' genomes. This will be one of the largest privacy questions that we will face in the twenty-first century, and it's essentially a question of ethics.

The point here is simply that our technology has leveraged our ethics in ways that we never saw in the past. Why is that? Isn't it largely because we spend tremendous amounts of effort in our educational system teaching about the nature of technology—and virtually no time at all talking about the moral, ethical consequences of that technology?

Yet, for all of our advanced systems and for all of our artificial intelligence, the decision-making stream continues to focus ever more pointedly, as it always has, on the thinking of one or two or half a dozen individuals sitting at the apex of that technology. That hasn't changed. What has changed is only the capacity to do terrific damage because of that decision making.

Fortunately, those structures can change—because the values system underlying the social systems can change. Futurist Earl Joseph suggests that, "as we gain new knowledge, values can be improved. Therefore, on the average, the deeper we penetrate the future, the better our values and ethics should become."

Recapturing a Sense of Standards

In the nineteenth century, one of the highest goals of Western nations was a sense of standards. We took our standards out into the rest of the world, colonized other regions, and imposed those standards. Were we tolerant of what we found there? Not at all. If the people whom we were trying to "civilize" didn't want to get "civilized," we went out and "civilized" them anyway! At the end of a gun, or however we had to do it, but we civilized them. Why? To bring them up to our standards.

By the 1960s, this attitude had shifted 180 degrees. Tolerance was what mattered most. As long as somebody said, "Yes, this is what I stand for, this is what I want to do," one was expected to be wholly tolerant of any conceivable value structure.

The job of the twenty-first century is not to forget the terrific progress we've made toward tolerance, because it has been invaluable in creating and incorporating a pluralistic society. At the same time, however, we must begin within that context to recapture a sense of the standards that in many cases appears to have been lost.

One of the places this lack of standards shows up is in the U.S. education system. Let me cite a few statistics. These are not statistics that tell you how awful it is that the United States somehow can't compete with the Japanese and the Germans on math and literature. These speak to the ethical sense of American students. Sixty-five percent of high-school students admit that they would cheat to pass an important exam. A similar percentage are ready to inflate their expense accounts when they enter the corporate world, or lie to achieve a business objective.

Remember, these are not merely students we're talking about.

They are, in fact, Western culture's middle managers in 2015 and its CEOs in 2030. These are the people who are going to administer *your* pension plans.

A Louis Harris poll for the Girl Scouts asked 5,000 American students where they would look to find the greatest authority in matters of truth. Where would they turn for that sense of authority? The answers that came back are very interesting. At the bottom are the media and the sciences. A few percentage points higher come parents and religion. Can you guess what the bulk of those students say is the greatest authority in matters of truth? "Me." The student himself or herself. These students tell us that there is no source of authority beyond their own experience. "I have not seen anyone out there that I can trust," they're saying. "I've got to go by my gut instinct. I've got to do whatever feels right, whatever turns me on, whatever is situational, relative, negotiable." That reply speaks volumes about the ethical standards that we are now seeing.

Tracking Value Shifts

Fortunately, as the century closes, this entire subject of ethics is becoming a very serious concern for an awful lot of people. That's why the Institute for Global Ethics was founded. It aims to track value shifts as we move into the next century.

The first issue of *Insights on Global Ethics*, our monthly newsletter, leads with a story from Mexico, looking at the Mexican public's changing attitude toward corruption. Mexico is no longer the business-as-usual, corruption-as-usual place we've all assumed it to be. There seems to be a groundswell of public opinion saying, "We can't live this way. We must change." Future issues will look at things like the question of marriage versus cohabitation in Sweden, the work ethic in Japan, and values education in Ukraine.

Of course, we could wait until the twenty-first century, and then we could read the results of these ethical changes in the economic and social data. Or we can get at them now and begin to track the values shifts that are already occurring. Why is that important? Because any meaningful social and political and economic change is preceded by a change in values. If we want to devote our energies to looking into the changes that are most going to dictate the future, we must look at the questions of ethics in the twenty-first century.

One thing seems clear: We will not survive the twenty-first century with the twentieth century's ethics. The dangers are simply too great—and the ethical barometer is simply too low.

Periodical Bibliography

The following articles have been selected to supplement the diverse views presented in this chapter.

Brian Bremner	"A Spicier Stew in the Melting Pot," *Business Week*, December 21, 1992.
Bill Clinton	"Education and Repairing the Family," *New Perspectives Quarterly*, Winter 1993.
Francis Fukuyama	"Immigrants and Family Values," *Commentary*, May 1993.
Daniel James	"To Cut Spending, Freeze Immigration," *The Wall Street Journal*, June 24, 1993.
Florence Karlstrom and Dick Sheen	"Families of the Twenty-First Century: For Better, or Worse?" *Futures Research Quarterly*, Summer 1993. Available from World Future Society, 7910 Woodmont Ave., Suite 450, Bethesda, MD 20814.
Christene Kene	"Generational Equity: Emergent Public Policy Concerns for the '90s," *Futures Research Quarterly*, Summer 1991.
Michael Marien	"Education and Learning in the Twenty-First Century," *Vital Speeches of the Day*, March 15, 1992.
David Orr	"Schools for the Twenty-First Century," *Resurgence*, September/October 1993. Available from Rodale Press, 33 E. Minor St., Emmaus, PA 18049.
Jeffrey S. Passel and Michael Fix	"Myths About Immigrants," *Foreign Policy*, Summer 1994.
PC World	"Online Commuting: Big Benefit for Business and Employees," May 1994.
Louis S. Richman	"Struggling to Save Our Kids," *Fortune*, August 10, 1992.
Richard W. Riley	"The Secretary of Education on Reinventing Education," *The Education Digest*, January 1994.
Wendy L. Schultz	"Culture in Transition: Alternative Futures of Immigration, Ethnic Composition, and Community Conflict Within the U.S.," *Futures Research Quarterly*, Winter 1993.
Thomas Toch	"Selling the Schools: Is Private Enterprise the Future of Public Education in America?" *U.S. News & World Report*, May 2, 1994.
Pete Wilson	"Securing Our Nation's Borders," *Vital Speeches of the Day*, June 15, 1994.

2 CHAPTER

Technological Change: How Fast and to What End?

AMERICA BEYOND 2001

Chapter Preface

Technological advancements are frequently acclaimed by many people as a boon to health, leisure, work, and other facets of life. Consider, for example, the historical impact of innovations such as airplanes, automobiles, computers, and medicines as well as their continued improvement.

It is often assumed that technology offers more of an opportunity for progress than a threat to humanity. Daniel Burris, author of *Technotrends: How to Use Technology to Go Beyond Your Competition*, introduces readers to "twenty-four new tools for the twenty-first century," including advanced compact discs, digital interactive television, and endoscopic surgery, which he believes will enable their users to "gain the decisive edge" in business and technology. Similarly, author McKinley Conway goes so far as to say, "Technology will become the top political and economic issue of the times, as it becomes clearer that scientific prowess is the key to leadership."

However, many others fear that powerful emerging technologies could bring untold harm in such areas as employment and personal privacy. According to Professor Ernest Braun at the Center for Technology Strategy in Britain, "It is clutching at straws if we believe that the wave of technological innovations related to information and communication technologies (ICT) will herald the beginning of a new economic upswing. The view that ICT is a destroyer of jobs is much more plausible." Cryptographer Whitfield Diffie sees privacy being continually under attack by "new technologies that will expose our secrets."

The effect on society of the increasing pace of technological innovation into the twenty-first century may be taken lightly by some but is of concern to many others. This effect is one of the issues debated in the following chapter on technological change.

"The time has come to make industrial competitiveness the basis for [developing critical technologies]."

Technology Can Secure America's Future

Andrew Pollack et al.

In the following viewpoint, a team of *New York Times* science and technology writers highlights emerging technologies that are likely to bolster America's economy in the future. Consulting with government, industry, and university experts, the writers compiled a list of ten critical and promising technologies that are ideal for investment to secure America's future. For the sake of brevity, three technologies—solar energy, supercomputers, and superconductors—are excluded. The writers include Andrew Pollack, William J. Broad, Barnaby J. Feder, John Markoff, and John Holusha.

As you read, consider the following questions:

1. According to experts cited by the authors, what should critical technologies address?
2. What do the authors believe are the possible applications for each technology?
3. What would be the benefits of a "gigabit network," according to the authors?

Trains that float above their tracks for a smooth, fast ride. Enormously powerful computers that will understand speech and help design new drugs. Motors the size of a dust speck, battery-powered cars, genetically engineered supercrops.

The coming decade [1990s] promises great progress on these and other technologies that have the potential to bolster the nation's economic well-being and help humanity. It also promises to be a decade of conflict as different industries argue for Government help in developing particular technologies. . . .

Lists of critical technologies have recently become quite popular. The Defense Department and Commerce Department have each made lists, [as well as] the White House Office of Science and Technology Policy. The Computer Systems Policy Project and the Aerospace Industries Association of America, two trade groups, have made lists for their respective industries. Other lists have been made in Japan and Europe.

The lists are similar to one another and to the *Times*'s choices. Semiconductors, biotechnology and advanced computing place on virtually all the lists. "The striking fact is the common ground out there from country to country and agency to agency," said Daniel F. Burton Jr., executive vice president of the Council on Competitiveness, a group of industry, academic and labor union officials that [has] its own list.

Winners and Losers

Government [has said it] should not be picking winners and losers. But some scientists and industry executives say such choices are inevitably, if implicitly, made whenever money is spent in one area and not another. And with pressures tightening on the Federal and industrial research and development budgets, such choices are likely to become even more necessary.

In the past, critical technologies were mainly those deemed necessary for national defense. But with the cold war subsiding, many executives and policy makers say the time has come to make industrial competitiveness the basis for the list.

Still others say that neither national security nor competitiveness is the appropriate standard. They say critical technologies are those that satisfy human needs, like pollution control and affordable housing, rather than technologies that help American companies sell more television sets.

"There's a real need for a compelling philosophy for investing in science and technology that motivates people without resorting to these base motives of helping ourselves and beggaring our neighbors," said Gary Chapman, executive director of Computer Professionals for Social Responsibility, a nonprofit group.

In compiling the list below, all the criteria were considered. The technologies are not ranked in order of importance. Unavoidably, some deserving technologies, including robotics and opto-electronics, were omitted. Some technologies on the list will undoubtedly turn out to be duds while technologies that cannot even be envisioned now will end up recasting the world.

Rotors and Gears for Tiny Robots

The saga of the incredible shrinking machine is expected to get a bold new chapter in the 1990's as scientists around the world perfect a new class of motors, sensors and mechanical devices so small that some would fit into the period at the end of this sentence.

The microscopic machines are seen as potentially having a wealth of medical, industrial and other applications. Japan has embarked on a 10-year, $200 million program to develop tiny robots that could be used for everything from surgery to inspecting nuclear power plants. Scientists at the University of Wisconsin are already making metallic gears so small several could rest on the head of a pin.

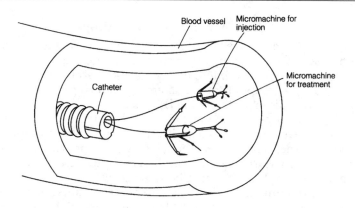

Micromachines tethered to a catheter treat a damaged blood vessel.

Look Japan, August 1993. Used with permission.

"There's no question it's going to be a multibillion-dollar field," said George A. Hazelrigg, an official of the National Science Foundation who oversees the Federal agency's financing of micromechanics. "It's going to grow very quickly.". . .

At Carnegie-Mellon University in Pittsburgh, researchers are trying to perfect a tiny biomedical sensor for measuring blood flow. At its heart is a small rotor with four blades, together about 300 micrometers wide, or the width of three human hairs.

It rotates as blood moves through it, allowing scientists to measure flow in coronary arteries.

In general, Dr. Hazelrigg said, an area of micromechanics already undergoing rapid commercial growth involves mechanical sensors that detect pressure, motion or vibration. Normally such sensors are fairly large and unreliable. But tiny ones now being built, he said, are potentially thousands of times smaller than traditional ones and hundreds of times cheaper, more reliable and more accurate. The Jet Propulsion Laboratory in Pasadena, Calif., he said, once used accelerometers on planetary probes that were the size of a shoebox. Now they are the size of a postage stamp and shrinking fast.

"They're 100 to 10,000 times more sensitive than the bigger ones," Dr. Hazelrigg noted. . . .

The National Science Foundation now supports more than a dozen American universities that do research in micromechanics, Dr. Hazelrigg said. Its annual budget for the work is about $2 million. Many American researchers would like to see the financing doubled, noting that Europe and Japan have launched ambitious efforts in the field. . . .

A New Ark of Beasts and Crops

In the 17 years since scientists first managed to splice genes from one species of living organism into another, billions of dollars have been poured into biotechnology research and development. Only a trickle of products emerged during the 1980's; a steady stream is expected in the [1990's].

Only a small percentage of the more than 100,000 genes that define humans have been definitively mapped. Work on plants and most other animals is not much further along. Genetic engineers are also searching for more precise, reliable and inexpensive methods to transfer genes between species.

Besides technical barriers, biotechnologists must also overcome regulatory and social problems, like resolving the conditions under which genetically engineered crop plants or animals can be released into the environment. The new technology will bring gain to some but pain to others. Some farmers fear that the use of genetically engineered growth hormones to raise milk production will simply drive small farmers out of business without providing long-term benefits to consumers.

Biotechnology's most conspicuous achievements to date have come in the medical sector. Many diagnostic compounds have been produced by genetic engineering, as have therapeutic products like human growth hormone, used to combat dwarfism. In the coming years, experts expect genetic engineers will create treatments for cancer, immune-system diseases, cardiovascular illnesses and other maladies. In some cases, the human body will be stimulated to defend or repair itself by gene therapy, the implantation of genetically altered cells.

While medical applications may seize most of the headlines, the technology may have equally dramatic effects on agriculture. Until now, plant and animal breeding have depended on choosing traits already present within a species' natural gene pool. Genetic engineering puts that process on fast forward by enabling gene splicers to induce valuable mutations instead of waiting for nature to produce them. . . .

A Merger of TV and Computing

The line between the computer and the television is blurring: increasingly, the computer can display video images and high-quality sound, while the television has grown from offering a one-way broadcast to a machine that can be used to compose, store and retrieve personally tailored programs.

On the one hand, this evolution gives the United States a new opportunity to re-enter the consumer electronics business after having lost the television market to the Japanese; on the other hand, Japan has a new chance to gain dominance of the personal computer industry.

High-definition television [HDTV] would permit movie-quality displays, though the screens must be large to perceive it. They would also let users store and manipulate images far beyond the ability of today's videocassette recorders. The technology is being pushed aggressively by both government and industry in the United States, Europe and Japan.

HDTV advocates say that developing advanced television systems for consumer markets could bring significant advances in related technological areas critical to future success in the entire electronics industry.

For example, HDTV may spark the development of a new generation of flat, lightweight video screens on which high-resolution color images can be formed. Called flat-panel displays, they are barely thicker than a heavy plate of glass and could replace the bulky cathode-ray tubes now used in desktop computers, televisions and other consumer electronics. Both start-up companies and large corporations like I.B.M. and Xerox have developed new flat-panel display technologies that match the best available in Japan. But still missing is a commitment on the part of United States manufacturers to finance the production of these displays on the scale necessary for consumer markets. . . .

Those who advocate even greater investment in HDTV argue that the HDTV industry could in time use more microprocessors and memory chips than the computer business does today, and as such it could become the driving force in the semiconductor industry. But if Japanese consumer electronics companies begin manufacturing systems that have computer features at today's television prices, they will probably take away some of the personal-computer market now dominated by American companies.

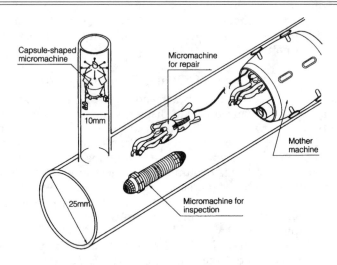

Various micromachines inspect and repair a section of pipe that is too small to allow human access.

Look Japan, August 1993. Used with permission.

"We've decided that the semiconductor industry is vital to national security," said William F. Schreiber, an electrical engineer who directed the Advanced Television Research Program at the Massachusetts Institute of Technology. "If we don't want it to be on welfare permanently we have to have a healthy consumer electronics industry.". . .

Reinventing Silicon Circuits

Microelectronic circuits embedded on pieces of silicon are the building blocks of modern electrical devices, from computers and communication equipment to consumer electronics goods. They are also critical components of weaponry, automobile-engine control systems to improve fuel efficiency and factory automation systems.

The performance of these vital components will continue to improve through the 1990's, rippling through the economy. The number of transistors that can be put on a chip will increase from about one million to close to 100 million. As that happens, more and more of the value of a computer will be contained in the chip. Complex chips, specialized for particular tasks, hold out the best hope of achieving long-sought goals like computers that can understand speech or interpret scenes.

The United States still leads in designs of clever circuitry but lags in the ability to manufacture chips. Sematech, the consortium financed by the Government and the semiconductor industry, is seeking to redress that imbalance. It is also trying to keep alive the endangered American manufacturers of chip-making equipment.

But Sematech alone, even if it is successful, will not be enough, experts say. A big problem for the United States is not technology but capital. Most American companies can no longer afford to build advanced manufacturing plants, which cost several hundred million dollars now and promise to keep getting more expensive.

Krishna C. Saraswat, an electrical engineering research professor at Stanford University, said one goal should be to use computer automation and other techniques to develop low-cost factories affordable by the small companies that often lead the industry in innovation. "If we can provide that opportunity, there will be many more companies willing to stay in business," he said. . . .

New Networks for the Nation

The "gigabit network" would make it possible to transmit computer data and video images among the nation's supercomputer centers, research laboratories and universities, as well as to businesses and homes. This network of fiber-optic cables, which would completely replace existing copper lines, is viewed by many scientists and executives as both a vital research tool and an essential part of the country's "information infrastructure" for the next century.

Despite vocal support from both Democratic and Republican legislators and from the [former] Bush Administration, Federal financing to develop a high-speed nationwide computer network failed in Congress in 1990. But this setback is probably temporary.

A gigabit network would permit researchers to share vast amounts of scientific and technical data. Doctors in their offices could view medical imaging animations produced by advanced diagnostic equipment in hospitals. A huge array of information, entertainment and business services would be created.

For example, a high-speed digital network could make the materials stored in the nation's best libraries instantly available to readers in thousands of community libraries around the country.

Or a home television viewer could choose to view whatever movie he or she wanted by selecting from a library of thousands of possible choices. In businesses, holding conferences by video, now expensive and inconvenient, would become commonplace, making it possible to minimize business travel. . . .

For example, one of the high-speed network projects now being coordinated by scientists at the California Institute of Technology would use the network to link different types of supercomputers separated by thousands of miles into a single machine many times more powerful.

Replacing the nation's copper telephone wiring with a network of fiber-optic cables would also have a dramatic impact on the nation's economy, say advocates like Al Gore. Just as the national highway system, constructed in the 1950's, brought about unexpected new economic activity all over the country, a national data highway could spawn dozens of research services and businesses. Both in Europe and Japan large efforts are under way to modernize older telecommunications networks to permit them to carry high-speed computer communications.

Researchers estimate that to install a similar network reaching into all of the homes and businesses that now have telephone service in the United States might ultimately cost $200 billion.

Instead of Metal, Novel Ceramics

To push beyond the present frontiers of technology, it will be necessary in many instances to develop materials with strengths and properties now unattainable.

Conventional metals cannot withstand the searing temperatures that would be encountered in the high speed travel, many times the speed of sound, likely to be attained by the next generation of jet engines and experimental aircraft. Projects like the National Aerospace Plane, which is to fly into space from an ordinary airfield, will require development of ceramics and ceramic-metal composites.

One hurdle, materials specialists say, is that most engineers are familiar with metals and may not be comfortable incorporating ceramics or composites in new designs. "The danger is that important technologies will slip through the cracks," said George H. Beall, a research fellow at Corning Inc.

The demands of projects like the one intended to double the power-to-weight ratio of jet engines by the year 2000 will force designers to consider new materials. "The rule of thumb is that 70 percent of the improvement in performance will come from new materials," said Karl Prewo, manager of materials sciences at United Technologies, which makes Pratt & Whitney engines.

"You are going to see a lot of replacement of metallic superalloys by ceramic matrix and carbon-carbon materials" in jet engines, Mr. Prewo said. The reason is "they have higher temperature performance and lighter weight." If the turbine in a jet engine can be made lighter, then the components supporting it do not have to be as robust, which improves power-weight ratio. . . .

Software Writing

As medical equipment, airplanes and weapons become increasingly computerized, errors in programming will increasingly have potentially fatal results unless ways can be found to produce software more quickly and reliably.

Although the cost of computer hardware continues to decline, program writing has not, since it is still a labor-intensive process. Not only is software becoming a higher share of total computing costs, but its development time is often the bottleneck that impedes full use of new computer technology.

Most big companies now spend far more of their data processing budget on software than hardware. Yet they also find themselves some two years behind in developing all the software they need. Programs can now be of extraordinary complexity, with millions of lines of instructions.

"The major issue for the software people is the enormous complexity we're trying to build into systems," said Larry Druffel, director of the Software Engineering Institute at Carnegie-Mellon University.

One solution would be better tools for helping programmers write programs automatically and check them for errors. A major gain in productivity could come from reusing software. A technique known as object-oriented programming, which allows software to be developed as small modules that can be combined in various combinations, holds promise of making reuse more common.

Experts caution that technical fixes alone won't do the job. Organization of people is crucial. Software development "needs to become more of an engineering discipline," said Victor R. Basili, professor of computer science at the University of Maryland. "It's treated too often as an art form, still."

New software and development tools are also needed to capitalize on new frontiers in computing. These include parallel processing to increase computer speed; distributed computing, in which tasks are spread over many small computers instead of one large one to save money; and multimedia computing, in which computers create and display images and sound as well as text and data.

Software has long been an American stronghold, but warning signs are on the horizon. Recent observations by Dr. Basili and others found that Japanese companies are often producing software with much lower error rates than American companies.

John Armstrong, vice president for science and technology at I.B.M., said, "It would be a mistake to conclude that we in the U.S. are uniquely good at software."

"The technologies created and disseminated by modern Western societies are out of control and desecrating the fragile fabric of life on Earth."

Technology Can Be Damaging

Chellis Glendinning

Chellis Glendinning is a New Mexico psychologist and author of *When Technology Wounds: The Human Consequences of Progress.* In the following viewpoint, Glendinning describes how the Luddites of nineteenth-century England opposed the introduction of new technologies by destroying machinery. The Luddites, Glendinning notes, believed these technologies threatened the bonds of family and community. Aligning herself with an emerging neo-Luddite movement instigated by scientists, thinkers, and activists, she warns that technological progress is "out of control and desecrating the fragile fabric of life on Earth." Glendinning argues that dangerous technologies—nuclear, chemical, television, and others—should be dismantled and replaced with technologies that have a benign effect on the earth.

As you read, consider the following questions:

1. According to Glendinning, what does technology consist of?
2. What do technologies tend to be structured for, in Glendinning's opinion?
3. Which technologies does the author believe are best for "life on Earth"?

Chellis Glendinning, "Notes Toward a Neo-Luddite Manifesto," *Utne Reader*, March/April 1990. Reprinted with permission.

Most students of European history dismiss the Luddites of 19th century England as "reckless machine-smashers" and "vandals" worthy of mention only for their daring tactics. Probing beyond this interpretation, though, we find a complex, thoughtful, and little-understood social movement whose roots lay in a clash between two worldviews.

The worldview that 19th century Luddites challenged was that of *laissez-faire* capitalism with its increasing amalgamation of power, resources, and wealth, rationalized by its emphasis on "progress."

The worldview they supported was an older, more decentralized one espousing the interconnectedness of work, community, and family through craft guilds, village networks, and townships. They saw the new machines that owners introduced into their workplaces—the gig mills and shearing frames—as threats not only to their jobs, but to the quality of their lives and the structure of the communities they loved. In the end, destroying these machines was a last-ditch effort by a desperate people whose world lay on the verge of destruction.

Barraged by Technologies

The current controversy over technology is reminiscent of that of the Luddite period. We too are being barraged by a new generation of technologies—two-way television, fiber optics, biotechnology, superconductivity, fusion energy, space weapons, supercomputers. We too are witnessing protest against the onslaught. A group of [University of California at] Berkeley students gathered in Sproul Plaza to kick and smash television sets as an act of "therapy for the victims of technology." A Los Angeles businesswoman hiked onto Vandenberg Air Force Base and beat a weapons-related computer with a crowbar, bolt cutters, hammer, and cordless drill. Villagers in India resist the bulldozers cutting down their forests by wrapping their bodies around tree trunks. People living near the Narita airport in Japan sit on the tarmac to prevent airplanes from taking off and landing. West Germans climb up the smokestacks of factories to protest emissions that are causing acid rain, which is killing the Black Forest.

Desperate Neo-Luddites

Such acts echo the concerns and commitment of the 19th century Luddites. Neo-Luddites are 20th century citizens—activists, workers, neighbors, social critics, and scholars—who question the predominant modern worldview, which preaches that unbridled technology represents progress. Neo-Luddites have the courage to gaze at the full catastrophe of our century: The technologies created and disseminated by modern Western societies are out of control and desecrating the fragile fabric of life on Earth. Like the early Luddites, we too are a desperate people seeking to protect the livelihoods, communities, and families we love, which lie on the verge of destruction.

What Is Technology?

Just as recent social movements have challenged the idea that current models of gender roles, economic organizations, and family structures are necessarily "normal" or "natural," so the Neo-Luddite movement has come to acknowledge that technological progress and the kinds of technologies produced in our society are not simply "the way things are."

As philosopher Lewis Mumford pointed out, technology consists of more than machines. It includes the techniques of operation and the social organizations that make a particular machine workable. In essence, a technology reflects a worldview. Which particular forms of technology—machines, techniques, and social organizations—are spawned by a particular worldview depend on its perception of life, death, human potential, and the relationship of humans to one another and to nature.

In contrast to the worldviews of a majority of cultures around the world (especially those of indigenous people), the view that lies at the foundation of modern technological society encourages a mechanistic approach to life: to rational thinking, efficiency, utilitarianism, scientific detachment, and the belief that the human place in nature is one of ownership and supremacy. The kinds of technologies that result include nuclear power plants, laser beams, and satellites. This worldview has created and promoted the military-industrial-scientific-media complex, multinational corporations, and urban sprawl.

Stopping the destruction brought by such technologies requires not just regulating or eliminating individual items like pesticides or nuclear weapons. It requires new ways of thinking about humanity and new ways of relating to life. It requires the creation of a new worldview.

Principles of Neo-Luddism

1. *Neo-Luddites are not anti-technology.* Technology is intrinsic to human creativity and culture. What we oppose are the *kinds* of technologies that are, at root, destructive of human lives and communities. We also reject technologies that emanate from a worldview that sees rationality as the key to human potential, material acquisition as the key to human fulfillment, and technological development as the key to social progress.

2. *All technologies are political.* As social critic Jerry Mander writes in *Four Arguments for the Elimination of Television,* technologies are not neutral tools that can be used for good or evil

Technology Has Failed Humanity

They hear the clank-and-whir of a garage-door opener and envision the obsolescence of skin-to-skin sex.

They see electronic books and imagine a planet encased in concrete, ruled by a handful of technological tyrants at computer-linked mega-corporations.

It's a vision of societal metamorphosis that has science fiction–fueled cyberpunks raising glasses of synthetic brain booster to toast the future: "Zoom!"

But a growing and increasingly vociferous group of skeptics say someone should have long ago hollered, "Stop!"

"Take a hard look at what technology has promised for the past 100 years—peace, universal health, economic equality, leisure, joy," says Jerry Mander, dean of what might be termed the neo-Luddite movement.

"Has it lived up to that?"

Most political, economic and historical observers will answer, "You bet"—at least relative to the way things used to be.

But neo-Luddites respond that society's perspective has been warped by surrounding technologies. They recite a litany of evidence—ozone holes, toxic pollution, disintegration of Eastern [European] nuclear reactors—to suggest that technological dependence may cause humanity to go the way of eight-track tapes.

Now, the skeptics say, another generation of gadgetry and techno-tinkering—from video-telephones to computerized smart bombs—has pushed society to a watershed. We'd better look hard, they say, before we take this flying leap into the new "mega-technologies" that will fundamentally alter human existence.

"We have a hard time imagining life before television or cars. We do not remember a United States of mainly forests and quiet," says Mander, author of the book *In the Absence of the Sacred: The Failure of Technology and Survival of the Indian Nations*.

"As we move into these larger and larger technological forms, we're dealing with the complete takeover of nature . . . and in the end, probably the destruction of humanity as well."

Bob Sipchen, *Los Angeles Times*, February 25, 1992.

---

depending on who uses them. They are entities that have been consciously structured to reflect and serve specific powerful interests in specific historical situations. The technologies created by mass technological society are those that serve the perpetuation of mass technological society. They tend to be structured for short-term efficiency, ease of production, distribution, marketing, and profit potential—or for war-making. As a result, they tend to create rigid social systems and institutions that people do not understand and cannot change or control.

As Mander points out, television does not just bring entertainment and information to households across the globe. It offers corporations a surefire method of expanding their markets and controlling social and political thought. (It also breaks down family communications and narrows people's experience of life by mediating reality and lowering their span of attention.)

Similarly, the Dalkon Shield intrauterine device did not just make birth control easier for women. It created tremendous profits for corporate entrepreneurs at a time when the largest generation ever born in the United States was coming of age and oral contraceptives were in disfavor. (It also damaged hundreds of thousands of women by causing septic abortions, pelvic inflammatory disease, torn uteruses, sterility, and death.)

Critiquing Technology

3. *The personal view of technology is dangerously limited.* The often-heard message "but I couldn't live without my word processor" denies the wider consequences of widespread use of computers (toxic contamination of workers in electronic plants and the solidifying of corporate power through exclusive access to new information in data bases).

As Mander points out, producers and disseminators of technologies tend to introduce their creations in upbeat, utopian terms. Pesticides will increase yields to feed a hungry planet! Nuclear energy will be "too cheap to meter." The pill will liberate women! Learning to critique technology demands fully examining its sociological context, economic ramifications, and political meanings. It involves asking not just what is gained— but what is lost, and by whom. It involves looking at the introduction of technologies from the perspective not only of human use, but of their impact on other living beings, natural systems, and the environment.

Program for the Future

1. As a move toward dealing with the consequences of modern technologies and preventing further destruction of life, *we favor the dismantling of the following destructive technologies:*

- nuclear technologies—which cause disease and death at every stage of the fuel cycle;
- chemical technologies—which re-pattern natural processes through the creation of synthetic, often poisonous chemicals and leave behind toxic and undisposable wastes;
- genetic engineering technologies—which create dangerous

mutagens that when released into the biosphere threaten us with unprecedented risks;

- television—which functions as a centralized mind-controlling force, disrupts community life, and poisons the environment;
- electromagnetic technologies—whose radiation alters the natural electrical dynamic of living beings, causing stress and disease; and
- computer technologies—which cause disease and death in their manufacture and use, enhance centralized political power, and remove people from direct experience of life.

Technology by and for the People

2. *We favor a search for new technological forms.* As political scientist Langdon Winner advocates in *Autonomous Technology*, we favor the creation of technologies by the people directly involved in their use—not by scientists, engineers, and entrepreneurs who gain financially from mass production and distribution of their inventions and who know little about the context in which their technologies are used.

We favor the creation of technologies that are of a scale and structure that make them understandable to the people who use them and are affected by them. We favor the creation of technologies built with a high degree of flexibility so that they do not impose a rigid and irreversible imprint on their users, and we favor the creation of technologies that foster independence from technological addiction and promise political freedom, economic justice, and ecological balance.

3. *We favor the creation of technologies in which politics, morality, ecology, and technics are merged for the benefit of life on Earth:*

- community-based energy sources utilizing solar, wind, and water technologies—which are renewable and enhance both community relations and respect for nature;
- organic, biological technologies in agriculture, engineering, architecture, art, medicine, transportation, and defense—which derive directly from natural models and systems;
- conflict resolution technologies—which emphasize cooperation, understanding, and continuity of relationship; and
- decentralized social technologies—which encourage participation, responsibility, and empowerment.

4. *We favor the development of a life-enhancing worldview in Western technological societies.* We hope to instill a perception of life, death, and human potential into technological societies that will integrate the human need for creative expression, spiritual experience, and community with the capacity for rational thought and functionality. We perceive the human role not as the dominator of other species and planetary biology, but as integrated into the natural world with appreciation for the sacredness of all life.

We foresee a sustainable future for humanity if and when Western technological societies restructure their mechanistic projections and foster the creation of machines, techniques, and social organizations that respect both human dignity and nature's wholeness. In progressing towards such a transition, we are aware: We have nothing to lose except a way of living that leads to the destruction of all life. We have a world to gain.

> *"A number of trends seem to converge on the year 2000 as a turning point when the IT [information technology] Revolution will become the dominant force governing modern societies."*

Information Technology Is Revolutionary

William E. Halal

The year 2000 signals the beginning of a new information millennium, according to William E. Halal. He argues that numerous trends in information technology since the 1970s—including more powerful computers, sophisticated software, and the growth of global communications networks—are likely to converge by the turn of the century and revolutionize the way Americans live and work. Halal warns that although information is a strategic resource, new technologies must be introduced cautiously because they always produce new dangers as well as gains. Halal is a professor of management science at the George Washington University School of Business and Public Management. A director of the World Future Society, Halal currently heads its World 2000 project.

As you read, consider the following questions:

1. How do neural networks function differently from traditional computer processes, according to Halal?
2. In the author's opinion, why are information services unlikely to replace direct human interaction?
3. What are the dangers of the information age, in Halal's opinion?

William E. Halal, "The Information Technology Revolution," *The Futurist*, July/August 1992. Reproduced with permission from *The Futurist*, published by the World Future Society, 7910 Woodmont Ave., Suite 450, Bethesda, MD 20814.

It has become a cliché to note the revolutionary impact of information technology (IT), but the real upheaval lies just ahead. If the number-crunching mainframe computers of the 1970s formed the childhood of IT, and the flowering of personal computers [PCs] during the 1980s marked its youthful adolescence, then the 1990s seem likely to see the passage of IT into adulthood. John Scully, chairman of Apple Computer, describes the future prospects this way: "We have been racing to get to the starting line. The really interesting stuff begins in the 1990s."

A number of trends seem to converge on the year 2000 as a turning point when the IT Revolution will become the dominant force governing modern societies. Far more powerful computers will be available, possibly using light waves and almost certainly using thousands of parallel processors. This vast new computing power will be used to operate highly sophisticated software that allows computers to do the work of experts, learn, talk, read handwriting, and serve as personal assistants. The current growth of networks, cellular communications, and fiber-optic cables should form the basis for a common information utility spanning the globe. And the use of computerized electronic services such as telecommuting, teleconferencing, electronic education, and electronic shopping will change the way we live and work.

A knowledge-based social order is now evolving in which homes, offices, schools, and communities become interwoven into a web of intelligent communication services offering unparalleled opportunities for accelerating scientific progress, economic development, education, and other revolutionary changes.

Computer Hardware

The power of computers resides basically in their ability to store and process information, and today vast leaps are under way in these fundamental capabilities.

A number of technologies are being developed to increase processing speed. Gallium-arsenide chips are commercially available, which allow speeds five to six times faster than silicon chips. Chips whose switching devices operate in a vacuum—thus offering no resistance to the flow of electrons—might each contain billions of such devices. And researchers are now learning how to store information at the molecular level in the chemical bonds between atoms; such "biochips" would pack the information storage power of DNA.

Optical disks, similar to the compact discs now used to record popular music, should offer continued huge increases in storage capacity. An optical disk today can store about 1,000 megabytes of data, which is more than sufficient to handle the contents of any multivolume encyclopedia. If present trends continue, entire libraries could soon be accessed electronically for little more than the cost of a few ordinary pop recordings.

The culmination of these developments may be the optical computer, which would operate with light waves. Such a machine could boost computing power by several orders of magnitude. While much of the scientific community is skeptical that optical computing can be developed in less than a generation, if at all, it should be remembered that all great advances have met such doubts. AT&T's Bell Labs expect to have prototype optical computers working near the year 2000, and 13 large Japanese electronic companies have teamed up with Japan's Ministry of International Trade and Industry to develop optical computers.

Stationary PCs will still be used in the year 2000 for technical work, but most people are likely to use small, portable computers like the "laptops" and "palmtops" now being developed. These should be user-friendly consumer electronic devices, almost like a smart TV remote control, connected to information networks through the same technology now used in cellular phones. Data, written text, newspapers, TV shows, movies, teleconferences, and a variety of other information could then be displayed in multiple high-resolution images projected on flat wall monitors. Other cheap, small computer chips are likely to be embedded in cars, home appliances, and other items.

The net effect is that "computing" will no longer be something one does primarily while sitting at a desk; rather, computers will be ubiquitous. Life will take place in a living landscape of interacting, intelligent machines that help us through our daily chores. David Nagel, head of Apple Computer's Advanced Technology Group, thinks this development will be "a real turning point in the way we live, work, and play."

Another important development is the growth of the information infrastructure. Integrated information networks will greatly expand the communications traffic flowing on space satellites. The fiber-optic cables now being installed by telephone companies are expected to reach most American homes and offices in the mid-1990s, allowing virtually everyone access to an enormous range of information and communications services. And open-system standards like the Integrated Services Digital Network (ISDN) should soon make it possible to create multimedia systems that link together all machines, data, voice, video, text, and any other type of information into one seamless whole.

Computer Software

Currently, sophisticated software is essentially built from scratch, with thousands of programmers working many years at a cost that usually runs into the tens of millions of dollars. But in a few years, this method may seem hopelessly archaic, rather like the quaint way we regard the building of the pyramids or Gothic cathedrals. Advances in automated software production should soon allow a software designer to simply stipulate the logic desired for a specific application; the actual programming would be carried out automatically as intelligent computers retrieve standardized packages of software and integrate them into a working whole.

News via the Internet

[When] the information capacity of the country is where it ought to be, I will be able to view any public meeting of Congress over the Net. And I will have artificial intelligence agents roaming the databases, downloading stuff I am interested in, and assembling for me a front page, or a nightly news show, that addresses my interests. I'll have the twelve top stories that I want, I'll have short summaries available, and I'll be able to double-click for more detail. How will Peter Jennings or *MacNeil-Lehrer* or a newspaper compete with that?

Michael Crichton, *New Perspectives Quarterly*, Summer 1994.

Alongside this crucial development is the rapid emergence of neural networks, which offer a fundamentally different approach to computing. Rather than relying on the brute number-crunching force of the old hierarchical computer architectures that used a single large processor, neural networks use many processors operating in a fluid, parallel networking mode that simulates the network of cells forming the human brain. Like the brain, neural networks organize information into patterns, assign different functions to different parts of the network, and can reorganize to adjust for failures of some components.

The speed at which neural networks are being developed is astonishing. In 1988, Nippon Electric announced the development of a four-processor PC selling for about $5,000 that can read text and voice inputs, use expert systems to solve problems, and learn from experience. Neural networks using thousands of processors are now being developed, and ones using as many as 1 million processors are expected to be working about 1995.

The more-sophisticated qualities of neural networks, combined with more-powerful hardware, should realize the exciting applications of artificial intelligence that have been promised for decades. These include quick and cheap solutions to tough scientific problems, automatic management of the burgeoning capital flows streaming through the global economy, personalized instruction on well-defined subjects, more-accurate and quicker diagnosis of medical illness, and all the other tasks needed to manage today's complex world.

Software advances will also help individuals navigate the ever more complex maze of information systems available. Intelligent software packages are being developed that function as a "knowledge assistant," "intellectual robot," or "slave" working on behalf of its "master."

Stored in an individual's portable PC and able to learn over time the unique way each master works, thinks, and decides, such an assistant could handle routine tasks automatically, search for needed information, respond to queries, and perform other such tasks. This computerized alter ego is likely to be given a name for easy reference—like Sam—and could even fill in for its master at meetings, much as a capable human assistant may do so now. Apple Computer introduced a "personal digital assistant" in 1993.

Information Services

The big question posed by the Information Technology Revolution is, What will all this powerful technology be used for?

In principle, most of today's social functions performed in person could be replaced by their electronic equivalents. For instance, a number of "electronic universities" now offer courses via interactive TV, computer conferences, and other media; the University of Maryland's University College announced in 1991 that it will offer the first degree program conducted electronically. An estimated 34 million Americans were working at home in 1991, and interest in telecommuting is growing rapidly.

Other information services now being adopted cover the entire span of human activity: electronic shopping, banking, trading securities, political polling and voting, home entertainment, corporate TV networks, teleconferencing, electronic house calls by physicians, psychotherapy practice via closed-circuit TV, electronic publishing, and even religious services conducted via computer conferencing systems.

The great potential of information services is highlighted by the fact that IBM and Sears have poured huge sums of time, money, and creative effort into launching Prodigy, which provides information services to the growing number of homes that now have computers. Prodigy has gained fairly wide acceptance, serving [nearly three] million subscribers. . . .

Social Interaction

Despite the growing use of information services, many people are ambivalent about replacing live social interaction with electronic exchanges. A 1987 survey of Honeywell employees found that 56% would continue to go to the office every day if given the choice of telecommuting, 36% would split their time between home and office, and only 7% would work at home exclusively. And a recent poll of experts revealed doubts about the widespread acceptance of teleconferencing, electronic shopping, and telecommuting even 15 years into the future.

Because people are social beings, information services are unlikely to *replace* direct interaction; rather, these services will offer a viable *alternative* to the real thing when more convenient. Road traffic is badly congested in most cities and growing worse, creating great incentives to find other options. As information services become more sophisticated and user-friendly, they will increasingly fill the need for that option.

Efforts are now under way to achieve a better match between social norms and the new information technologies. A good example is the compromise now evolving between working at the office and working at home. Employers want to spare their workers long trips to urban offices, yet often they feel uncomfortable allowing them to work at home. One solution is the "telework center," a satellite office that allows employees to work near their neighborhoods. Pacific Bell has been operating two such centers in California for years, Hawaii has created a center in a suburb of Honolulu for use by employees of local firms and government agencies, and similar centers are being used in European countries and Japan.

Social Transformation

As the new information technologies and services find increasing use, they may usher in a dramatic social transformation. The possibility of conducting most social functions electronically means that there will cease to be any good reason why one cannot locate an office, home, school, or other facility virtually anywhere. Thus, science-fiction author Arthur C. Clarke, who lives in Sri Lanka, is deeply involved in American society thanks to his electronic connections.

The new option of interacting globally is beginning to dramatically alter the way the world works. Multinational corporations are now able to conduct their business around the world with ease, and this global scope of business activity is primarily responsible for the recent emergence of a global economy. Today's rapid integration of financial markets, for instance, is making it possible to buy or sell securities using an ordinary PC, on any stock market in the world, around the clock.

Family life may also be revolutionized as education, shopping, work, and other activities are brought into the home. The home may even recover its traditional role as a center of production, as it was during the long history of agricultural societies. If this occurs, we may see a resurgence of cohesiveness in family life, neighborhoods, and cities as people devote more time and interest to their local communities; at the same time, they would be intimately connected to the outside world through powerful information networks.

Another important change is that electronic relationships are even now beginning to shift the locus of power in modern societies. Authority figures can always use computers to dominate subordinates, of course, but information systems naturally tend to drive power, initiative, and control down to the bottom of large institutions.

Before computerization, the Industrial Age demanded conformity to decisions flowing from the top of a hierarchy in order to keep the production lines running. But now, the Information Age encourages the creative use of knowledge because the need to solve tough new problems is becoming the central function of a high-tech, global economy. As management expert Peter Drucker says, "Leadership throughout the developed world no longer rests on financial control or traditional cost advantages. It rests on brain power."

This downward and outward spread of power is basically why communism collapsed in 1990 and why free markets are spreading throughout the world with such enthusiasm. The same transformation of power structures can be seen in capitalist nations as large corporations are decentralizing into small, semiautonomous units; each of these "internal enterprises" collaborates among its employees, suppliers, and other stakeholders, even including competitors.

The Virtual Community

The result of these trends is likely to be a society governed not by hierarchical pyramids, but by constantly changing pockets of collaboration within a web of social/information networks spanning the globe. To identify this development with a sharply focused label, we might extend the tradition in computer circles of defining "virtual machines," "virtual reality," and other ethereal new realms of computer behavior into the social domain— the "virtual community."

People in far-flung nations today commonly use jet travel, cheap long-distance phone calls, fax, computer networking, and other high-tech capability to engage in virtually any type of social and working relationship around the world: business deals, professional collaboration, scientific research, and the like.

This newly emerging phenomenon of electronic interaction goes beyond the idea of the "global village," which focused on a sense of global awareness created by the advent of mass media

95

like TV. The virtual community transcends mass communications to provide *electronically mediated relationships* that actually turn the earth into a single global community.

To carry this line of thought further, a close similarity exists between the information networks now forming a virtual community and the brainlike quality of the computer architecture emerging for the future—neural networks. If the individual operating a computer can be thought of as analogous to a single nerve cell, then the emerging web of information networks operated by billions of educated people around the world becomes analogous to a massive "global brain" possessing the capacity for an unprecedented form of "global intelligence."

Managing the New World Order

The emergence of some form of global intelligence highlights a subtle but distinctive change that should occur when the Information Technology Revolution arrives shortly after the year 2000. Although people in advanced nations like the United States and Japan have been speaking about the Information Age for years now, they are in fact still living in service societies.

It is commonly claimed that 70% of the labor force in such nations work in "services and information," but this figure obscures the crucial distinction between service work and knowledge work. The dominant activity in these societies consists of providing personal services such as merchandising goods, operating restaurants and hotels, teaching, financial services, and the like, which occupy roughly 40% of the labor force. Only 30% are engaged in information-based activities such as scientific and industrial research, journalism, communications, higher education, and strategic problem solving.

Although the knowledge-producing sector is still relatively small, it should grow to exceed the service sector by about the year 2000. This crossover point will mark the beginning of a genuine knowledge-based social order, a global system that is primarily concerned with the creation, analysis, and distribution of new knowledge for the purpose of solving the difficult challenges looming ahead.

Over the next 30 to 40 years, world population seems almost certain to shoot up to at least 10 billion people, all of whom will want to live as affluently as Americans, thereby placing a huge additional load on the environment that is even now unable to sustain the present level of industrialization. Add to this the need to contain a world of exploding cultural diversity, technological complexity, and demands for local autonomy, and we have the makings of an historic breakdown in present techno-economic-political systems.

From an evolutionary perspective, then, the purpose of the

Information Technology Revolution may be to create some type of global information system capable of managing the "New World Order."

New Dangers

The Information Technology Revolution offers enormous promise, but new technologies always introduce new dangers as well as gains. As we become deeply reliant upon information systems that are so powerful and complex as to almost defy comprehension, much less control, great costs must be paid in human diligence.

For instance, ensuring computer security, personal privacy, and protection against destructive intrusions (such as viruses) will require far greater care and ingenuity as information systems become more pervasive. Even small unintended failures can be catastrophic. In 1991, a software bug consisting of three lines of faulty computer code brought down the Washington, D.C., telephone system, effectively crippling the U.S. capital for several hours. How much more damage could be accomplished by a skilled person who wished to wreak havoc with the large information systems that run the military, airports, financial markets, and other strategic functions?

And as information becomes the primary resource in a knowledge-based economy, far greater attention must be devoted to its equitable distribution if the world hopes to avoid creating an underclass of "information have-nots." One of the primary reasons that the United States is in economic decline is that an out-moded educational system has left most American youngsters functionally ill-equipped to cope with a high-tech society.

Perhaps the toughest challenge will be to develop effective means for finding our way through the looming avalanche of data that even now threatens to engulf us. It is supremely ironic that people living in the Information Age feel more, rather than less, ignorant: An overabundance of knowledge leaves us with a heightened awareness of all that is unknown, even as we struggle through masses of data to find the information we need.

But despite these drawbacks of the Information Age, remarkably bright possibilities lie waiting around the turn of the millennium. Human progress has been made very slowly and with great struggle throughout the long advance of civilization, and now a great surge forward seems likely as science and technology harness the power of information that has heretofore been largely unrealized. Whether we like it or not, the genie of knowledge is finally being released from its bottle.

"All the talk about 'future shocks', 'third waves', 'megatrends' and 'post-industrial' societies must now be taken with a large pinch of salt."

Information Technology Is Not Revolutionary

Tom Forester

In the following viewpoint, Tom Forester maintains that information technology has not been the revolutionary force that forecasters of the 1960s and 1970s predicted. He argues that the anticipated transformation of the workplace, home life, and the education system due to advances in computer and communications technology has not materialized. According to Forester, forecasters who predicted such change were too utopian in their visions; they failed to foresee that computers—due to their fallibility and their potential for misuse by people—would create unexpected problems. Forester was a professor at Griffith University's School of Computing and Information Technology in Queensland, Australia.

As you read, consider the following questions:

1. What percentage of American and European workers work at home full-time, according to Forester?
2. What problems are caused by the complexity of computers, according to the author?
3. What is "infoglut," according to Forester?

Excerpted from Tom Forester, "Megatrends or Megamistakes?" *Computers & Society*, October 1992. Reprinted with permission.

What ever happened to the Information Society? Where is the Information Age? What, indeed, happened to the "worker-less" factory, the "paperless" office and the "cashless" society? Why aren't we all living in the "electronic cottage", playing our part in the push-button "teledemocracy"—or simply relaxing in the "leisure society", while machines exhibiting "artificial intelligence" do all the work? . . .

The truth is that society has not changed very much [since the 1970s]. The microchip has had much less social impact than almost everyone predicted. All the talk about "future shocks", "third waves", "megatrends" and "post-industrial" societies must now be taken with a large pinch of salt. Life goes on for the vast majority of people in much the same old way. Computers have infiltrated many areas of our social life, but they have not transformed it. Computers have proved to be useful tools—no more, no less. None of the more extreme predictions about the impact of computers on society have turned out to be correct. Neither Utopia nor Dystopia has arrived on Earth as a result of computerization. . . .

The Workplace in the "Leisure Society"

Since so many of the early predictions about the social impact of IT [information technology] envisaged dramatic reductions in the quantity of paid employment and/or large increases in the amount of forced or unforced leisure time available to the average person, work and leisure would seem an appropriate starting point for an assessment of the actual social impact of IT.

First, the microchip has not put millions of people out of work—although it is steadily eroding employment opportunities. Mass unemployment has not occurred as a result of computerization chiefly because the introduction of computers into the workplace has been much slower and messier than expected for a variety of financial, technical and managerial reasons. . . .

Second, the vast majority who are in the workforce appear to be working harder than ever. There is very little sign of the "leisure" society having arrived yet! According to one survey, the amount of leisure time enjoyed by the average US citizen shrunk by a staggering 37 per cent between 1973 and 1989. Over the same period, the average working week, including travel-to-work time, grew from under 41 hours to nearly 47 hours—a far cry from the 22 hours someone predicted in 1967! Note that these increases occurred just as computers, robots, word processors and other "labour-saving" gadgetry were entering the workplace. . . .

We are still awaiting the "workerless", "unmanned" or "fully-automated" factory. The "factory of the future" remains where it has always been, somewhere in the future. Take industrial robots, for example: analysts confidently predicted that the US robot population would top 250,000 or more by 1990. The actual figure was 37,000—and some of these had already been relegated to training centres and scrap metal dealers. . . .

John Branch/*San Antonio Express News*. Reprinted by permission.

The "paperless" office now looks to be one of the funniest predictions made about the social impact of IT. More and more trees are being felled to satisfy our vast appetite for paper, in offices which were supposed by now to be all-electronic. In the US, paper consumption has rocketed 320 per cent over the past 30 years, ahead of real GDP [gross domestic product], which has gone up 280 per cent. In absolute terms, this means that US consumers gobbled up 4 trillion pages of paper in 1991, compared with only 2.5 trillion in 1986—about the time that word processors and personal computers were becoming really popular. The two most successful office products of recent times—the photocopier and the fax machine—are of course enormous users or generators of paper, while technologies which do not use paper—such as electronic mail and voice mail—have been slow to catch on. . . .

Where Is the "Electronic Cottage"?

One of the most pervasive myths of the IT revolution is that large numbers of people will "soon" be working from home, shopping from home and banking from home. The appealing notion of the "electronic cottage" was first made popular by writers such as Alvin Toffler (who gave a new verb to the English language—to "toffle", as in "waffle"). The general idea was that the Industrial Revolution had taken people out of their homes—and now the IT revolution would allow them to return. It has since become a recurring theme in the literature on the social impact of computers and has become firmly implanted in the public consciousness as an allegedly widespread social trend.

The only problem with this attractive scenario is that it is not happening. There is very little evidence to suggest that increasing numbers of people are working from home full-time, although some professionals are doing more work at home using their "electronic briefcase". Most surveys would seem to indicate that only about 10 per cent of the total workforce in the US and Europe work from home full-time on a variety of tasks, just as they have always done. . . .

Thus it seems that many commentators have overestimated the capacity for IT-based gadgetry to transform domestic lifestyles. The argument that developments in consumer electronics, computers and telecommunications will dramatically alter the nature of economic and social activity in the home is not supported by the available evidence. Despite the arrival of microwaves, food processors, VCR's, CD players, big-screen TV's, answering machines, home faxes, word processors and portable phones, home life remains basically the same. Moreover, a succession of revolutionary "homes of the future" incorporating various "home automation" systems have been built in the US and Europe in recent decades, but by and large they have left consumers cold. . . .

The same sort of miscalculation has been made in relation to schools. There is as yet not much sign of the "classroom revolution" taking place and the idea of human teachers being replaced by automated teaching machines still sounds just as fanciful as it always did. A recent OTA (Office of Technology Assessment) report in the US pointed out that classrooms have changed very little in the last 50 years. . . .

Why Technology Predictions Go Wrong

Obviously those industry analysts, forecasters, academics and writers who have made predictions in the past which have turned out to be completely wrong do not tend to publicize their own mistakes, let alone examine in public just where and why they went wrong. But recently two writers have attempted to explain why so many technology forecasts go awry.

Steven Schnaars re-examined major US efforts to forecast the future of technology and found they had missed the mark not by a matter of degree, but completely. For example, top scientists and leading futurists in the 1960's had predicted that by now we would be living in plastic houses, travelling to work by personal vertical take-off aircraft, farming the ocean floors and going for holidays on the moon. Robots would be doing the housework, working farms, fighting wars for us, and so on. The best result of these forecasts was a success rate of about 15 per cent. Most others failed miserably—chiefly, says Schnaars, because the authors had been seduced by technological wonder. They were far too optimistic both about the abilities of new technologies and the desire of consumers to make use of them. The forecasts were driven by utopian visions rather than practicalities and hard realities. An especially common mistake of the 1960's predictions was to assume that existing rates of technological innovation and diffusion would continue. Schnaars thus comes to the astonishing conclusion: "There is almost no evidence that forecasters, professionals and amateurs alike have any idea what our technological future will look like".

Likewise, H. Brody went back and looked at the forecasts made by leading US market research firms about the commercial prospects for robots, CD-ROM's, artificial intelligence, videotex, superconductors, Josephson junctions, gallium arsenide chips, and so on. In almost every case, he found that the market researchers had grossly exaggerated the market for each product, sometimes by a factor of hundreds. The main reason for this appallingly low level of accuracy was that the researchers had mostly got their information from vested interests such as inventors and vendors. A second lesson was that new technologies often did not succeed because there was still plenty of life left in old technologies. Consumers in particular were loath to abandon what they knew for something that offered only a marginal improvement on the old. Predictions based on simple trend extrapolation were nearly always wrong and forecasters often neglected to watch for developments in related fields. They also failed to distinguish between technology trends and market forecasts and they greatly underestimated the time needed for innovations to diffuse throughout society.

Unintended Consequences and New Social Vulnerabilities

The IT revolution has created a whole new range of problems for society, problems which were largely unexpected. Some arise from the propensity of computers to malfunction, others arise from their misuse by humans.

As complex industrial societies become more dependent on computers, they become more vulnerable to technological failure because computers have often proved to be unreliable, insecure and unmanageable. Malfunctioning hardware and software is much more common than many (especially those in the computer industry!) would have us believe. There is little doubt that we put too much faith in these supposedly infallible machines. Computers are permeating almost every aspect of our lives, but unlike other pervasive technologies such as electricity, television and the motor car, computers are on the whole less reliable and less predictable in their behaviour. This is because they are discrete state digital electronic devices which are prone to total and catastrophic failure. Computer systems, when they are "down", are completely down, unlike analog or mechanical devices which may only be partially down and are thus still partially usable.

Popular areas for computer malfunctions include telephone billing and telephone switching software, bank statements and bank teller machines, electronic funds transfer systems and motor vehicle licence databases. . . .

Computers enable enormous quantities of information to be stored, retrieved and transmitted at great speed on a scale not possible before. This is all very well, but it has serious implications for data security and personal privacy because computer networks are inherently insecure. . . .

No Impact on Productivity

Economists who make their living analyzing business efficiency have consistently found that the information technology revolution has had no measurable impact on the overall productivity of American industry. . . .

Although productivity—measured as output per worker—remains higher in the United States than in other countries, it has simply failed to improve significantly as a result of the computer revolution.

Jonathan Weber, *Los Angeles Times*, March 8, 1992.

Computer systems are often incredibly complex—so complex, in fact, that they are not always understood even by their creators (although few are willing to admit it!). This often makes them completely unmanageable. Unmanageable complexity can result in massive foul-ups or spectacular budget "runaways". For example, Bank of America in 1988 had to abandon a $20 million computer system after spending five years and a further $60 million trying to make it work! . . .

Complexity can also result in disaster: no computer is 100 per cent guaranteed because it is virtually impossible to anticipate all sources of failure. Yet computers are regularly being used for all sorts of critical applications such as saving lives, flying aircraft, running nuclear power stations, transferring vast sums of money and controlling missile systems—and this can sometimes have tragic consequences. . . .

The Misuse of Computers

As society becomes more dependent on computers, we also become more vulnerable to the misuse of computers by human beings. The theft of copyright software is widespread, while recent, well-publicized incidents of hacking, virus creation, computer-based fraud and invasion of privacy have been followed by a rising chorus of calls for improved "ethics" in computing and new laws to protect citizens from computerized anarchy.

It can be argued that the "information" or "knowledge" society cannot possibly flourish unless better protection is offered to individuals and companies who generate wealth from information. . . .

The IT revolution has also made it easier to put people under electronic surveillance and it has increased the likelihood of individuals' having their privacy invaded. D. Burnham pointed out that IT enables governments and commercial organisations to store vast amounts of "transactional data", such as details of phone calls, financial payments, air travel, and so on. From these, a composite picture of an individual's friendships, spending habits and movements can be built up. New IT gadgetry makes it much easier to spy on people with hidden bugs and other eavesdropping devices, to gather information by, for example, illicit phone taps, and to directly monitor the performance of employees with videos and computers. Electronic databases containing vital medical, financial and criminal records—which are often inaccurate—have been accessed by unauthorized users. As David Linowes and D.H. Flaherty argue, this creates a major problem of how to protect privacy in "information" societies—a problem which the law has been slow to tackle.

New Psychological Maladies

The IT revolution has brought with it a number of psychological problems associated with computer-mediated communication. These have implications for both organisational productivity and human relationships. One major problem is that of "information overload" or so-called "infoglut". This arises because modern society generates so much new information that we are overwhelmed by it all and become unable to distinguish between what is useful and what is not-so-useful. In essence, it is a problem of not being able to see the wood for the trees. For example, 14,000 book publishers in the US release onto the market 50,000 new titles every year. There are now at least 40,000 scientific journals publishing more than 1 million new papers each year—that's nearly 3,000 per day—and the scientific literature is doubling every 10–15 years. Clearly, it is impossible for any one individual to keep up with the literature, except for very small areas. . . .

Improvements in IT enable us to gather, store and transmit information in vast quantity, but not to interpret it. But what are we going to do with all that information? We have plenty of *information* technology—what is perhaps needed now is more *intelligence* technology, to help us make sense of the growing volume of information stored in the form of statistical data, documents, messages, and so on. . . .

In commerce and in government, it is alleged that infoglut is affecting decision-making to such an extent that some organisations now suffer from "analysis paralysis". Managers and administrators become overloaded and prevaricate by calling for more studies, reports, etc, instead of actually making a decision. But as someone once said, "waiting for all the facts to come in" can be damn frustrating if the facts never stop coming. . . .

There is also serious concern that media infoglut is having a damaging effect on society—in particular the younger generation. As James Chesebro and Donald Bonsall show, the television set is on in the average American household for 7 hours and 7 minutes a day. In addition, recorded video tapes are watched for a further 5 hours 8 minutes a week on average (1987 figures). Young Americans can also tune in to any of 9,300 radio stations in the US, on one of the 5.3 radios in the average American household. In these and other ways, the typical American encounters no less than 1,600 advertisements each day. By the age of 17, the average American child would have seen over one-third of a million ads. It is little wonder that US academics are talking about America "amusing itself to death", its collective mind numbed by video-pulp, 10-second sound bites and 30-second video clips. . . .

A second set of problems concerns the way some people use the new computer-based communication technologies and how they relate to other people as a result. For instance, some managers have been diagnosed "communicaholic" because of their obsessive desire to keep in touch and to constantly communicate using their car phones and fax machines. Some have allegedly become "spreadsheet junkies", playing endless what-if? games on their computers, or "e-mail addicts" spending hours sending and answering trivial e-mail messages. But does this "hyper-connectedness" mean that they are doing their jobs any better and are they making wiser decisions? . . .

Putting Humans Back in the Picture

We have seen that many of the predictions made about the impact of computers on society have been wide of the mark, primarily because they have accorded too great a role to technology and too little a role to human needs and abilities. At the same time, there have been a number of unanticipated problems thrown up by the IT revolution, most of which involve the human factor.

Perhaps the time has come for a major reassessment of our relationship to technology, especially the new information and communication technologies. After all, haven't manufacturers belatedly discovered that expensive high-tech solutions are not always appropriate for production problems, that robots are more troublesome than people and that the most "flexible manufacturing system" available to them is something called a human operator? Didn't one study of a government department conclude that the only databases worth accessing were those carried around in the heads of long-serving employees? And is it not the case that the most sophisticated communication technology available to us is still something called speaking to each other? One conclusion to be drawn from this is that technological advances in computing seem to have outpaced our ability to make use of them.

Computers have also de-humanized many social activities ranging from commercial transactions to hospital care. Human interaction has tended to decline in the computerized workplace. ATMs [automatic teller machines] have de-personalized banking. Even crime has been de-personalized by the computer—pressing a few keys to siphon-off funds is not the same as bashing someone over the head and running-off with the cash! To many, the military conflict in the [Persian] Gulf resembled a giant video game and even became known as the "Nintendo War". There is also little doubt that many computer scientists and other computer enthusiasts have low needs for social interaction and seem to relate better to their machines than they do to other human beings—the so called "nerd" syndrome. Further, computers have speeded up the pace of life, leaving little time for calm reflection and contemplation. This can lead to "techno-stress", fatigue, anxiety and burnout. Most people now know that slow is healthier, but there is little evidence that people are slowing down. Perhaps we should go back to basics and first decide what we really want out of life—a decent home, a satisfying family life, a reasonable standard of living, a clean environment, an interesting job with a healthy workstyle—and then direct technology toward these simple, human ends. It would be nice to think that our schools and colleges are helping make future generations more aware of the choices and the possibilities, rather than fatalistically joining in the uncritical, headlong rush toward an ill-defined and ill-thought-out high-tech future.

"Third Wave societies—with economies based on information, communications and technology—run at hyper-speeds."

Technology Rapidly Changes Society

Alvin Toffler and Heidi Toffler

Alvin Toffler and Heidi Toffler are among the world's best known futurists, and are the authors of such books as *Future Shock* and *War and Anti-War: Survival at the Dawn of the 21st Century*. In the following viewpoint, the Tofflers argue that the world has evolved from one of agrarian and industrial societies to one including technological societies. The Tofflers' opinion is that a "group of societies that increasingly do the world's economically relevant 'knowledge work'" is developing, and that America can protect its vital interests in the future by understanding this change and planning strategically.

As you read, consider the following questions:

1. Why are nations becoming less important, in the Tofflers' opinion?
2. What is the paradox produced by "third wave" societies' dependence on connections to the outside world, according to the authors?
3. According to the Tofflers, how do the vital interests of first, second, and third wave societies differ?

Alvin Toffler and Heidi Toffler, "Societies at Hyper Speed," *The New York Times*, October 31, 1993. Copyright ©1993 by Alvin and Heidi Toffler. Reprinted by permission of the authors.

W_{hy} doesn't America know where it is going? U.S. foreign and military policy is swerving like a drunken driver without a map. It shows no clear grasp of our vital short-term national interests—let alone an understanding of the long-term shape of the global system.

We need to start by understanding that the old world map is obsolete—that the global system would be in revolutionary upheaval even if the Soviet Union still existed. We are undergoing the deepest rearrangement of global power since the birth of industrial civilization.

Until very recently, world power was bisected—industrial societies on top, peasant-based societies on the bottom. But the rising importance of goods and services based on sophisticated knowledge and high technology—from computer software and news services to genetically enhanced seeds—has created a third layer, a group of societies that increasingly do the world's economically relevant "knowledge work."

Of course, this transition is not yet clear because nowhere is it complete. Even Japan and the United States, whose economies are the most technically advanced, still have large and politically potent smokestack sectors in which low-skill labor prevails. China, Brazil and India, mainly agrarian, have large industrial economies with pockets of high technology. But these overlaps should not blind us to the powerful forces that are shaping the global system of the next century.

Global Systems

As global competition drives the advanced economies deeper into high-skill, information-intensive production and distribution, they transfer more and more of their unskilled muscle-based jobs to agrarian countries like China or, for that matter, Mexico.

Nations like Japan, the United States and Singapore are neither agrarian nor industrial. Their work forces are predominantly white-collar. Societies are media-drenched. Economies rely on complex electronic infrastructures—like the data superhighway central to the battle [between cable TV giants QVC and Viacom] for control of Paramount Communications. [Viacom acquired 75 percent of Paramount's shares in February 1994.] This digital structure is needed to handle the information that is the most basic raw material of tomorrow's economy. It is to the emerging high-technology nations what roads and ports were to the emerging industrial nations.

But nations, as such, are becoming less important. Powerful transnational businesses are creating information networks that "bypass the nation-state framework," in the words of Riccardo Petrella, director of science and technology forecasting for the European Community.

Regions are also growing in power. Mr. Petrella continues: "By the middle of the next century, such nation-states as Germany, Italy, the United States or Japan will no longer be the most relevant socioeconomic entities and the ultimate political configuration. Instead, areas like Orange County, California; Osaka, Japan; the Lyon region of France; or Germany's Ruhrgebiete will acquire predominant socioeconomic status. The real decision-making powers of the future . . . will be transnational companies in alliance with city-regional governments."

Technological Change Eliminates Some Jobs, Expands Others

Percent Employment Change, 1992–2005

Computer operators	–39%
Billing, posting, and calculating machine operators	–29%
Telephone operators	–28%
Typists and word processors	–16%
Bank tellers	–4%

Five Fastest-Growing Occupations Requiring a College Degree, 1992–2005

Computer engineers and scientists	112%
Systems analysts	110%
Physical therapists	88%
Special education teachers	74%
Operations research analysts	61%

Source: Bureau of Labor Statistics.

Another type of unit is also growing in importance: thousands of transnational organizations—Greenpeace, for example—are springing up like mushrooms to form a new "civil society."

Add to these components of the new global system world religions like Roman Catholicism and Islam, plus fast-multiplying media networks like CNN that cross (and blur) borders, and it is clear that the world system built around neatly defined nation-states is being replaced by a kind of global computer, with thousands of diverse components plugged into a three-level motherboard.

At one level, agrarian countries are hardly connected to the system, with few links to the outside world other than the countries that serve as markets, and they operate at a leisurely "clock speed." At a second level, industrial nations move faster and are more connected to the global system.

But what we call "third wave" societies—with economies based on information, communications and technology—run at hyperspeeds. And they require an amazing number of connections with the outside world. In 1930 the United States was a party to only 34 treaties or agreements with other countries; today, with the world's most knowledge-intensive economy, it is party to more than 1,000 treaties and tens of thousands of agreements.

This produces an overlooked paradox: a very strange world in which the most powerful and most accelerated countries are the ones most tied down by external commitments, the least free to act independently. This explains why a [General Muhammad Farah] Aidid in Somalia or a junta in Haiti could run rings around the United States.

These widening differences in the trisected global system also change each nation's list of vital interests. For "first wave," or agricultural, economies, the essentials for survival are land, energy, water for irrigation, cooking oil, food, minimal literacy and markets for cash crops or raw materials. Their natural resources and farm products are their chief salable assets.

States in the second wave, or industrial tier, still rely on cheap manual labor and mass production, with concentrated, integrated national economies. They need high inputs of energy per unit of production. They need bulk raw materials to keep their factories going—iron, steel, cement, timber, petrochemicals and the like. They are the home of a small number of global corporations. They are major producers of pollution and other ecological problems. Above all, they need export markets for their mass-produced products.

Third Wave Economies

Third wave economies, the newest tier of the global system, have sharply different vital interests. Unlike agrarian states, they have no great need for additional territory. Unlike industrial states, they have little need for vast natural resources of their own, as Japan and Singapore demonstrate.

These societies still need energy and food, of course, but they also need knowledge convertible into wealth. They need access to, or control of, world data banks and telecommunications networks. They need markets for products and services that depend on knowledge: financial services, management consulting, software, television programming, banking, economic intelligence and all the technologies on which these things depend.

They need protection against the piracy of intellectual products. And as for ecology, they want the "unspoiled" agrarian countries to protect their jungles, skies and greenery for the "global good"—sometimes even if it stifles development.

When we take all these changes together—differences in the

110

types of units making up the global system, in their connected-ness to that system, in their speed and in their vital interests—we arrive at a transformation more revolutionary than anything caused by the end of the cold war.

The Emerging World and U.S. Policy

It is an emerging world in which great powers may decline, tiny states may become shooting stars, nonstates dominate many decisions and advanced technologies and weaponry may turn up in the remotest corners of the planet. This is the arena in which tomorrow's wars—and the efforts to stop those wars—will be fought.

U.S. policy will continue to swerve drunkenly across the globe until its business and political leaders study this road map of to-morrow and develop long-range strategies to advance America's truly vital interests on a trisected planet.

> *"Technology does change society, but on a time scale of decades, not years. Looking back, the pace of change can seem almost glacial."*

Technology Slowly Changes Society

Nicholas Wade

In the following viewpoint, Nicholas Wade argues that enthusiastic proponents of technology give the public an incorrect impression that all technological change is relevant and that it happens quickly. While some technologies do affect society, according to Wade, the process by which these technologies develop—and the pace at which they influence society—is gradual, spanning decades rather than years. Pronouncements about the significance of technological discoveries and innovations need not be believed until the impacts of such advancements on society are visible, Wade concludes. Wade is a writer for the *New York Times Magazine*.

As you read, consider the following questions:

1. What reason does Wade posit for the acceptance of technological optimists' overpromises?
2. What are some examples of technology's slow pace of changing society, according to the author?
3. What examples does Wade give of technologies that have been "just around the corner"?

Somehow the technology that's due tomorrow always seems far more profound and revolutionary than the high-tech products that arrived today. Any moment now, the information highway will link computers and their owners in a worldwide network.

Genetic engineers, made wise with the fruits of the Human Genome Project, will repair the body's frailties and enhance its better qualities. Nanotechnologists, the masters of the subminiature, will craft microscopic machines to navigate the bloodstream, plumb leaks and remove plaque.

Tomorrow's Technology

It's easy to locate the source of this enthusiasm. The people responsible for promoting tomorrow's technology can seldom be sure of the time scale of development, yet they must assure their nervous backers of the fastest feasible delivery. Thus the panorama of almost all new technology that's visible for the next 20 years is foreshortened in common perception as if it were all about to happen immediately. In fact, new technology is usually arduous to bring into being, since the steps leading from basic science to practical technology to acceptable product can each require heroic effort.

The imminent wonders of genetic engineering, for example, have been touted since gene splicing was invented in 1973; 20 years later, genetically engineered drugs are just beginning to appear in any quantity. Similarly, for a decade experts have been forecasting the presence of a computer in every home, but only now, after growing far more powerful and much cheaper, are the machines at last arriving there in serious numbers. The future shock that Alvin Toffler breathlessly warned of in his 1970 book has been more of a slow hiss than a sonic boom.

Despite the string of broken delivery dates, the technological optimists still promise a cornucopia of marvels poised to move markets and transform living patterns. The overpromises are quickly swallowed, perhaps because the expectation of high-tech miracles helps modern societies endure the pain of adjustment as one industry wrenchingly displaces another.

Technology: Snail's Pace of Change

But in fact, new technology tends to arrive at a snail's pace, for a host of mundane reasons that, if too much dwelt on in advance, would burst the bubble of hope and delusion on which much human progress depends. Consider the Human Genome Project, a grand leap of imagination that can be counted on to change our lives, though not in the present century. Those long gibberish jumbles of A's, T's, G's and C's [organic bases] of which DNA sequences consist do indeed contain the complete genetic instructions for making an organism. Yet even the plain

113

text of evolution's instruction book is still almost as mystifying as a computer program written for an unknown computer. The full genetic sequences of much simpler organisms, including the AIDS virus, have been worked out, but biologists are still far from translating that knowledge into antidote.

Even when the basic science is in place and is converted into drugs or devices, the products may still fail on the market or require years of costly experimentation. Ampex invented the videocassette recorder for professional recording in 1956 but it took Japanese engineers at Sony and JVC 20 years of tinkering to make the VCR a household product. Success also requires insights into the strange whims of consumers. The first Betamax had a playing time of one hour, long enough to record the average television program, but the VHS standard prevailed largely because it could record for twice as long. For companies dominated by engineers, these are hard lessons to learn. "It's a humbling experience for technologists to discover you can make a lot more money on a pager just by changing colors," George Fisher, former chairman of Motorola, has said.

True, some technologies do develop at a headlong pace—but usually during a specific phase of predictable refinement like that which is transforming computer memory chips and microprocessors. As Andrew Grove, chief executive of Intel, explained to the *Financial Times*, "We have to gobble up our older children—our current microprocessors—before the competition does. We intend to move as fast as we can, ripping up the road behind us." Grove's words are a vivid illustration of Joseph Schumpeter's dictum that capitalism is a process of "creative destruction" that keeps economic structures in a state of incessant revolution. Yet even with new generations of memory chips and microprocessors appearing every few years, the utility of the computers that depend on them has evolved more gradually. For most people it still makes more sense to keep a checkbook than to use a computer bookkeeping program.

"Just Around the Corner"

Then there are the technologies that are perennially just around the corner: synfuels (whatever the world price of oil, synthetic oil always costs $2 more per barrel); fusion energy (which has been getting closer and closer for years, but whose advocates promise no practical application before 2050); superconducting wires for ferrying frictionless electricity; faster computer chips made from gallium arsenide instead of silicon. The information highway is another flight of fancy that may take years to accomplish everything its backers claim. On-line services are not for everyone. Prodigy has grown slowly despite the prodigious efforts of its sponsors, I.B.M. and Sears. It's no wonder, really. At first it's a thrill to sign on to a computer bulletin board and converse with chance strangers from any part of the country. After a few sessions, though, the interchange brings to mind Oscar Wilde's lament, "The brotherhood of man is not a mere poet's dream: It is a most depressing and humiliating reality."

Technology does change society, but on a time scale of decades, not years. Looking back, the pace of change can seem almost glacial. The VCR, the microwave oven, the telephone answering machine, the fax machine—these gadgets make life more comfortable, but they have hardly transformed it. Modern electronics as a whole may have brought revolutionary changes, but their impact has been felt only bit by bit since the transistor was invented in 1947.

Still, an ironclad conspiracy of interests holds that imminent technological change is about to transform our lives. Investment bankers, stock analysts, publicity agents, journalists, economists, politicians—almost everyone whose business is to think ahead has an interest in making the future sound exhilarating. It's all good fun, but these many enjoyable wonders needn't be fully believed until seen.

> *"Farmers working in offices? Surgeons 'operating' from thousands of miles away? Welcome to work in 2010."*

Information Technology Workers, 2010

Andy Hines

Information technology will be the primary focus of many workers' jobs in the early twenty-first century, Andy Hines argues in the following viewpoint. Hines describes ten job categories to illustrate how different types of workers in 2010 may do their jobs. The categories include farmers, police officers, salespeople, and scientists. Hines maintains that four main information technologies will have revolutionary effects: computer networks, imaging technology, massive data storage, and artificial intelligence. Hines is a planner with Coates and Jarrett, Inc., futurist consultants in Washington, D.C.

As you read, consider the following questions:

1. On what two levels will information technology affect future workers, according to Hines?
2. What will "knowbots" do, according to the author?
3. What role does Hines predict teachers will play in the future?

Andy Hines, "Jobs and Infotech Work in the Information Society," *The Futurist*, January/February 1994. Reproduced with permission from *The Futurist*, published by the World Future Society, 7910 Woodmont Ave., Suite 450, Bethesda, MD 20814.

Farmers working in offices? Surgeons "operating" from thousands of miles away? Welcome to work in 2010.

Information technology—infotech for short—consists primarily of computing combined with telecommunications and networking. Infotech also includes expert systems, imaging, automation, robotics, sensing technologies, and mechatronics (microprocessors embedded in products, systems, and devices). These interconnected technologies are moving out of the office and across the landscape to reshape how workers do their jobs—on farms, in offices, in factories, in hospitals, and in classrooms. By the year 2010, infotech will effect many positive changes, making many jobs more challenging and rewarding, but it may also lead to job loss, depersonalization, or boredom.

A fundamental underpinning for infotech will be the use of digital signals over fiber optics, supplemented by satellite and wireless technologies. Making systems and technologies compatible will expand their use and will depend on the ability of political leaders to reach a consensus on standards.

The Effects of Infotech

However, infotech will affect workers on two levels: First, it will be an important tool that lets workers do more of their job through an intermediary, such as a personal computer or expert system. Second, infotech will change the nature of jobs because organizations will redesign jobs to take advantage of such capabilities. In speculating about future farmers, for example, we must consider that such technology will reshape farming.

To understand the effects of infotech, let's look at 10 job categories selected to represent a broad range of workers and workplaces in the year 2010. We will assume that state-of-the-art equipment will be highly available in these fields in the year 2010 and will try to anticipate the more-important effects on workers and their daily routines.

• *Farmers will become farm managers.* Farmers will primarily work indoors, where information will come to them. Farmers will oversee extensively automated smart farms. Sensing technologies will feed data into computers, which will analyze soil conditions, plant health, degree of ripeness, fertilizer mix, and moisture content. The seeds of these smart farms already exist: bar codes now identify individual cows and provide information about their health status; the codes are read by feeding machines, which then decide the proper feed mixture for the animal.

Farmers will identify more closely with professional managers than with the family farmers of today. By 2010, farmers will perform market analysis, develop independent weather forecasts, and maximize growing conditions and output. They will enter instructions into computers, which will then transmit instructions to field equipment.

Data visualization will be particularly important for converting the massive amounts of information into manageable form. Imaging technology will present data in attractive, easy-to-grasp pictures, rather than tables and charts of numbers. And while automation will be necessary for all but small farms, there will be room for farmers to customize applications to suit their working style.

Armed with Information

• *Police officers will be well armed—with information.* The bane of police officers' existence—paperwork—will be transformed by electronics. Police officers and detectives will hunt for clues in databases instead of searching door to door. DNA sampling will supplement fingerprints. Automated traffic-management systems will smooth traffic flows and identify offenders. Officers will be able to prepare for arrests and courtroom appearances by accessing computer files from headquarters with a keystroke or voice command.

The squad car will be a mobile crime lab in close contact with a crime technology center. This rapid access will help the officer on the street make decisions quickly. An officer in trouble will be able to summon nearby patrol cars with a shirt-pocket or wrist-based personal communicator.

Electronically monitored house arrest may be more prevalent in the future. If a criminal violates his or her electronic parole, a central crime technology center will use satellite-based global-positioning systems to locate and signal the closest officer.

• *Utility workers will oversee automated operations.* Automation will eventually make jobs such as meter reading obsolete. Instead of human meter readers, utility supercomputers will exchange data with traditional meters or with buildings' energy-management systems.

In utility plants, workers will use virtual reality in overseeing automated operations: A worker will manipulate an image of a part needing repair while tele-operated robots and equipment carry out the worker's commands. Workers still needed in the field to maintain transmission lines and respond to emergencies will use palmtop computers to obtain plant specifications on maintenance and repairs. However, even field workers might need to spend only one or two days a week at field sites.

Fast Service

• *Consultants will provide fast and timely advice.* The management consultant—far more common in the knowledge-based economy of 2010 than today—will benefit from computer networks, personal communicators, videoconferencing, e-mail, and faxes. The consultant's primary task—providing tailored and timely expertise—relies heavily on managing and manipulating information. Systems that sort through large amounts of information will become invaluable.

Artificial-intelligence software agents, or "knowbots," will search through networks of databases for the desired information and deliver it either on an ongoing basis or for a specific task. For example, a consultant may ask for all the information on private waterworks in Europe for the last five years. The knowbot will present options with prompts such as "Would you like abstracts or full records?"

Responding to client requests rapidly will give the consultant a competitive advantage. Personal communications technology will allow consultants to be accessible around the clock; their clients will reach them at a single phone number no matter where they go. Organizations and individuals will have to negotiate a balance between free time and work time, as some consultants may resent intrusive contacts outside the office.

Reach Out and Touch Someone—Electronically

• *Salespeople will pioneer the mobile office.* Salespeople will convert their cars or vans into mobile offices. The salespeople of 2010 will have little use for an office at headquarters. They will increasingly work on the road and at their customers' offices. Sales vehicles will be equipped with portable cellular phones with voice recognition, digital faxes, notebook computing, and perhaps built-in videoconferencing capability.

Technologies will make it possible to transmit orders directly from the customer's site to the factory. Many routine meetings will be by videoconference, freeing salespeople for more face-to-face sales calls. E-mail or voice mail will handle less-urgent communications.

Images will become increasingly important for selling. Customers will want to see what they are buying and then try it out by using simulations. Salespeople will need strong information skills to supplement their people skills.

• *Scientists will expand their horizons.* The scientists of 2010 will work more easily in large groups, as infotech connects them with colleagues working on similar problems around the world. Bringing scientists together will lead to exponential advances in knowledge. There will be much less "reinventing the wheel," as new knowledge is made available faster.

A key in 2010 will be videoconferencing and groupware—software that enables workers in different locations to share the same information on their computer screens. The longer-range goal will be technologies allowing scientists to work on problems simultaneously or share the workload with colleagues in different locations. Individual scientists will see the work space of others, enabling them to ask questions such as "John, look at window five of my screen. What do you think that DNA strand there is doing?"

• *Doctors will team up.* Far more than today, the physicians of 2010 will work in teams that include technicians, nurses, and therapists, as well as other physicians. Consulting with colleagues and expert-system assistants will become routine. Expert systems will supplement and enhance the physician's skills, filling knowledge and skill gaps, providing advice for complicated procedures, and doing routine diagnoses. These systems will be a great boon to places short of doctors and to hospitals short of staff.

Computerized Shipping

Advancing technology means that complexity is accompanied by simplification. Truck loading and routing become more complex as these processes are analyzed, computerized, and conducted in ever more efficient ways. But on the loading docks workers using hand-held computers make fewer decisions than in the past. Nor do they need computer literacy. They need only the ability to recognize numbers. And in most cases the passing of the computer's electric eye over a bar code renders even number recognition unnecessary.

Peter Shaw, *National Review*, January 18, 1993.

Expert systems will diagnose routine conditions without consulting physicians. Patients may dial up an expert system online or by phone, feed in their medical history with a smart card, and receive a diagnosis.

Infotech will also link physicians in remote areas with nearby high-tech centers. A logical, though hardly inevitable, solution to higher health-technology costs will be to share the resources through such links. The rural physician may not have massive data storage capability on site, but would be able to tap into larger databases elsewhere. Videoconferencing technologies will enable live assistance from one or more physicians for more-difficult procedures. A heart specialist in London could observe an operation in San Francisco and provide needed advice to the surgeons.

Coordinators and Facilitators

• *Factory workers will guide robots.* Automation will continue to decrease the share of workers involved in manufacturing. One result will be "dark areas"—sections of a factory with no people and therefore no lighting or other features needed by human workers. Usually, however, workers will be on hand to monitor and maintain robots and other equipment.

There will still be opportunities for creative work. Designing, monitoring, and maintaining the automated systems will be primary functions of factory workers or engineers. Workers will continually adjust automated systems to provide the flexibility and customization necessary for market success.

Computer-aided design and computer-assisted manufacturing systems will tie all branches of a factory into design. As designers consider their options, they may query the financial people on the costs of option A versus option B. Similarly, they may consult the human-resources department to see if workers with the required expertise are available. Exchanges like the following may become commonplace: "Sorry, Sue, but the two people you need for procedure one are tied up with another project until next month. We can provide the help you need for the second procedure. Video me at my desk when you decide. I e-mailed Mark that you may need him soon."

• *Pilots will become flight supervisors.* The chief functions of the future pilot will be to coordinate the plane's on-board technologies with air-traffic control and headquarters and to reassure passengers during a flight. Electronic-data interchanges and global-positioning satellites will combine to improve communications to and from the plane.

Airlines will seek to improve travel efficiency with just-in-time principles. They will track the plane and talk with pilots in transit to coordinate loading and unloading, refueling, and maintenance checks just in time. Pilots will still file flight plans and perform weather and maintenance checks. They will also be ready to take over in the rare case of a systems failure.

Virtual-reality systems will be important training tools. Simulations will replace much of the expensive need for actual flight experience. The virtual-reality environments of 2010 will be real enough to provide a satisfactory substitute.

• *Teachers will facilitate learning.* The teacher of 2010 will rarely spend a day lecturing, but will be primarily a facilitator and coach. Teachers will act as intermediaries between students and the world of information, helping students draw on resources around the globe.

A teacher will help students tap into educational programs customized for their particular needs. The teacher will coach students through video lectures, educational television programs, and artificial-intelligence-based programs. Only occasionally will teachers instruct classes themselves. Instead, they will be freed up to deliver the personalized instruction critical to educational achievement.

The artificial-intelligence tutor will become a valuable assistant, providing the individualized instruction that a teacher with 20 or more pupils does not have the time for. Learning can take place at the student's pace.

Common Patterns in Infotech

There are four primary conclusions that can be drawn about the effects of infotech on workers:

• *Practically no one will be exempt.* Infotech will change the nature of jobs and how workers do their jobs, affecting all the workers considered here, and probably 90% of the work force, by 2010.

The infotech revolution will not be confined to the office, where its primary effects are being felt today. Infotech is spreading across the full spectrum of workplaces. Similarly, it will not be restricted to the 60% of today's work force that is grouped in the information sector. It will become more difficult to distinguish an information worker from a non-information worker, as there will be few tasks that will not involve infotech.

Most workers in 2010 will be primarily information workers who incidentally make widgets, sell clothes, and grow corn. The worker's primary activities will be gathering, creating, manipulating, storing, and distributing information related to products, services, and customer needs.

• *Technologies will compete against each other.* The scope and importance of effects from infotech will not be uniform. The technologies themselves are at varying stages of development. Some technologies are just taking off and will advance considerably over the next 15 years or so, therefore having strong effects across the board. Other technologies, however, will not be as far along in development. Virtual reality, for example, will be a high-impact technology beyond 2010, but workers will just be starting to feel its effects before then. Other technologies are more mature. E-mail, voice mail, and fax, for example, will not advance much beyond today's capabilities and will therefore have less impact out to 2010.

Some technologies will directly compete with one another. Personal communicators, for example, will compete with cellular phones. The two may split the market for wireless communications by 2010, or one may win out.

• *The "Big Four" information technologies—computer networks, imaging technology, massive data storage, and artificial intelligence—will have revolutionary effects.* These key technologies will reshape today's occupations and become vital tools for most workers. The Big Four technologies are already important today, and their use will expand dramatically as people learn to use them more skillfully and effectively.

Networks will become indispensable for sharing and communicating information. National "information highways" of computer networks are in the early stages. The final step will be linking the national networks to create the global village of electronic networks, making it possible to communicate with anyone, anywhere, anytime. *Imaging technology* will make information more user-friendly and will enable the rapid transmission of images, which is still a bottleneck today. *Massive data storage systems* will handle the expansion of information, which will be stored electronically in readily accessible, attractive, and concise formats. This will help workers to deal with the problem of information overload. *Artificial-intelligence systems*, including expert systems, knowbots, and machine vision, will become partners with workers, although sometimes they will replace workers.

• *Implementation strategies will determine whether information technologies are a boon or a bane to workers.* The positive or negative effects of information technologies on workers by 2010 will hinge largely on how the systems are set up. Strategies will range from empowering workers to eliminating them. These technologies can automate dull, routine tasks and create more-challenging jobs; they can also cut costs, cut jobs, and onerously monitor worker performance. No matter what the implementation strategy, infotech will replace many jobs and radically alter others. . . .

The infotech revolution is still in its infancy today. But for workers, the old saying "you ain't seen nothin' yet" is probably fair warning.

Scenarios for Infotech Workers, 2010

• *The Farmer.* Harry looks over the visual representation of his farm on the screen. "Show me the soil moisture map," he commands the farm-management system, which coordinates field sensors with the computer system. A barrage of colors come up on screen. "Too much red," he observes. Red is the color representing dangerously low levels of soil moisture. He wistfully recalls last season's blue map, which resulted from record rainfalls.

Harry activates his expert-system assistant. "What are my options?" he asks. Three choices appear on the screen:

A. Divert water from purple areas (acceptable levels of moisture).

B. Borrow or purchase water from Johnson, who borrowed 1,000 gallons two years ago.

C. Purchase water from the municipal supply.

Harry dials up his weather forecasting service and asks for the next month's forecast. "More dry weather," he complains aloud. He decides that he will ask Johnson for some water and contract for the rest from the municipal water supply. He taps into the videotex service run by the county. It is an on-line bidding service. As Harry suspected, rates are up due to the drought. He winces and bids for the water he needs. The electronic-data-interchange service notifies him of the price and asks for his approval. Harry reluctantly adds his electronic signature.

• *The Police Officer.* Testimony of Officer Nina Padula before the Seventh District Court, August 29, 2010: "My squad car's computer alerted me at 2:45 p.m. on May 7, 2010, that a Quick-shop had been held up just two minutes previously. I was in the area and quickly spotted two young men running down the street with a bag. I ordered them to halt, advised them of their rights, and scanned their fingerprints into the computer. The computer searched the National Criminal Database and within seconds advised me to arrest the suspects, since they were in violation of their electronic house arrest. I was warned that they had a history of violence and I took the appropriate safety procedures, stunning the suspects and fully activating my body armor."

Science and Education

• *The Scientist.* A team of scientists headed by Lara Radinsky appears to be close to the breakthrough long sought by the bioremediation field: the demonstration of a new genetically engineered microorganism that will attack many of the plastics buried in landfills around the world.

"Teamwork was the key," says Radinsky. "We had scientists in Indonesia, Mexico, Germany, and China working on the project around the clock."

At first, some scientists had worried that the multinational team might have a hard time integrating its findings, but the bugs were worked out. "The godsend was our new computer-supported, cooperative-work software," says Radinsky. "Findings from each team member were immediately available to the others. As a result, we never lost perspective of the project as a whole."

• *The Teacher.* Samantha arrives at Shaker Elementary and urgently advises Mr. Wheel that she is ready to move on to the next level of her geography program. Wheel smiles and brings the quiz up on Samantha's screen. He is amazed at how eager the kids are to learn since the new computer-assisted instruction programs arrived. . . .

Wheel observes that Samantha called up the country screen six times and the pictures screen only once. He gives her the okay to move on to the next level and advises her to be ready for the science lesson, in which a local scientist will give the students a tour of the lab by videoconference.

"*Criminal organizations of the twenty-first century will continue to use violence and wealth . . . but they will also increasingly use knowledge to enhance the power they already have.*"

Information Technology Criminals, 2010

Richter H. Moore Jr.

Information technology in the twenty-first century will enhance the power of criminal organizations, argues Richter H. Moore Jr. in the following viewpoint. Moore contends that the predicted cashless society of the future will prove no impediment to drug trafficking, as credit cards can easily replace cash in drug transactions. He believes information technology will lead to many new types of crime, such as sophisticated high-tech theft and extortion using computer viruses. Moore predicts that corporate computer hackers will be prime aids in illegally obtaining intellectual property and technology. Moore, a former president of the Academy of Criminal Justice Sciences, is a criminal justice professor at Appalachian State University in Boone, North Carolina.

As you read, consider the following questions:

1. How might criminal organizations use satellites in the future, according to Moore?
2. According to the author, what new areas of crime are criminal organizations likely to enter in the future?
3. According to Moore, what is the "nuclear mafia"?

Richter H. Moore Jr., "Wiseguys: Smarter Criminals and Smarter Crime in the Twenty-First Century," *The Futurist*, September/October 1994. Reproduced with permission from *The Futurist*, published by the World Future Society, 7910 Woodmont Ave., Suite 450, Bethesda, MD 20814.

Organized crime has invaded the Information Society. With today's satellites, telecommunications, video technology, and computers, the world of information is open to everyone, and the ability to use information—to turn it into knowledge—is a source of power.

Criminal organizations of the twenty-first century will continue to use violence and wealth (their most common sources of power in the twentieth century), but they will also increasingly use knowledge to enhance the power they already have. The top guns of twenty-first-century criminal organizations will be educated, highly sophisticated, computer-literate individuals who can wield state-of-the-art information technology to the best advantage—for themselves and for their organizations.

Targeting Financial Institutions

One of the top targets of twenty-first-century organized crime will be financial institutions. In the last quarter of the twentieth century, organized crime has become a major international financial force. Profits from drug trafficking have built major cartels and international conglomerates, with financial power rivaling many of the world's major corporations. Drug entrepreneurs blithely write off "business" losses greater than some countries' entire budgets. They use their illegal profits to establish giant financial empires, which usually include some major investments in legitimate businesses. Their dabblings in legitimate activities give these operators knowledge of the vulnerabilities of financial institutions. And insiders might be lured by opportunities for great wealth to hook up with criminal organizations.

Banks will be handling increased amounts of customer information valuable not only to them, but to criminal organizations as well, so criminal organizations of the future will routinely place their own operatives in financial institutions, or develop contacts with those already there. These "moles" will provide information such as computer passwords and access codes, which will allow criminal organizations to invade without casting suspicion on their insiders. To further elude detection, pairs of insiders could work in different parts of the organization— perhaps even in different countries.

Hijackings on the Information Highway

Some futurists predict that the developed world will become a cashless society within the first quarter of the next century and that this will solve the problem of drug trafficking. Unfortunately, the criminal organizations of the future will be ready for a cashless society. Their electronic, financial, and legal experts will simply establish new ways of doing business.

In drug trafficking, for example, the street dealer who today collects cash for his transactions will be able to accept "plastic," and the buyer will be provided with an adequate credit line with which to make purchases. The seller of illegal goods and services can use a legitimate business operated by the crime group as a means of recording the sale. The sale of drugs may show up as merchandise on the records of a restaurant, bar, or convenience store.

Computer extortion will be a steady moneymaker for criminal organizations of the future. The introduction of a virus into the computers of a multinational corporation could be disastrous. The loss or vandalism of computer data could result in a complete work stoppage or, if related to an assembly line, to defective products. Tomorrow's viruses will be even subtler and more vicious than today's. They will be able to attack mainframes and even destroy hardware without being detected.

Theft in the new century will far exceed anything in the old in terms of sophistication and specialization. Already we see harbingers of what is to come: For example, high-tech airplane guidance systems worth more than $100,000 each were stolen in the spring of 1992 by a crime ring operating at Kennedy International Airport in New York and sold to a drug cartel for use on narcotics-smuggling planes. In the years ahead, all sorts of high-tech gear, such as medical equipment stolen from hospitals, will be sold on the increasingly international black market.

Manipulating Identities

Criminal organizations will hire the most-skilled computer hackers to penetrate targeted institutions. These hackers will change bank records, credit accounts and reports, criminal-history files, and educational, medical, and even military records. The hackers will also sell identity-manipulation services to those who need a new persona but cannot get one legitimately. Anyone's private records may be invaded, copied, deleted, or removed for criminal purposes.

Future criminals may also be able to manipulate a person's genetic identity—a feat that will be increasingly desired, because of the growing use of genetic identification. Already genetic identification is being used by the U.S. military to assure that there will be no more "unknown soldiers." By the twenty-first century, genetic-based records will include a birth-to-death dossier of a person and will be *the* method of criminal identification.

However, with further advances in genetic engineering, an individual's genes may become manipulable in such a manner as to change the structure of his or her DNA. If so, criminal organizations will likely steal computer records of DNA to provide new identities for their own people or to clients who need one. These new identities will not only include the "paper identity" (birth certificate, driver's license, etc.), but—through bioengineering—the "physical identity" as well, including a DNA pattern that matches the individual being impersonated.

Building a Facade of Legitimacy

Criminal organizations worldwide currently use their profits from illegal activities to buy legitimate businesses. The Colombian drug cartels are thought to have major portfolios that include substantial holdings of stock in many of the *Fortune* 500 companies. Japan's premier criminal organization, the Yakuza, is believed to have major stock and real estate holdings around the world, including substantial investments in the United States. And the Mafia has long invested in legitimate business enterprises.

By the next century, criminal organizations will not only own shares of multinational corporations, but manage them as well. Such a company will not be concerned with distinguishing between legal and illegal means of gaining an advantage over its competitors. A corporate computer hacker could be assigned to illegally obtain the technology, plans, formulas, intellectual property, and experimental information of the competitor. Data can be stolen outright or simply manipulated in a manner that causes major problems for the victim, such as placing incorrect information in a database or obstructing data.

Satellites will be yet another tool for tomorrow's criminals. Today, satellites make possible instantaneous communications all around the world; they also allow people and products to be tracked and help identify the best site for a particular activity and the location and extent of a competitor's holdings. Satellite-imaging information services and communications networks are increasingly available on the commercial market. By the next century, criminal organizations will be able to afford their own satellites. For example, a drug cartel could hire its own team of scientists to launch a satellite that could be used as a secure information network for the cartel's drug trafficking and money laundering operations. Such systems could also be used to track couriers and shipments and act as an early-warning system spotting drug-enforcement agency operations.

With major organized-crime groups around the world already working together, it is likely that more than one group will become involved in the use of these satellite systems. Some organized-crime groups already have state-of-the-art equipment and communications systems, most of which puts law-enforcement technologies to shame. There is no reason to believe criminal organizations will not keep up with the latest, most-sophisticated technology. Their money will enable them to buy whatever they need to make themselves as invulnerable as possible.

Satellite systems could conceivably be adapted to seize and redirect military weaponry, such as rockets or guided missiles, to use against government or law-enforcement forces.

Growing Sophistication

The twenty-first century will see growing sophistication of criminal organizations, which will all be tied into larger networks devoted to meeting the public's demand for illegal goods and services. Technology and communications will allow crime networks to operate more efficiently and with greater impunity.

Garison Weiland. Reprinted by permission of the artist.

Sports gambling in the twenty-first century will be truly global. With their own satellite communications networks, criminal organizations will be able to operate from sites where law-enforcement agencies are sympathetic. Sporting events worldwide, from horse racing to school sports, will be fixed. In 1992, authorities discovered a $1-billion gambling ring operating out of the Dominican Republic that was involved in fixing sporting events in the United States. As criminal organizations refine and expand their networks, the Dominican ring will appear to have been a very small beginning.

Prostitution rings will use modern technology to coordinate global activities. The trade in young women from Africa, India, Pakistan, China, Thailand, and the Philippines for Yakuza and Chinese Triad brothels in the Far East will likely increase and expand into the Western Hemisphere, especially South America.

Organized-Crime Activities

Criminal organizations will also use their high-tech networks and information-based power to move into new areas, such as trafficking in newborn infants, sold to childless couples. If kidnapping fails to supply the market adequately, pregnant women may be seized, labor induced, and the child taken. Given false documentation, stolen children may appear in the official records as the natural children of the individuals who bought them.

Fetuses are also becoming important in medical research and in treating certain conditions such as Parkinson's disease. Since religious, social, and political constraints restrict the supply, fetuses may also become subject to unlawful trafficking.

Waste disposal is another activity that may be increasingly pursued by crime organizations. Governments have not been—and will not be—willing to make the effort to fully enforce their own environmental regulations or to provide the personnel to do so. This leaves the door open for criminal entrepreneurs to provide waste-disposal services in violation of local laws. They will not hesitate to haul away toxic materials for illegal and dangerous dumping if the price is right. The Mafia has hauled hazardous industrial waste from New York and New Jersey and illegally dumped it in North Carolina. They have also dumped dangerous hospital waste in the Atlantic Ocean, and some of it has washed up on beaches.

An even more menacing opportunity for criminal entrepreneurs lies in the vast quantities of arms and nuclear materials that have become available with the shattering of the Soviet army and bureaucracy. Arms sales within the former Soviet republics are booming. Well into the twenty-first century, there will be a surplus of Soviet weapons. And more arms will flow from the downsized Western military forces. Criminal organizations will be able to supply the private armies of worldwide criminal networks, terrorists, hate groups, questionable regimes, independent crime groups, and individual criminals.

To make matters worse, a "nuclear mafia" has developed in the last two decades. Groups can acquire nuclear materials, mostly by theft, and then make them available to any regime or group with the money to purchase them. Germany has become the center of nuclear smuggling. According to one official, the problem is becoming so bad that Germany is in danger of becoming the global emporium for nuclear smuggling. By the next century, criminal groups will likely develop the ability to make nuclear weapons. Nuclear extortion will not only be a tool of irresponsible governments, but of criminal establishments as well.

Infiltrating Governments

In the years ahead, criminal organizations will control the governments of many countries, either directly or indirectly. In the new states of the former Soviet Union, organized-crime groups are tied closely to governments and essentially control economic systems. In other countries, such as Nigeria and Colombia, criminal organizations have virtually paralyzed the government. If members of the organization are arrested and tried, they receive special treatment and continue to run their organizations from prison.

The individual who becomes a part of a criminal organization in the twenty-first century will do so not because it's the only route to success, but because it offers the best opportunity for achieving wealth and power.

As members of criminal organizations become more educated, they will become more attuned to the ways of politics. They will become actively involved to assure that their interests are protected. Gaining greater power, they will become a force that world society will have to recognize and deal with.

Scenario: Crime in the Year 2010

As her beeper sounded, Security Chief Susan Willis knew that it was another attempt to infiltrate the databases of Global Chips, the world's premier computer company, located in Seattle, Washington.

We have made great strides in protecting our databases from intrusion, Willis thought as she headed for her office. From the announcement in 2006 of the period-size or "dot" computer chip with mainframe information capacity, efforts by industrial spies, criminal entrepreneurs, and sophisticated computer hackers to obtain Global's secrets had multiplied.

Willis had been busy at Global over the years, meeting the challenges of outside data theft, infiltration of the company by data thieves, and virus-planting saboteurs. One of her first projects for the company was the "Eyes Only" access system in 1999. In the last decade of the twentieth century, data theft from U.S. computer companies was particularly rampant. Her

"Eyes Only" system used a retina-identification scanner to allow a person access to a computer. Only authorized individuals, whose retina patterns were stored in the computer, could obtain access. Since retina patterns cannot be duplicated, such a system is absolutely secure.

Willis had worked with one of the firm's founding members, Cassandra Winter, to develop the portable retina scanner, which could be plugged into any computer in the world. It was this development that first put Global Chips on the map and made the company's initial fortune. The "Eyes Only" system was now used worldwide to protect access to computer databases and had substantially reduced the theft of data and virus-based sabotage.

But spies and members of global criminal enterprises continued to try to infiltrate Global and break into its computers. Willis was pleased when Cassandra Winter had developed a nanocomputer that used the dot chip. This nanocomputer was so small and powerful that it could be implanted into an individual's brain and used to detect lying, disloyalty, theft, and other actions contrary to the best interests of the company or the country.

The ultimate nanocomputer—the "MiniGiant"—was the result. When tested on Global employees, the MiniGiant discovered six infiltrators: a Yakuza member working for a major Japanese computer manufacturer; a Russian mafia member with a doctorate in miniaturization; a Chinese government agent; a Hong Kong Triad member; a German operative for the Sicilian mafia; and a member of the Cali drug cartel with an MBA from Harvard.

From the beginning, the MiniGiant had been a boon to companies infiltrated, but not yet taken over, by members of criminal organizations. Legitimate businesses could now compete better against criminally controlled or infiltrated enterprises, protecting their trade secrets with the tools that Global had developed.

Arriving at her office, Willis sat down at the computer. After identifying herself through the retina scanner, she was immediately put on-line. "Identify the individual who is attempting to gain access to the system," she commanded the computer. Immediately a world map appeared on the screen with an arrow pinpointing Japan. Then the screen changed and showed a picture of a major Japanese computer manufacturer in an industrial park just outside of Tokyo.

"The party seeking to break into my database is located on the second floor, left rear corner of the plant," said the computer, now showing a schematic diagram of the building. "The individual is using a model 9001XJ computer over phone line 069JA-9208612 in this attempt at breaching my security."

Willis smiled, pleased by this new detection system—not yet made public—which let you know both who and where your enemies were.

"Computer, allow him access to the system and direct him to the directory designated 'False Trail,'" she said. The computer complied, baiting the intruder with access to information that would lead him to believe that he had tapped into plans for one of Global's new products. But unbeknownst to him, this "new product" would not function. However, the spurious information had been so cleverly prepared that the Japanese firm would spend a fortune on getting it to market.

Mission accomplished, Susan Willis thought as she settled back in her chair.

Periodical Bibliography

The following articles have been selected to supplement the diverse views presented in this chapter.

Robert U. Ayres "Technological Trends," *National Forum*, Spring 1994. Available from PO Box 16000, Louisiana State University, Baton Rouge, LA 70893.

Laurent Belsie "Myths Litter the Information Highway," *The Christian Science Monitor*, July 6, 1994. Available from One Norway St., Boston, MA 02115.

Samuel E. Bleecker "The Virtual Organization," *The Futurist*, March/April 1994.

Kristene B. Detienne "Big Brother or Friendly Coach? Computer Monitoring in the 21st Century," *The Futurist*, September/October 1993.

John Diebold "The Next Revolution in Computers," *The Futurist*, May/June 1994.

Peter F. Eder "Privacy on Parade: Your Secrets for Sale!" *The Futurist*, July/August 1994.

Al Gore "The National Information Infrastructure," *Vital Speeches of the Day*, February 1, 1994.

Herbert Kaufman "The Emergent Kingdom: Machines That Think like People," *Futures*, January/February 1994.

Jerry Mander "Tyranny of Technology," *Resurgence*, May/June 1994. Available from Rodale Press, 33 E. Minor St., Emmaus, PA 18098.

Joseph P. Martino "Technological Forecasting: An Introduction," *The Futurist*, July/August 1993.

Norman S. Mayersohn "The Outlook for Hydrogen," *Popular Science*, October 1993.

John D. Morgan "Strategic Materials for the Future," *Futures Research Quarterly*, Winter 1991. Available from 7910 Woodmont Ave., Suite 450, Bethesda, MD 20814.

Scientific American "Communications, Computers, and Networks," September 1991.

David C. Wyld, Sam D. Cappel, and Daniel E. Hallock "The New Eugenics? Employers and Genetic Screening in the 'Risk Society,'" *Futures Research Quarterly*, Fall 1992.

What Will Become of America's Economy?

AMERICA
BEYOND
2001

Chapter Preface

During the early 1990s, up to two-thirds of Americans indicated through opinion polls that America is "on the wrong track." Many questioned whether the American dream of each generation's living better than the previous one could continue. Indeed, this dream is being sorely tested by such factors as a declining standard of living, corporate downsizing, global competition, and anxiety over the funding of such entitlements as Social Security and Medicare.

Surveying public attitudes about the future, researchers James Patterson and Peter Kim, authors of *The Day America Told the Truth*, reported that 77 percent of Americans believe "the rich will continue to get richer and the poor poorer." The prevailing belief many polls find among Americans is that future standards of living will be lower than those of post–World War II baby boomers, who, in turn, fear a long-term decline in their own standard of living.

However, according to Kevin Phillips, author of *America Extrapolated*, most of Americans' gloom derives from an excessive dose of "extrapolationism." He advises, "When everyone is telling everyone else how a trend will continue uninterrupted on its current trajectory, don't bet on it." Looking back on projections proven wrong by time, Phillips finds that "the pathways of history are littered with the corpses of extrapolators whose projections caught up with them." Others agree that Americans are prematurely losing faith in, or abandoning, the American dream. According to consumer researcher Fabian Linden, the wealth inherited by baby boomers, improved housing and labor markets for post–baby boomers, and continued low interest rates for both groups promise to sustain Americans' standard of living.

Standards of living will be of concern to present and future generations. The authors in this chapter examine trends affecting America's economic future.

"This whole fantastic new economy is absolutely laden with opportunity if we . . . are smart enough to get with the program rather than put a brake on it."

The Global Economy Is Real

Tom Peters

According to many experts, America is becoming increasingly integrated into a global economy. In the following viewpoint, Tom Peters agrees, arguing that new technologies have increased the importance of information and reduced the role of large-scale industrial processes in production, signaling the end of the Industrial Revolution. Peters predicts that information-based, export-oriented business and increased international trade will transform America as well as other nations. Peters is the author of *In Search of Excellence, Thriving on Chaos,* and *Liberation Management* and president of the Tom Peters Group, a management training firm in Palo Alto, California. This viewpoint is adapted from his speech before Congress in July 1993.

As you read, consider the following questions:

1. How does Peters compare the economies of America and Japan?
2. What does the author mean by "reengineering"?
3. In Peters's opinion, why is American education so critical in the global economy?

From Tom Peters, "Surviving and Thriving in the Emerging Global Economy," *What's Next: A Newsletter of Emerging Issues and Trends,* Fall 1993. Reprinted with permission.

We are in the middle of change that is revolutionary. And if there is a revolution going on out there in the way business is done and economies are developed, then it suggests that a revolution had better be going on here, as well!

The end of the Industrial Revolution came approximately January 17, 1992. On that day the stock market value of software superstar Microsoft, then tallying $2 billion in annual turnover, shot past that of General Motors, with $124 billion in annual turnover. A *New York Times* writer declared at about the same time that "Microsoft's only factory asset is the human imagination." If ever you wanted a symbolic event that said the age of brawn and lifting metal and digging holes had been replaced by the age of brains, that has to be it.

Economic Renaissance

I am so phenomenally excited about what is going on in the world that I can't see straight. We are in the middle of an economic renaissance the likes of which the planet has not seen. Sure we have to compete like crazy to keep up with the Japanese and Asians, but how can you be anything but excited to watch this all happen.

When I was in Asia recently, my wife and I decided to take three weeks and hang out and sort of smell the place. I came back with a head that was exploding. This is a civilization busting loose. [Congressmembers] and Bill Clinton are struggling to keep our generation of 150,000 jobs a month going while 150 million people are going to be added to the Chinese workforce before the end of this decade. Let me tell you, they ain't all making sandals. Many are, in fact, programming computers and doing sophisticated systems work. I think this whole fantastic new economy is absolutely laden with opportunity if we in Sacramento, Albany [state capitals of California and New York, respectively], and Washington, DC, as well as the entrepreneurial capitals of the world are smart enough to get with the program rather than put a brake on it.

I ended up with a few days in New Zealand and Australia. In Australia, against all odds, a labor party was just re-elected despite 11 percent unemployment. They were fundamentally re-elected on a plank of getting rid of most of the social benefits package they had put in place over the last 50 years. It is sort of a last ditch effort to get Australia focused away from Europe and on to Asia and into the business of competing not just with the Japanese but with that phenomenal explosion of talent, energy, and effort going on in Indonesia, Malaysia, Singapore, and Taiwan.

Quite simply, we are in a new economy. The same thing is true basically all around the world. The car is a classic example.

Depending on how you do your counting, essentially there are something like 200 or 300 computer chips in the average car today. For all practical purposes, an automobile is a bunch of seats, a bunch of tires, and a computer.

I got in a lot of trouble a while back when I said the US has seven of the ten leading media companies in the world. I'd rather have seven of the ten leading media companies in the world than two of the three leading automobile companies. Time-Warner is getting together with US-West; Microsoft and Time-Warner and Telecommunications Inc. are getting together. There is a multi-trillion dollar industry called computer-software-cable-telecommunications-publishing-entertainment that nobody knows anything about.

Competing in the Global Economy

Bill Clinton [once] declared that "open and competitive commerce will enrich us as a nation. . . . It spurs us to innovate. It forces us to compete, it connects us with new customers. It promotes global growth without which no rich nation can hope to grow more wealthy." For years, the president stated, we had not been preparing ourselves fully for the brutal competition of this new post–Cold War global economy, letting the agenda of the future slide, enjoying today at the expense of our children's tomorrow.

Ronald H. Brown, *The Washington Times*, September 21, 1994.

Another point is one that is beautiful and scary in equal measures. All nations share the same strategy. Should you go to Malaysia, Malaysia has the same strategy as Silicon Valley in the US [a region of California that is a national center of high-tech manufacturing]. Malaysia does not want to make sandals either. Malaysia's strategy is high value–added, knowledge-based, exportable economy. Japan's strategy is high value–added, knowledge-based, exportable economy; Australia's is high value–added, knowledge-based, exportable economy. What do we have here in the US? Precisely the same.

Sometime [soon], the average gross domestic product (GDP) per capita in Singapore, now called the intelligent island because they figured out that fiber optic highways were important even before Al Gore did, the average per capita income in Singapore will go past that of Great Britain.

US Productivity and Services

Let us never forget that we still come at this business with an advantage. The US is as close to being in the catbird seat as you can possibly be on any number of dimensions. The productivity figures for the US as you adjust them to a purchasing power basis, which is, after all, what economies are all about, puts us in the driver's seat. It puts us in the driver's seat in two-thirds of manufacturing and in virtually the entire area of services, where most Americans are now employed. Some 94 percent of Americans are working in industries that are more productive than Japanese industries.

What is happening in Japan? What is happening in Japan is children go broke faster than their parents. The Japanese shot up out of nowhere; they have come significantly close to closing the gap with us, and then they slowed down.

We weep, and we mourn. Yet *Fortune* magazine reported that in the world there are 55 computing companies with over $1 billion in revenue. The US has 42 of them. We are hardly at the storm.

The next point I want to make, and I think this is terribly important when you consider investment strategies and so forth, concerns the service sector. The service sector, much as it has been maligned by "they are all flipping hamburgers," is an absolute national treasure. If you read the front page of the press, you would think that everyone in the US is making hamburgers and everyone in Japan is making automobiles. The fact of the matter is 75 percent of us are in the service sector, and about 70 percent of the Japanese are in the service sector. And there isn't much difference except their service sector is going to occupy as many of their people as ours does.

A report turned out by McKinsey [and Co. business consultants] said we are absolutely dominant in the *new* services and soft manufacturing sectors—and we must take care to understand the source of our success. And said the study, the source of our relative success in service is that we are radically deregulated compared to the service sectors in Japan or Germany. We have these phenomenal leads in productivity in banking, telecommunications, and general retail. The service sector is making a ton of money for us.

How many people realize that we are running a $95 billion so-called deficit, and the service sector is generating a $60 billion positive trade balance, netted out to $35 billion. But $35 billion in a $6 trillion economy also is not precisely the end of the world. You would think it's the end of the world the way we act.

Change, Change, and More Change

We are in the midst of a once-every-several-hundred-years change. If you don't feel totally confused about what is going on, you are out-of-touch. And I mean that in the kindest sense of the word.

Another point is—as messy and as uncomfortable as it is—the

message is churn. The success of the American economy since the very beginning of time is business failure as much as business success. If you are looking for one single secret to Silicon Valley, let me tell you what that secret is. Failure. We have got a higher rate of business failure than any other 1300 square miles in the world economy today. For every [computer designer] Steve Jobs for whom we write a biography, there are 75 other people who are just as intelligent, work just as hard, mortgage their house, borrow themselves dry, and fail and are never heard of. Silicon Valley is outrageously exciting because things are stopping, and people are going out of business, and people are coming into business, and it is sheer madness. From 1965 to 1989, the US created 45 million new jobs, while the Japanese could muster 14 million and the Europeans could muster 10 million. Job creation does not come from adding people to the payroll of General Motors or IBM.

Head-to-Head Confrontation

Economic competition, as [economist] Lester Thurow sees it, has moved from complementary niches, determined in the past by the uneven resources of the trading countries, to a head-to-head confrontation among near equals. The "great wall" that protected U.S. industry—an educated work force, technological preeminence, and, above all, cash for investments—has slowly eroded; America's highest-paying jobs, and ultimately its standard of living, have become vulnerable to assaults from abroad. The key to competitive advantage in the next century, Thurow argues, now lies in overarching strategies for organizing the productive capacities of nations and perhaps of entire continents.

Robert C. Crawford, *Technology Review*, October 1992.

Big company job loss has barely begun. Some of you may have read in the press, there is a term sweeping the business management literature, it is called "reengineering" which basically means once you have gotten rid of the hierarchy you have to hook the company together again so that people work together as teams. One of the reengineering gurus said if we did it right, reengineering would cost us another 25 million jobs.

How overstaffed are our big companies? London's *Financial Times* reported, "IBM to cut British headquarters staff from 2,500 to 90." In our sizable corporations like American Express, General Motors, IBM and so on, we are talking about overstaffing levels that, taken as a whole, still run in the millions. If you are going to move fast, if you are going to innovate fast, if you are going to stay close to your customers, you don't do it out of a 47-story tower loaded with bureaucrats who only know how to say no.

Job destruction will continue to go on in the service sector and the manufacturing sector and our biggest firms. This is on net good news as long as the private sector can create the offsetting jobs. We went through it first. Go to Japan now; they are panicked about the same thing we were panicked about ten years ago—getting lean, getting mean, and figuring out where to send the bureaucrats to pasture.

The mid-sized companies and the small companies are our salvation. Yes, there are crummy jobs in small businesses, but if you look at the statistics as a whole, small companies have more than their fair share of high wage jobs. When we say small company, we equate small company with low pay, no benefits, and second-rate work. There is some of that going around but, in fact, the small business sector is key.

The next major point that I want to make is to emphasize the obvious, we are in a brain-based society. When we talk about GATT [General Agreement on Tariffs and Trade], when we talk about NAFTA [North American Free Trade Agreement], the issue is not rice. The issue is the dramatic economic transformation of the world, and the US will maintain its lead in the world to the extent that it exchanges lower valued jobs for higher valued jobs. The possibility of hiding [now] is just zero.

Education Haves and Have-Nots

All of that leads to the point that "education-R-us." From 1968 to 1977 in the US, average inflation-adjusted family income went up 20 percent. And the rising tide lifted all boats. If you were a high school dropout, you got your 20 percent; if you were a college graduate you got 21 percent. We are dealing with a country with 250 million people ten years later. The information age is in bloom: high school dropouts lost 4 percent, and college graduates, on average, gained 48 percent. That is the basis for social revolution. The Industrial Revolution brought us Karl Marx, the Information Revolution is going to bring us another Marx. In what form he or she will appear, the impact she or he will have, I don't know. But I do know that we are talking about a gap between haves and have-nots based purely on education that is stunning and unprecedented in the history of the US.

To put it mildly, the program of education must be reinvented. The one disastrous mistake we can make is to copy the Japanese K-12 [kindergarten through twelfth grade] system at exactly the time the Japanese are getting fed up with their K-12 system. This is the time to produce creativity, not the time to remember long lists of kings and queens and princes and archdukes.

I would add one other thing, one final point on this topic of education and knowledge, and that is guard our universities as if they were the most precious jewels that we've got. If the world wants into Berkeley, Stanford, Dartmouth, Penn, and MIT, and so forth, then it tells you something. If this is a brain-based economy, then to the extent we can keep our great, research-based universities and our community colleges going, we are a lot better off. That is the place where we are absolutely unconquerable. There is no single place where the US has a more dramatic lead over the Germans, Chinese, Japanese, Swiss, and Malaysians.

Change Means Growth

I would just reiterate—there is no place to hide. If we hide, if we don't do GATT, if we don't do NAFTA, if we hide in this little place and pretend that the world is not changing, if we continue to make low value-added products, we will watch ourselves deteriorate over time. It is a big world; it is a dramatically changing world. And the more open the borders, the faster we can shut down the parts of the economy that ought to be shut down. Look at those numbers: 48 percent real income increase if you had a college degree and a drop of 4 percent if you were a high school dropout. What we need to do, what we want to do is get as many Americans as we can into the higher education, higher value-added jobs.

I know you [congresspeople] get into trouble if you even take a half a day off on a junket outside the US, but you have to hang out and smell what is going on in places like Asia. It is not "sandal and thong" country. The world is making software in Bangladesh or India. Apple has a major software design center and not because it is cheap, but because it is damn good! And that is the nature of the competitive challenge we face.

Whether a corporation of the US, the Senate, or what, the American tone has to be a tone of growth, of openness, of expansion over the long haul.

"No one disputes that modems and airplanes and faxes are making markets more interknit. But let's not get carried away."

The Global Economy Is Largely Myth

Alan Farnham

The extensive size and impact of the global economy are more myth than reality, argues Alan Farnham in the following viewpoint. Farnham contends that the global economy is little different now than in the nineteenth century in terms of trade in goods and services and the international flow of capital and labor. One significant difference, according to Farnham, is the speedier transmission of business information. While he does not believe they are inevitable, Farnham describes changes companies may undergo in the future if a global economy does evolve, including international alliances that will create "Trillion Dollar Enterprises" and the ability of companies to succeed globally. Farnham is an associate editor of *Fortune* magazine.

As you read, consider the following questions:

1. In what way are many companies not as global as they appear, according to Farnham?
2. What are the impacts of the global economy on services, according to the author?
3. According to Farnham, what are the advantages of a "Trillion Dollar Enterprise"?

By the shores of Flathead Lake, Lester Thurow—economist, MIT professor, and Montana native—sat down and explained, in a video made a while back for the Missoula Economic Development Corp., why Montana is a great place to do business. Many reasons, probably, you could guess yourself. But not this: Montana is part of the Pacific Rim. How? It's connected to that economy by airplane and modem. You'd be making a mistake to think of Montana as just, well, Montana—146,000 square miles of grain, sheep, mines, and an occasional espresso bar—when in fact it is *Montana*—anteroom to Osaka and gateway to the global economy.

Baloney? Yes, and of an especially ripe and lustrous kind. No one disputes that modems and airplanes and faxes are making markets more interknit. But let's not get carried away. Montana's status as a Pacific Rim economy would seem forever compromised by its being on the right-hand side of Idaho.

Many of today's highest-profile global corporations, looked at from certain angles, don't appear much more global than Montana. Wrigley, Coca-Cola, Ford, Time Warner, and others do indeed produce and sell an increasing number of products worldwide, and with great finesse. But boards of directors in both U.S.- and foreign-owned global corporations remain almost exclusively a native affair. Cyrus Freidheim, vice chairman of Booz Allen & Hamilton points out that at major U.S. corporations, the same percentage of board seats were held by foreign nationals in 1991 (2.1%) as were held ten years earlier. At Asian corporations, says Freidheim, "foreign board members are as rare as British sumo wrestlers." Similarly, stock ownership is almost always concentrated in the home country.

Yet a truly global economy is emerging, and with it, a truly global corporation. The advent of these two will affect where you live, what job you hold, and even what hours you sleep (not past 3 a.m. if you want to take a breakfast teleconference with Tunisia). To discern the outline of the future, however, one must peer through the hype. Our goal is to pierce those clouds, describe the beauties within, and not succumb to globaloney anywhere along the way.

The Global Economy

What is the global economy? Asked this appallingly basic question, MIT professor Paul Krugman isn't insulted, since, he says, he suspects most people now brandishing the phrase have no clue what it means. Krugman, author of *Peddling Prosperity*, defines the global economy concretely: trade in goods; a much smaller trade in services; the international movement of labor; international flows of capital and information. "That's it," he says. "There is no more mystical sense in which we have a global economy."

What aspects of today's economy are unprecedented? Hardly any. Says Krugman: "We are living in a world which is about as integrated, give or take a few measures, as the world of the 19th century." Trade in goods and services is only slightly larger now, as a fraction of gross world product, than it was before 1914. Measured against GDP [gross domestic product], U.S. imports are only slightly bigger now (11%) than they were in 1880 (8%). Yes, 1880. Labor mobility is lower, too, due to restrictions on immigration.

Capital mobility? It's greater than it was in the 1960s, but, except for the movement of short-term money, it's smaller than it was in the years before World War I. Says Krugman: "If you were to ask what fraction of the savings of mature European countries was being invested abroad back then, it was a much higher share than anybody invests now. Great Britain ran an average annual current-account surplus of 4% of GDP for the 40 years before World War I, as big as the peak Japanese surplus of the 1980s."

Information Flow in the Global Economy

One significant difference: the speed with which huge volumes of information can be transmitted and received. The increase in speed may actually be less significant than differences in content: You could telegraph somebody instantly in the 19th century, but you couldn't fax her a set of working drawings.

"I was weaned on a fax machine," says David Montague, whose bicycle company, Montague Corp., designs its unique folding mountain bikes in Cambridge, Massachusetts, makes them in Taiwan, and sells most of them in Europe. Businesses like his, which must send design changes back and forth between three continents sometimes daily, would not be possible without the information technology that is at the heart of the new economy.

Nu Skin International, a Utah-based direct-sales company, uses a computer network and special software to help its 300,000 independent distributors sell personal care and health products in any of eight countries where the company has a sales license.

The company follows a multilevel marketing model; that is, a distributor receives a commission on his own sales as well as a share of commissions generated by the salespeople he recruits and by salespeople later recruited by his enlistees. But no matter how complex or how international a distributor's "tree" of commissions, he gets paid instantly. Renn Patch, international vice president, gives an example: If a sales trainee recruited by a distributor in Texas moves to Japan and sets up her own sales force, the Texan gets commissions on the Japanese sales. If one of the Japanese then moves to Mexico to help crack open the Mexican market, a share of the Mexican commissions winds its way back to Texas, too, by way of Japan.

Another difference between the global economies of old and ours today is the growth in services. Since most services, like the haircut you got last week, cannot be traded, says Krugman, "the shift to a service economy is the big force running counter to globalization." Does this mean that the 80 million or so people working in service jobs can ignore what happens in the global economy? John Cavanagh, co-author of *Global Dreams*, says the answer depends on what sort of service work you do. If you're employed in the 85% of services that aren't tradable— restaurants, retailing, wholesaling, for example—you can shrug and say, "Eh? Global, schmobal." But if yours is one of the growing number that *are* tradable—consulting, law, accounting, transportation, banking, and construction, to name a few big-ticket examples—better renew your subscription to *Le Monde* ["The World," a French daily newspaper].

The Global Competition Myth

Almost nobody—in business or government—would disagree with this statement: "Today America is part of a truly global economy. To maintain our standard of living, we must learn to compete in an ever tougher world marketplace. That's why high productivity and product quality have become essential. We need to move the economy into high-value sectors that will generate jobs for the future. And the only way we can be competitive is if we forge a new partnership between government and business."

The problem is: It's baloney. In reality, there is almost nothing to our fixation with national competitiveness, or its central idea— that every country is like a giant corporation slugging it out against rivals in global markets. The U.S. and Japan are simply not competitors in the same way that, say, Ford competes with Toyota. Any country's standard of living depends almost entirely on its own domestic economic performance, and not on how it performs *relative* to other countries. That's not just my view; it's what most economists think.

Paul Krugman, *Fortune*, March 7, 1994.

Even services not traded are exposed indirectly. Garry Jacobson, whose company, Malloy Electric, repairs and services electric motors in Sioux Falls, South Dakota, says, "People keep buying more and more of these cheap, Red Chinese motors, so we have to learn how to repair them. Either they bring them in or they just throw them away and buy a new one, which costs us." Subtly or not, the world creeps in.

Krugman predicts that "come the millennium, everything will be tradable. We'll put on our virtual-reality helmets and be able to supply anything to—or buy anything from—anybody in the world. That doesn't seem to be happening at breakneck speed. I don't think the world ten years from now will be one where the service sector has broken wide open to international trade. Fifty years from now? Maybe."

Evolution of the Global Economy

Besides, nowhere is it written that the global economy must thrive and prosper, growing ever more borderless and transparent. It could instead go *phhhht*. Absent the facilitating influence of information technology, the world of 1913 had many of today's earmarks of globalism, including multinational companies whose linkages spanned the world. That's why the bottle of aspirin in your cabinet is labeled Bayer. The pharmaceutical industry in the U.S. was almost entirely German-owned. But shoot the right archduke, and such fragile conceits break.

Says Krugman: "The idea that technological and economic trends are so powerful now that political forces can't derail them is nonsense." Capitalism's triumph in the Cold War notwithstanding, the main lesson of 20th-century history is that politics usually gets the drop on economics.

Assuming, however, that no wars or other retrograde political events interrupt the current march toward the future, how might the global economy evolve? What changes might that evolution prompt in corporations? *Fortune* uncovered several provocative speculations.

Globalization of Corporations

Cyrus Freidheim of Booz Allen thinks the competing interests of nationalism and globalism will bring forth what he calls the Trillion Dollar Enterprise—a world-girdling organization that would operate more like a political federation than a corporation. Because of its huge size, no industry could field more than a few of these. In communications, a TDE might arise from an alliance between AT&T, Sony, Deutsche Bundespost Telekom, and six other equally large players. All would retain local ownership and governance but would ally to accomplish difficult or expensive missions—say, building a global interactive video broadcasting system.

What advantages would such an organization possess? Apart from the obvious ones of shared talent and resources, the alliance could avoid running afoul of antitrust laws, since each company would still be independent. And since each would retain its local identity, the alliance would enjoy a political advantage in home markets. It could raise capital in each market and could escape restrictions, such as those in Brazil, that compel foreign-owned manufacturers to buy only local components.

Each player's independence, however, would mean the alliance would be ticklish to run. Freidheim says managers would need to acquire skills "important to the diplomat and politician," such as cultural sensitivity and a talent for discerning shared interests. "This is not the sort of executive the Western world has been growing," he says. Business schools offering courses in cross-cultural team building should do land-office business.

Freidheim's isn't the only model, of course. Thomas Malone, professor of information systems at MIT, envisions a proliferation of companies at the opposite end of the size spectrum from Freidheim's TDEs. These one-person companies would link up on a specific project. They might, for instance, be independent engineers in several countries collaborating by computer to design a car's electrical system.

To prevent theft of intellectual property, each would have to sign nondisclosure and noncompete agreements with the others. Malone thinks present attitudes toward such agreements will change. "Many of the people who resist the notion of legal protection for such property now, especially in the software world, do so because they see these contracts as favoring big companies. In fact, it may be just the opposite. More effective intellectual property protection may be necessary for the proliferation of viable small firms."

In such a world, where sets of collaborators could be in constant flux, reputation will count for much. *Is he trustworthy?* could be the all-important question. Once word got out you'd robbed another person's mental poke, you might as well hang up your mouse.

Caution for Businesses

How will globalization affect the way services and products are marketed? The combination of instant communications and a convergence of taste—among, say, teenagers in different countries—could mean, for example, that when a movie hits, it *really* hits; and when it bombs, it bombs atomically. Once somebody in Peoria declares *Last Action Hero* a dud, marketers will not be able to palm it off in Bali as "the picture all America is talking about."

Perhaps, as we near the end of our contemplation of the future, a note of caution should be sounded. Taking a local business global will continue to be hard—harder than any novice can imagine. Someone with a ringside seat on that process is David Helin, an expert on international expansion for FIND/SVP, a market research company in New York City. All day long, clients call him to ask questions about going global, flushed with excite-ment at the prospect. Most quickly change their mind. Of every 100 clients who express interest, fewer than 10, once they know the realities, try it.

But press on: There's a prize waiting for those who do. People who succeed in going global, says author John Cavanagh, "truly have a fabulous global menu to pick from: where to work, where to consume, where to travel. For them, globalization has opened up a remarkable world."

It's David Montague's world. Montague, the global bicycle en-trepreneur, wouldn't run his business any other way. True, he does have to get up now at 5 a.m. to talk to Germany. But man-ufacturing and selling in different markets, he thinks, makes his business—and his workers' jobs—safer: He's not dependent on any one economy.

Measured not just in money but also in tastes and sights and adventures, his life is richer than if he had stayed rooted to a single spot. He likes taking a gondola to the airport (in Venice) and flying over the Alps at night. Shopping the world for the smartest talent and cheapest prices, he also eats better than he would in Newton, Massachusetts. Recalling lunch in Venice, he says, "Boy, do they know pasta." Now, having savored the global economy, he figures he could run his business from any city, anywhere—even Missoula.

"Entitlements are actually the soundest part of the budget!"

Entitlement Programs Are Sustainable

Daniel Patrick Moynihan

Entitlements are the collective federal programs (such as Social Security, Medicare, and Medicaid) that provide guaranteed benefits, mostly to the poor and the elderly. In the following viewpoint, Daniel Patrick Moynihan argues that entitlements are the most solvent part of the federal budget—Social Security, Medicare, and Unemployment Insurance each receiving more revenues than benefits disbursed. Moynihan opposes suggestions to cut Social Security benefits and maintains that, with certain adjustments, the system will be sustainable well into the twenty-first century. Moynihan is a Democratic senator from New York.

As you read, consider the following questions:

1. How did the term "entitlement" originate, according to Moynihan?
2. In Moynihan's opinion, how does Social Security help the budget deficit?
3. Why are objections that workers receive greater Social Security benefits than they contributed no longer valid, in the author's opinion?

It's become somewhat popular in the nation's capital—in some circles, anyway—to talk about the need to cut federal spending for entitlements. You may ask, What exactly is an entitlement? Well, truthfully, I wondered myself and recently did a little noodling around to find out.

Defining Entitlements

As best I can determine, the term has two meanings. The first is rather technical and would be the meaning intended by professional budgeteers in the Congressional Budget Office or the Office of Management and Budget. In this context, "entitlement" refers to so-called mandatory spending, mostly in the form of payments to individuals. Such spending is called mandatory because the money goes to whoever is eligible for a given program, automatically. Congress does not decide how much to spend every year on entitlement programs, as it does on, say, defense spending.

Specifically, in the words of the Congressional Budget Act, entitlements are

> payments (including loans and grants), the budget authority for which is not provided for in advance by appropriation Acts, to any person or government if, under the provisions of the law containing such authority, the United States is obligated to make such payments to persons or governments who meet the requirements established by such law.

That's the technical definition.

I mentioned another definition. It is simpler, if more surreptitious. I admit that this definition is one I have inferred, rather than found somewhere. But I feel that "entitlement" is a code word for Social Security.

Of course, proposals to cut Social Security benefits are nothing new. But such proposals have never succeeded because Social Security is too popular. What was needed, apparently, was a new term for what we were talking about. Hence, "entitlements."

As a matter of principle I do not agree with attaching the entitlement label to Social Security. The term does not capture the essence of the program, which is its contributory nature. Robert M. Ball, the former Commissioner of Social Security who has dedicated his life to the system, has made the point nicely:

> [The word "entitlement"] seems to put all the emphasis on getting something and none on the obligations one must fulfill before rights are established under [Social Security and Medicare]. "Entitlement" sounds as if you have a right to something just because you were able to survive to 65 or 62. . . . That is not the idea behind Social Security and Medicare.

Poking around, I learned that "entitlement" appears to have its origin in lawyerly conceptions of welfare; in a 1965 *Yale Law*

Journal article, Charles A. Reich, LL.B., stated: "The idea of entitlement is simply that when individuals have insufficient resources to live under conditions of health and decency, society has obligations to provide support, and the individual is entitled to that support as of right." In 1970 the Supreme Court, in *Goldberg v. Kelly*, relied on this article to find that welfare recipients have certain Constitutional rights with respect to their entitlements, such that the government cannot cut off their benefits without notice and an opportunity for a hearing.

And so it was officially established that welfare is an entitlement.

Now I have nothing against welfare. But Bob Ball is perfectly correct in pointing out that welfare is not the idea behind Social Security. Never has been. Social Security was envisioned from the beginning as a social-insurance program. People would establish eligibility for Social Security through their work and contributions. Workers' contributions are even identified on their pay stubs as "FICA"—Federal Insurance Contributions Act. Notice that the whole idea of contributory insurance is neatly avoided by the word "entitlement."

Social Security Solvency

Entitlement programs alone are [not] responsible for the deficit and skyrocketing national debt.

Each entitlement program should be reviewed and, if necessary, reformed *separately*; arbitrary across-the-board cuts should never even be considered. Social Security, off-budget and building a huge reserve, will stay solvent until about 2029. Most experts agree there is plenty of time to reform Social Security to maintain its solvency beyond that year as well.

Horace B. Deets, *Modern Maturity*, November/December 1994.

But why would one advocate cutting Social Security benefits to begin with? The argument seems to go like this: Social Security accounts for nearly 20 percent of federal spending ($320 billion of 1994's $1.5 trillion budget). We have a budget deficit of $220 billion. We can't eliminate a deficit of this size if we put 20 percent of federal spending off limits.

The flaw in this argument is that it overlooks the fact that Social Security had a $60 billion *surplus* in 1994. The system is so well funded that annual surpluses will continue for many years. The surplus was expected to be $70 billion in 1995 and rise to $100 billion by 1999. The Social Security Trust Funds' reserve will reach nearly $3 *trillion* by 2020.

Clearly, Social Security is not causing the budget deficit. In fact, surplus Social Security revenues are invested in U.S. Treasury bonds and in this way actually help finance the deficit! The deficit is in the non–Social Security part of the budget. Cutting Social Security benefits would thus not actually address the underlying deficit problem—it would just produce a larger surplus to help mask the problem.

The same holds true of other so-called entitlement programs. For example, Medicare had a surplus of $3.4 billion in 1994, and the Unemployment Insurance Trust Fund took in $2.2 billion more than it paid out in benefits and administration. Entitlements are actually the soundest part of the budget!

Contributions and Benefits

Once in a while I hear another argument in favor of cutting Social Security benefits: that Social Security recipients receive five or ten times the amounts they paid into the system. I looked into this one as well. In fact, I held Finance Committee hearings on the subject in March of 1993.

We learned that indeed workers who retired in the past received or are receiving benefits of greater value than the Social Security taxes they and their employers paid (accumulated with interest). But the experts also testified that for workers retiring now and in the future, this will no longer be true. A worker who has paid the maximum into the system and retires in 1994 can expect to just break even. This will hold for the average contributor in just a few years. The Social Security system has "matured," as the actuaries might say. Yet it has done so without our recognizing it.

The Social Security Board of Trustees' 1994 report indicates that the system is solvent through 2029. Sure, we may have to make some adjustments in the next 20 years. Bump up the contribution rate a little. We made such adjustments in 1983 based on recommendations of the bipartisan National Commission on Social Security Reform, on which I served. That is the way to consider changes in Social Security—up front and in the proper context. And as a result of our work in 1983, Social Security is doing just fine.

"The picture that [the Commission's findings] paint is unsettling."

Entitlement Programs Are Not Sustainable

Bipartisan Commission on Entitlement and Tax Reform

In the following viewpoint, Congress's Bipartisan Commission on Entitlement and Tax Reform questions the long-term viability of the federal government's entitlement programs—including Social Security, Medicare, and Medicaid—and warns of a catastrophe in the making. It predicts that by the year 2030, entitlement spending will consume all federal tax revenues unless appropriate policy changes are made. The commission members believe that unless the federal government acts soon, America's future generations will face the brunt of an entitlement crisis. The ad hoc commission, which was headed by U.S. senators Robert Kerrey of Nebraska and John Danforth of Missouri, issued its final report in December 1994.

As you read, consider the following questions:

1. How much have private savings fallen since the 1960s, according to the commission?
2. According to the authors, how could an aging population strain some entitlement programs?
3. How could the poverty rate for the elderly substantially increase, according to the commission?

From the Interim Report of the Bipartisan Commission on Entitlement and Tax Reform, Sen. J. Robert Kerrey, chrmn., August 8, 1994.

Throughout America's history, each succeeding generation has enjoyed the promise of a better standard of living. The goal of this Commission [the Bipartisan Commission on Entitlement and Tax Reform] is to help maintain that promise—to help secure for America's children a standard of living that is better than that which we enjoy today. To achieve this goal, the Commission will assess the need for entitlement and tax reform and make specific recommendations for reform to the President.

These findings are the Commission's first step in achieving its goal. The findings describe the economic future that will confront Americans during the first quarter of the 21st century if the nation fails to act. The picture that they paint is unsettling. The findings are not, however, a prediction of the future. They are merely the product of current budget policies if our course is not changed.

A better future for America can be secured if the country embarks on the course of long-term reform. We can help Americans save and invest in themselves and the country. We can make the essential public investments in our workers and our children. And we can maintain the strength of vital government programs that support and protect many Americans.

Government Action Now

Finding #1: To ensure that today's debt and spending commitments do not unfairly burden America's children, the government must act now. A bipartisan coalition of Congress, led by the President, must resolve the long-term imbalance between the government's entitlement promises and the funds it will have available to pay for them.

• Although the short-term fiscal outlook has improved, the long-term situation requires immediate attention. For the short term, the federal deficit is projected to average 2.5% of the economy, its lowest level since the 1970s. After 1998, however, federal spending is projected to grow faster than revenues, which will cause federal deficits to rise rapidly.

• In 2012, unless appropriate policy changes are made in the interim, projected outlays for entitlements and interest on the national debt will consume all tax revenues collected by the federal government.

• In 2030, unless appropriate policy changes are made in the interim, projected spending for Medicare, Medicaid, Social Security, and federal employee retirement programs alone will consume all tax revenues collected by the federal government. If all other federal programs (except interest on the national debt) grow no faster than the economy, total federal outlays would exceed 37% of the economy. Today, outlays are 22% of the economy and revenues are 19%.

Finding #2: To ensure the level of private investment necessary for long-term economic growth and prosperity, national savings must be raised substantially.

• Countries that save and invest more grow faster and have more rapid improvements in the standard of living of their citizens. In the United States, declining private savings and large government deficits limit investment, productivity, and economic growth.

• Since the 1960s, private savings have fallen from more than 8% of the economy to about 5% today. At the same time, government deficits have increased from less than 1% of the economy to more than 3% today.

• As a result, the supply of savings available for private investment, "net national savings," has dropped from more than 8% of the economy to less than 2% today. This restricts American productivity and growth.

Projected Federal Health Care Spending

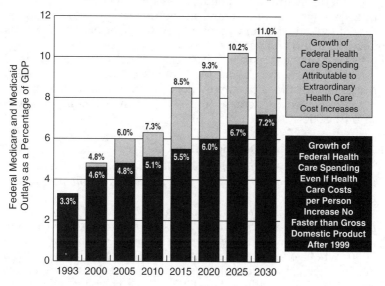

Source: Social Security Administration, 1994.

Finding #3: To ensure that funds are available for essential and appropriate government programs, the nation cannot continue to allow entitlements to consume a rapidly increasing share of the federal budget.

• Entitlement spending and interest on the national debt together consume more than 60% of federal outlays today (47% for entitlements and 14% for interest), double the percentage of just 25 years ago.

• The Congressional Budget Office projects that entitlement spending and interest payments together will exceed 70% of total federal outlays by 2003 (58% for entitlements and 14% for interest).

• By 2003, unless appropriate policy changes are made, less than 15 cents of every dollar the federal government spends will be available for non-defense discretionary programs that can raise productivity and contribute to economic growth.

Finding #4: To be effective, any attempt to control long-term entitlement growth must take into account the projected increases in health care costs.

• The growth of public and private health care costs poses an immediate problem that must be addressed. The Commission's recommendations will depend largely upon Congress's actions on health care.

• Federal health care spending has been increasing at annual rates averaging 10% or more during the early 1990s, far in excess of overall economic growth. Private sector health care costs have increased comparably.

• If the increase in health care costs is not restrained, federal spending on Medicare and Medicaid is projected to triple as a percentage of the economy by 2030. Federal health care spending is projected to increase from 3.3% of the economy today to 11% by 2030.

Demographic Changes

Finding #5: To be effective, any attempt to control long-term entitlement growth must also take into account fundamental demographic changes.

• *America's population is growing older because of longer life expectancies and the aging of the baby boom generation.* Today, there are almost five working-age persons for each person over 65. In 2030, when today's workers have retired and today's children are in their prime working years, the Social Security Trustees project that there will be fewer than three working-age persons for each person over 65.

• *The aging of the population will strain major entitlement programs,* making it difficult to provide health and income security to seniors and disabled citizens. Even if the extraordinary increases in health care costs were eliminated after 1999 (so that costs for each person of a given age grew no faster than the economy), federal outlays for Medicare and Medicaid would still double as a percentage of the economy by 2030. The aging of the population drives combined Medicare, Medicaid, and

Social Security spending from about 8% of the economy today to about 14% of the economy in 2030.

Finding #6: To respond to the Medicare Trustees' call to action and ensure Medicare's long-term viability, Medicare spending and revenues available for the program must be brought into long-term balance.

• Medicare provides an important source of health security for the nation's seniors and disabled persons.

• *Medicare Hospital Insurance (HI).* The Public Trustees conclude that the Medicare HI program "is severely out of financial balance and is unsustainable in its present form." Medicare HI outlays already exceed tax revenues dedicated to the program and are rapidly depleting Trust Fund assets. The Trust Fund is projected to run out of money by 2001.

• In the long run, the situation gets even worse. By 2030, unless appropriate policy changes are made, projected Medicare HI outlays will exceed 8% of the payroll tax base, while dedicated tax revenues will remain around 3%.

• *Medicare Supplementary Medical Insurance (SMI).* The Public Trustees urge "prompt, effective, and decisive action" to ensure the long-term financing of Medicare SMI. Today, about 75% of Medicare SMI spending is funded from general revenues, while about 25% is from premiums paid by beneficiaries.

• In the long run, unless appropriate policy changes are made, the Trustees project that Medicare SMI outlays will rise from just over 1% of the payroll tax base today to more than 7% by 2030.

Restoring Balance

Finding #7: To respond to the Social Security Trustees' call to action and ensure the long-term viability of Social Security, Social Security spending and revenues available for the program must be brought into long-term balance. Any savings that result should be used to restore the long-term soundness of the Social Security Trust Fund.

• Social Security is an important source of support for many of the nation's citizens. Today, the poverty rate for senior households is about 13%, but without Social Security, it could increase to as much as 50%. Social Security provides 90% or more of the total income for almost half of the senior households below the poverty line. Half of all American workers do not have employer-provided retirement programs and must rely upon Social Security and their own savings.

• The Public Trustees believe that "legislative action is needed to ensure the long-range financial integrity of the [Social Security] program."

• Once the baby boom generation begins to retire in 2010, the cash flow surplus from Social Security will rapidly decline. By 2013, Social Security benefit payments will exceed the tax revenues dedicated to the program. After 2013, the cash flow shortfalls in Social Security will cause the total federal deficit to increase rapidly unless appropriate policy changes are made.

• The Trust Fund is projected to run out of money in 2029. Unless appropriate policy changes are made, projected outlays will be about 17% of the payroll tax base, while dedicated tax revenues will remain about 13% of payroll.

• Congress and the Executive Branch have faced long-term problems with Social Security in the past and have acted in a bipartisan manner to restore stability to the system, most recently in the 1983 Social Security legislation.

> Are these the shadows of the things that Will be, or are they shadows of the things that May be, only? . . . Men's courses will foreshadow certain ends, to which, if persevered in, they must lead. . . . But if the courses be departed from, the ends will change. Say it is thus with what you show me!
>
> —Charles Dickens, *A Christmas Carol*

America can change course. If the government acts soon, it can ensure that future generations are not unfairly burdened with today's debt and spending commitments. It can ensure public and private investments that are needed for America's future prosperity. And it can ensure the solvency of the Medicare and Social Security Trust Funds that are an important source of support and security for many Americans.

"As long as the European and Japanese economies are guided by industrial policy, we will continue to fall behind our international competitors."

America Needs an Industrial Policy

Hazel Henderson

Hazel Henderson is a futurist and the author of *Paradigms in Progress: Life Beyond Economics*. In the following viewpoint, Henderson argues that the United States must end its inefficient economic and industrial practices to thrive in the future global economy. Henderson's proposals include a national industrial policy to revamp an industrial base plagued by waste, obsolescence, and the unsustainable use of resources. She contends that such a policy is needed for America to remain competitive with Europe and Japan.

As you read, consider the following questions:

1. In Henderson's opinion, why will macroeconomic measures not help the economy?
2. According to Henderson, how could a shift in the tax burden benefit America?
3. In what ways do Americans support a new international role for the nation, according to the author?

Hazel Henderson, "Restructuring the Economy for the 1990s," *Positive Alternatives*, Winter 1992, ©1992 by the Center for Economic Conversion, Mountain View, Calif. Reprinted with permission.

In the 1990s, as we Americans face up to our relative economic decline in the world, economic conversion of the U.S. military sector will become a central issue.

The excesses of recent years, which have mortgaged our economy, swelled our budget deficit, and weakened our banking and insurance sectors, will, at last, force a national debate over re-prioritization.

But this much-needed debate over post–Cold War priorities could be forestalled, if the congressional budget process continues in gridlock, with such heavy-handed (and ill-conceived) palliatives as the current, arbitrary, separate caps on domestic, military, and foreign categories.

At present, the economy continues to sag, drifting dangerously between crises in the S&Ls [savings and loans], banking, and other heavily indebted corporate sectors from retailing to airlines. Calls for the old macro-economic "snake-oil"—income tax cuts, capital gains tax cuts, and investment tax credits—miss the economic mark by a considerable distance. Such across-the-board measures do not address the need to re-structure and re-prioritize. In any case, they work too slowly and are all predicated on creating jobs. Yet in today's global economy, there is almost no relationship between job creation in the United States and these macro-economic measures to spur investment.

Corporate managers and investors will happily take tax cuts and credits and continue to invest their capital where it will earn the highest return, whether in the high-flying stock markets of Mexico or in European bonds yielding higher returns than U.S. Treasury notes.

Targeted tax relief could only help if specifically earmarked for U.S. job creation. Or, we could shift the tax burden from income and employment, by taxing pollution, as we tax other "sins" such as alcohol and tobacco. Such a policy would create huge new revenue streams for government, and also discourage the unsustainable economic practices so characteristic of our economy.

Re-Structuring the Economy

What is needed is a long-overdue national debate over how to re-structure our economy for the 1990s and for a "new world order." Americans have always believed that there was no need to bite the bullet when it came to setting priorities, since the laissez-faire economists hold that the "invisible hand" [a term coined by eighteenth-century economist Adam Smith to describe the harmony of the process of supply and demand] of the market guides the decisions between bombers and schools, tanks and health care, or SDI [Strategic Defense Initiative] and safer airlines. The other siren song of Keynesian economists was

162

that no hard choices need be made, since we could instead rely on deficit-financed growth to make the pie bigger and avoid those nasty issues about sharing the slices.

All of this economic theorizing assumed that resources would always be available at the right price; that Nature could keep on re-processing our industrial wastes; that disparities in power, need, wealth, and income were irrelevant; and that our domestic economy would remain insulated from the roller coaster of the global economy. Today, all these assumptions are threadbare and predictably, our economic decline continues, due (among other factors) to our energy inefficiency, our bloated military sector, and an industrial base built on waste, planned obsolescence, and unsustainable rates of resource depletion.

Trading Places

The lack of a national industrial policy in the United States today is the main reason that Japan and the United States are, in [the Economic Strategy Institute's] Clyde Prestowitz's phrase, "trading places" in terms of wealth and technological prowess. Call it whatever you want—industrial policy, economic strategy, competitiveness policy or a defense-science policy—we need one and can no longer afford to have it blocked by economic ideologues.

Our political leaders tell us that we don't need an industrial policy, even though Australia is the only nation in the Pacific with which we have a favorable balance of trade. We also hear that our government is incapable of formulating one because bureaucrats cannot pick the industries of the future. But industrial policy does not mean picking winners. It means supporting those enterprises that look promising, just as the National Science Foundation and the National Institutes of Health do not pick the sciences and drugs of the future but do support those that the best-informed think are important.

Chalmers Johnson, *Los Angeles Times*, March 25, 1991.

The United States must consciously re-structure its economy. Surprisingly, polls indicate that, while politicians may fiddle, trying to please their favorite special interests, the American people are ready for re-structuring and new institutions to deal with today's global realities, and that they are way ahead of their leaders in re-visioning America's role in a "new world order."

In a survey by the Americans Talk Issues Foundation, 68 percent of those polled agree that the U.S. should reduce its dependence on imported oil, 59 percent would support a 5 percent tax on imported oil to discourage excessive consumption, and 92 percent support the U.S.'s "using its position to get other nations to join together to take action against world environmental problems." Furthermore, 70 percent support a proposal first made by the U.N.'s Brandt Commission in 1980, to "monitor and tax international arms sales, with the money going to famine relief and humanitarian aid."

As long as the European and Japanese economies are guided by industrial policy, we will continue to fall behind our international competitors in sector after sector, unless we proceed with the kind of re-structuring that Americans say they support—whether or not economists call it "industrial policy." Those more strategically planned societies are moving, like the twelve nations of the European Community, to even closer economic alignment.

Of course, the United States has had its own "industrial policy" for decades—our defense budget, which helped create our misshapen economy of today. Perhaps it's time for the laissez-faire boys to admit that the "invisible hand" has always been our own. After all, blaming the "invisible hand," like blaming God for one's troubles, is very disempowering. Acknowledging the facts, then, could be a significant step towards empowerment, and a significant step as well in the process of repairing the languid American economy.

"The irony is that just as the Japanese are fleeing national business management, some Americans are edging toward it."

America Does Not Need an Industrial Policy

Karl Zinsmeister

In the following viewpoint, Karl Zinsmeister argues that Bill Clinton's modeling of U.S. industrial policy after Japan's is misguided because Japan's policy has little to envy or copy. The history of failures of Japan's industrial policy should be a warning to America, the author concludes. Zinsmeister lives in Ithaca, New York, and is editor-in-chief of *American Enterprise* magazine, a publication of the American Enterprise Institute, a conservative research and education organization in Washington, D.C.

As you read, consider the following questions:

1. In Zinsmeister's opinion, how did the Japanese auto industry reach its current level of excellence?
2. How have government policies harmed Japan's financial sector, according to Zinsmeister?
3. According to the author, over what industries has Japan's government relaxed control?

Karl Zinsmeister, "The Great Industrial Policy Hoax," *The Wall Street Journal*, March 10, 1993. Reprinted with permission of *The Wall Street Journal*, ©1993 Dow Jones & Company, Inc. All rights reserved.

President Clinton, stressing the need to "copy our competitors," is devising an expansive U.S. industrial policy. His main model is Japan. Unfortunately, the president doesn't seem to understand the true strengths of the Japanese economy—or its underreported weaknesses. The fact is, Japanese industrial policy offers very little to envy or copy.

The Popular Fable of MITI

In popular fable, the grand intelligence behind Japan's economic miracle has been the Ministry of International Trade and Industry. In the aftermath of World War II, MITI bureaucrats used their broad powers to distribute Japan's limited commercial resources and assign tasks for rebuilding the shattered economy. Right from the beginning, though, MITI's economic enterprising brought misdirections.

In the 1950s, for instance, MITI worked vigorously to force the Japanese automobile industry into a single company because planners were certain multiple domestic competitors would only weaken each other. Fortunately, ministry officials were unable to strong-arm private manufacturers into accepting their vision of one, two, or (by 1961) "at most" three Japanese auto firms. Today Japan has nine auto builders—and fierce competition among them has driven the industry to its current levels of excellence.

At about the same time, MITI was pushing other companies to avoid what it viewed as a dead-end in electronics. In 1953, a small company named Sony asked to buy transistor-manufacturing rights from Western Electric. MITI was not impressed with the technology, or with Sony, and didn't want to squander scarce foreign currency on either. Permission to make the purchase was refused, and a great enterprise would have been lost had it not been for Sony founder Akio Morita's persistent badgering of other bureaucrats until he got the go-ahead.

Meanwhile, MITI was leading other sectors of the Japanese economy down paths that would lead to disappointment and wasted resources.

Take the steel industry. In the United States, Japan's steel industry is commonly thought of as a MITI triumph. It has actually been a net drag on national income. After a giant, force-fed buildup during the 1960s and 1970s, many of Japan's blast furnaces have fallen idle. Tens of thousands of steelworkers have been laid off over the past decade, and costly but underutilized plants have been scrapped. MITI's expensive crusades to build up the aluminum and nonferrous metal industries were an even worse debacle.

MITI's attempts to target "industries of the future" have misfired far more than they have succeeded. Efforts to build up

Japan's aircraft and aerospace industries have produced only inferior products at absurd prices. Decades-long attempts to jump-start the biotechnology industry have been equally disappointing. MITI's Sunshine Project, which was intended to achieve breakthroughs in alternative energy sources, was fruitless.

MITI also made a mess of Japan's oil industry. Ministry mandarins enforced what has been called the world's worst national oil policy, resulting in huge costs to government, consumers and business alike plus a very weak set of energy companies. MITI floundered in similar ways in the petroleum-based chemical making industry.

Another MITI disappointment is the computer industry. Though the sector was first targeted nearly three decades ago, most Japanese products continue to be also-rans, in little demand outside their sheltered domestic markets. Nimbler American companies set almost all industry standards, and have used superior technology and manufacturing to take back submarkets—like printers, hard drives and palmtop computers— that were once believed to be slated for Japanese dominance.

One of MITI's most ambitious programs, the Fifth Generation Computer Project, inspired much fear in other countries when it commenced in 1981. The ten-year effort coordinated the work of eight companies in a new government laboratory. Its widely trumpeted goal was to produce the world's first thinking, "artificially intelligent," computers. The project has fallen far short of its aims, however, having produced no fundamental technical advances or marketable products.

Follies of Japan's Ministries

MITI isn't the only agency that has failed at industrial policy.

Take shipbuilding. Starting in the 1950s the Transport Ministry used tariffs and other measures to build up the world's largest yards and highest-volume industry. By the late 1970s, though, world-wide overbuilding and changing cargo patterns had turned the facilities into white elephants. Because they were following government incentives instead of market signals, Japan's shipbuilders monumentally miscalculated the demand for and profitability of their product. The losses were huge.

Another folly engineered by the Ministry of Transport was the national railway. The railway is known to most Americans for its impressive high-speed "bullet trains." What is less well appreciated is that until it was finally privatized in 1987, the agency had thousands of feather-bedded employees, poor service, strikes, overcrowding and losses that averaged more than $20 million a day. Some $279 billion in debt ended up on the public books, a burden to be carried by taxpayers for decades. There is a warning in this for Mr. Clinton, who has spoken often of his plans to have the government build high-speed rail lines in this country.

Government coddling has also made Japanese airlines extremely inefficient. Until 1986, government-run Japan Airlines (JAL) held a monopoly on overseas flights and All Nippon Airways had a virtual monopoly on domestic flights. Tickets were so costly that relatively few Japanese could afford to fly. When JAL was finally privatized in 1987, its managers found that the cozy regulatory cocoon they enjoyed for so many years left them ill-prepared for fierce global competition. Today JAL is one of the world's highest-cost carriers, and its share of travel to and from Japan has fallen by one-sixth. American carriers, which honed operations after being released from government regulation about a decade earlier, are far more competitive on the major trans-Pacific routes.

The Great Economic Lesson

The great global economic lesson of the last generation is that earnest centralized management—even in as mild a form as existed in post-War Japan—always will bring less prosperity than open market competition. It will be a tragedy if the [Clinton] administration, in the name of aiding American "competitiveness," ignores that vital lesson here at home.

Karl Zinsmeister, *Policy Review*, Spring 1993.

Telecommunications, similarly, has been stifled by the government's embrace. Although the national telecom monopoly, Nippon Telegraph & Telephone, is at last being privatized, it is still mostly state-owned and not very efficient. Phone calls cost 50% more in Japan than in the United States, and service is much less innovative. Cellular phones, for instance, have only just recently caught on, due to clumsy regulation by the Ministry of Posts and Telecommunications.

Then there is the financial sector. Ministry of Finance doting has kept Japan's banks, life insurance companies and stockbrokering firms in an inefficient backwater state, and in the past several years many institutions have careened toward insolvency. Government policies are also directly responsible for the collapse of Japan's stock market and for the disastrous speculation in land and real estate markets that has made homes up to ten times more expensive than in America.

The farm policies of the Ministry of Agriculture can only be characterized as a fiasco. Japanese consumers must pay twice as much for food as Americans as a share of family income. In a time of damaging labor shortages in Japan, 9% of the workforce is tied up in farming (vs. 3% in the United States). And large amounts of prime urban land are locked away in inefficient cropping instead of being used for desperately needed housing or commercial buildings.

Privatization and Deregulation

The list of industrial policy failures goes on and on. It is striking to note that many of Japan's feeblest industries are those that have been subsidized by the government. Many of its strongest businesses—such as home electronics, cameras, robotics, precision equipment, pianos, bicycles, watches and calculators, numerically controlled machine tools, and ceramics—developed without help from MITI or other agencies. Japan achieved its economic miracle not because of government planning but in spite of it.

The Japanese understand this and have started to discard their industrial policies, privatizing the national railway, the national airline, and the telephone monopoly. Deregulation of the oil-refining industry and banking and financial services has begun. The once tightly controlled retail and distribution sector is seeing some relaxation. And numerous government tariffs are being removed or lowered. The irony is that just as the Japanese are fleeing national business management, some Americans are edging toward it.

"A highly regimented economy is precisely where we are most likely to wind up."

America's Economy May Become Intensely Regulated

Alfred L. Malabre Jr.

Alfred L. Malabre Jr. is a former senior editor of the *Wall Street Journal* and the author of *Beyond Our Means: How America's Long Years of Debt, Deficits and Reckless Borrowing Now Threaten to Overwhelm Us*, published in 1987 and excerpted here. In this viewpoint, Malabre argues that America is living "beyond its means" from overborrowing and overconsumption and will suffer economically. Here, Malabre accurately discounts the emergence of deflation or hyperinflation by the end of the 1980s and forecasts the recession of the early 1990s. Malabre stresses that the most likely long-term scenario for America is "a new era of intensifying governmental regulation over the economy."

As you read, consider the following questions:

1. What warning does Malabre give about monetary debt owed to U.S. institutions?
2. Why is the government regulation scenario most likely to occur, according to Malabre?
3. In the author's opinion, how can individual investors succeed in a climate of regulation?

How will it end? Where does our postwar extravagance, our increasing propensity to live beyond our means, finally lead us? And how should we manage our affairs so as best to cope with whatever troubles lie ahead?

Economics isn't really the dismal science as [historian] Thomas Carlyle suggested. More accurately, it has become the hopeful science. Its practitioners carry on their trade in the hope that through adroit economic management, prosperity can somehow be engendered and preserved. . . .

Fiscal stimulation assuredly has served from time to time to spur economic activity. The Federal Reserve's sporadic efforts to attune monetary growth to the economy's capacity to expand have surely proved beneficial on occasion. There's clearly something to be said for supply-side measures that may encourage, even slightly, sound entrepreneurial endeavor.

Beyond Our Means

Such considerations must be weighed, however, against the larger fact that we have lived now for too long far beyond our means. We have overborrowed and overconsumed and overpaid ourselves, and all the while we have been investing far too little in the machinery and brick and mortar that ultimately must accompany whatever economic progress we may manage to achieve in coming years. The fault lies not with any particular brand of economics but in our American tendency to live the good life whenever and wherever possible. What remains to be considered is the road ahead, what to expect now.

There's no tidy answer, only a general sense of the eventualities, and it rests not so much on economics as on simple common sense. In brief, the jig is about up and, for all the accumulated wisdom of all the eminent economists of the various schools, painless extrication from our predicament just isn't going to be possible. To be sure, the economic bind that now grips us will be broken in time—perhaps far less of it than anyone now imagines—but only through an intense amount of economic dislocation and downright pain. Just what degree of pain is unclear, but it will arrive, one way or another.

However the bind is broken—through inflation or deflation or otherwise—living standards will suffer, in some households more than in others. Unemployment will mount. Most importantly, financial obligations will be disregarded on a massive scale, for there will be no orderly way to liquidate debts. Perhaps this will happen through default of debt at all levels. Perhaps it will occur through currency debasement during a time of rapidly accelerating inflation. Or perhaps it will happen as a result of crisis legislation, such as a decision to repay Treasury securities coming due at considerably less than full value. Any one of these tactics, or possibly some combination, would be sufficient to erase much or all of the awesome burden of debt that has accumulated in the postwar era and that now presses down on us. . . .

If a painless resolution of our difficulties is not possible—and that seems the outlook—what are the likelier scenarios? How will the predicament be resolved?

Hyperinflation Scenario

The most frequently mentioned resolution—but in my view not a very probable one—is the so-called hyperinflation scenario. . . .

The sort of hyperinflation that could erupt in the U.S. within the next few years—and by hyperinflation we mean yearly rates of price increase at least in the high double-digit range—would stem in part from explosive monetary expansion. In addition, however, it would derive from a further sharp increase in the buildup of debt. Borrowing, much of it unwise and not re-payable, permeates today's American economy. . . .

Clay Bennett. Reprinted by permission.

How could hyperinflation develop in the U.S. between now and, say, the end of the 1980s? How likely is it?

To tackle the last question first, I would give it a probability

172

rating of perhaps 20 percent. As to the reasons, much of the debt suffusing today's economy is of questionable quality and unlikely to be repaid—at least in money that's worth anything remotely close to the value of [the late-1980s'] dollar. This applies to debt owed U.S. banks by overextended third world countries, to debt owed American and foreign investors by the U.S. government, to debt owed U.S. mortgage lenders by homeowners, farmers, and business enterprises of countless variety. Much of this debt simply cannot—will not—be repaid in anything like the currency value that lenders anticipated when the loans originally were negotiated.

However, it's possible that overextended borrowers could handle their debt-servicing obligations if they could repay in vastly cheaper dollars. The dollar's value, of course, hinges to a large extent on supply-and-demand forces. Thus, the Federal Reserve has the power to drive down its value by flooding the economy—and indeed the world, since the dollar is a global currency—with money. One incentive would be to help the Treasury service its huge debt burden. . . . The Fed [Federal Reserve] may simply decide that ballooning the money supply—and thereby chancing runaway inflation—represents the least painful way to try to cope with deepening economic trouble. . . .

Deflation Scenario

This brings us to the next possible scenario—deflation. I would assign deflation a likelihood of perhaps 30 percent. Deflation is what the U.S. experienced in the 1930s. Prices actually go down when deflation strikes; it's not to be confused with disinflation, a far less painful circumstance, under which inflation merely abates, as happened in 1983–84. . . .

Could the monetary authorities possibly cope, for example, if a wave of third world repudiations happened to hit simultaneously with a new rash of loan defaults by oil-drilling companies and farmers? I doubt it. . . .

Compounding Debt

The deflation scenario also takes into account the distressing mathematics of debt compounding. Taken as a whole, public and private debt in the U.S. exceeded [in the mid-1980s] $7 trillion and through the magic of compounding, . . . total debt could well reach some $57 trillion by 1995 and, again through compounding, $448 trillion by 2015. It's unreasonable to suppose that the Fed or any other governmental or private institution could contain the trouble that would inevitably arise in such a debt-burdened future. . . .

The role of compounding is apparent, among other places, in the federal debt situation. Interest obligations on the federal debt are rising faster than national income can possibly expand each year, and national income of course ultimately supplies federal revenues. This means that interest costs must rise as a percentage of national income. Let's assume that the average interest rate on federal debt outstanding is 12 percent and that additional federal borrowing will also be financed at 12 percent. Let's also assume that future growth of national income is expected to average 9 percent annually, of which 5 to 6 percent will represent simply inflation. These assumptions are all reasonably close to the actual outlook foreseen by many economists in 1985. Under these circumstances, income would double every eight years, while federal debt would double every six years. Looking further ahead, income would double three times in the next twenty-four years, but debt would double four times. In the process, the federal budget deficit would rise with recent trends from 4 percent of gross national product, where it has ranged of late, to about 8 percent, and the national debt would rise from about one third of GNP [gross national product] to two thirds. "The arithmetic of deficit finance becomes rather dismal," remarks Jerry L. Jordan, the former presidential adviser.

The swelling debt burden is by no means the only consideration in the deflationary scenario. The price of oil is another. Robert Horton, managing director of British Petroleum Corp., touched on this concern when he warned an oil industry conference in London in mid-1985 that a prolonged "collapse in the oil price would trigger a major financial crisis, requiring the Federal Reserve to launch a lifeboat the size of the QE [Queen Elizabeth] 2." Even if the Fed were able to launch such a lifeboat, there surely would be lengthy bureaucratic and legislative delays, perhaps covering weeks. Again, deflation could threaten.

Government Regulation Scenario

The reason I've assigned the deflation scenario no more than a 30 percent probability, however, is that I'm convinced such gloomy forecasters as Julian Snyder—and he is only one of many deflationists—tend to underestimate Washington's power. I believe that there's a 50 percent chance that our economy will avoid both hyperinflation and the sort of severe, prolonged deflation outlined above, and instead will enter a new era of intensifying governmental regulation over the economy. This may seem a peculiar forecast when the Republican party appears to be winning converts from the Democratic ranks. Yet a highly regimented economy is precisely where we are most likely to wind up as a result of our efforts to deregulate, particularly in the financial markets, and to pare taxes and in general unleash free enterprise. Not immediately, perhaps, but very possibly before the 1980s are out.

How might all this happen?

My guess is that first off, the economy will lapse into yet another recession that perhaps will arrive before the end of Ronald Reagan's second term, which expires in January 1989. That certainly is what experience suggests. Because of the rigidities and excesses that have built up over the postwar era and that now permeate our economy, the next recession will quickly deepen. Business failures will rapidly mount. . . . The federal-budget deficit will swiftly worsen as revenues diminish; this will complicate governmental efforts to stimulate a sagging economy.

Deflation will be beckoning, to be sure. But I don't believe that it will really settle in, at least not for very long. And not because the Fed will be pumping up the money supply at a swift pace—which, I expect, it will be doing to a degree. Deflation, as it occurred during the Great Depression, won't take hold because the government, however reluctantly at first, will be stepping in across the entire economic landscape—not just through the Fed. . . .

As the government becomes ever more deeply involved in the economy's workings, in the marketplace, how will the various difficulties now confronting us be resolved? How will the oppressive burden of debt be lifted? How will the budget deficit be narrowed? How will the banks be rescued as borrowers by the millions fail to service their obligations?

My guess is that government debt will be repaid—and the deficit effectively erased—in a manner tantamount to default—or confiscation. Holders of Treasury securities coming due may be told, for instance, that unless their bills, notes, or bonds are rolled over, Uncle Sam will pay only a specified fraction of face value. Interest payments on such securities may also be capped. This would amount, of course, to repudiation of a large part of the federal debt and would require legislative action. But that could come swiftly under such dire conditions. Nationalization of the banking system would no doubt be a part of the operation. As long ago as October 1984, William Isaac of the FDIC [Federal Deposit Insurance Corporation] warned a New York banking group of the need for "greater market discipline" in banking and suggested that Uncle Sam might eventually have to supply the restraining influence through outright control of the institutions.

An Uncheerful Prospect

Our main matter of concern, then, isn't hyperinflation or deflation but the prospect of greatly increased governmental control over all aspects of economic activity. This is what the future seems to hold. And we shouldn't be overly surprised. After all, if one looks back not just a few decades but over the centuries, increasing governmental involvement in economic affairs is an overriding pattern. The recent years of freer and freer markets may well be remembered in the late 1990s as only a pleasant but foolish interlude—an aberration—in a transcendent long-term trend.

In the sort of business climate that could well emerge, the Federal Reserve Board could lose its present independence and be placed under the firm thumb of the White House. All banks, indeed all thrift institutions, could wind up being nationalized. Foreign trade and capital transactions most likely would be government managed. Wages and prices would largely be set by people in Washington. Tax rates would be far higher than now and enforcement far stricter. Corporate managers would be under rigid governmental supervision that would make today's regulations seem blissfully relaxed.

All in all a new era would be upon us, a far less carefree one, whose roots trace back to the earlier decades of overindulgence. It's not a cheerful prospect, but it's a likely one.

How can investors protect themselves if this scenario does unfold? There's really little that can be done. If hyperinflation were the likeliest prospect, one could readily hedge against it by investing in such tangibles as gold and real estate. If deflation were highly probable, bonds of top-rated companies and even cash would be in order. But the prospect of spreading governmental control over the economy—over our lives—is another matter. Black markets become more attractive, of course. The so-called underground economy—off-the-books transactions, which may actually have diminished in recent years with the reduction in tax rates—receives a new life. Legally, however, there's little that individual investors can do to protect themselves against an encroaching Washington presence. Legislation is always unpredictable, but luck and pull in the federal power centers become supremely important. One can seek a freer investment climate abroad if international investing is allowed, which is doubtful. But where to invest abroad? The next recession won't be limited to these shores but will spread and in the process spur the growth of government regulation abroad as at home.

The Keys to Success

The best investment, under such circumstances, will be in one's affiliations. Individuals employed by large, powerful organizations with governmental ties and clout will surely fare far better than the self-employed person who hopes to build enduring financial independence through hard work and ingenuity.

The dream of the Reagan years and earlier—that we can go on indefinitely living beyond our means—will at last be dead as the government extends its influence. Uncle Sam will be everywhere, and a key to investment success will be one's ability to bend or circumvent the rules and traverse the underground economy.

The Reagan goal of uninhibited self-help and self-interest will be a memory. But we will have begun, for the first time in a very long time, to live within our means—under much duress and not nearly as comfortably as we might have done had the proper belt-tightening been undertaken decades ago. But that's another story, one that sadly never happened.

"What new postindustrial world are we moving toward?"

Economic Scenarios: From Boom to Collapse

Kenneth Labich

In the following viewpoint, Kenneth Labich outlines four scenarios for America's economic prospects leading up to the twenty-first century. Labich maintains that most forecasters' predictions fall into one of four scenarios: full-scale boom; lower, steady economic growth; little or no growth; and economic disaster. Labich contends that only a minority of forecasters predict the extreme economic changes, with most anticipating low, steady growth. Labich serves on the board of directors of *Fortune*, a biweekly business magazine.

As you read, consider the following questions:

1. According to Labich, what are the signs optimists point to in the first scenario?
2. How will the corporate sector change in the second scenario, according to forecasters cited by Labich?
3. On what basis does futurist Barry Minkin foresee an economic disaster, according to the author?

Chances are that the current decade has not been particularly kind to you. . . .

How and when will the economy fully recover? Or if the economic landscape is undergoing not merely a slow change in seasons but instead a fundamental structural transformation, what new postindustrial world are we moving toward? Since so much rides on the answers, social and economic forecasters across the U.S. are busily charting scenarios of how the future may play out—in many cases alternative scenarios. Governments and major corporations base long-range plans on such scripts, which at their best raise a host of "what if?" questions. They should raise such questions for you. While anything can happen, most forecasters come down on one of four scenarios for the years up to the millennium.

Boom Times

No. 1: Up, Up, and Away. . . . A small minority of forecasters say the rest of the Nineties will bring a full-scale boom, with much lower unemployment and economic growth averaging 5% to 6% annually. These optimists base much of their analysis on the economy's strengths—particularly low interest and inflation rates—plus signs that consumers and business, while turning away from Eighties-style financial profligacy, haven't given up on spending, this time spending based on a more secure foundation of saving and investing.

David B. Bostian Jr., chief strategist at the Wall Street brokerage firm Herzog Heine Geduld, points to studies that show corporate debt has fallen to about 40% of cash flow and consumer installment debt has dropped from 18.5% to 15% of disposable income. Says Bostian: "In the Eighties, taking on debt for pure consumption and speculation was a stupid thing to do. But one of the fundamental traits of the human species is that we learn from our mistakes."

With others who share his rosy vision, Bostian is especially keen on Bill Clinton's announced plans to funnel billions into high-tech information, environmental, and transportation investments. He observes that pollution cleanup is already a $100-billion-a-year business worldwide and argues that it could mushroom to $1 trillion by 2000. . . .

Bostian is convinced the U.S. will emerge from the Nineties far stronger than current global competitors. He is particularly bearish on Japan's prospects, citing that country's limited natural resources and a rigid social structure that undervalues women's economic contributions. He figures enhanced U.S. competitiveness will lead to strong export gains, lush corporate profits—especially for capital goods manufacturers—and a strikingly robust stock market. Says Bostian: "I think the Dow Jones average could reach 5000 by 1995, and I would not be surprised to see the Dow at 10,000 by the turn of the century."

Consumer Spending

Fabian Linden, executive director of the consumer research center at the Conference Board [business think tank], is similarly enthusiastic about the decade ahead, but for different reasons. Linden foresees startling demographic shifts over the next few years that will lead to a surge in consumer spending power. He cites the fact that a great many more Americans will be entering their peak earning years of 35 to 55—peak, at least, if their experience is anything like preceding generations. He asserts, too, that a lot more is going on to plump up people's wallets. As the last of the baby-boomers marry, says Linden, relatively affluent childless couples will account for about 60% of new households. At the same time women's salaries will continue to increase as more of them move into more demanding jobs. . . .

A Better Tomorrow?

Throughout our history, we have dreamed of a better tomorrow, confident that we could face the challenges that lie before us. Americans, as individuals and as a nation, are preoccupied with being the best. But our confidence that our nation is the best has waned considerably. The 25th anniversary of the July 20, 1969, landing on the moon came at a time of national introspection. When Baby Boomers were asked which nation would be the leading economic power in twenty years, only half (51%) chose America—only half. In a survey of Ivy League students, ostensibly America's brightest, if not best, just 54% answered "America" to the same question.

Frank Luntz and Ron Dermer, *The Public Perspective*, September/October 1994.

Harry S. Dent Jr., a management consultant and futurist, makes much of beefed-up consumer spending power in his sunny book, *The Great Boom Ahead*. He believes that the good times arrive like clockwork as each new generation of consumers progresses up a predictable curve of earning and spending, until its consumption peaks between ages 45 and 49. He contends the inevitable result of the 78-million-strong boomer crowd, now between 28 and 46, making the trip will be a massive increase in consumer demand—he calls it a spending wave—that . . . will lift the economy to unparalleled heights by the end of the century. . . .

These wonders are possible in Dent's world because all that increased spending power will be joined by a surge of new technologies—an innovation wave—that will send salutary ripples throughout the economy. Past generations came up with clusters of crucial inventions that prompted major economic growth spurts. The Abraham Lincoln generation brought railroads, the telegraph, and basic steel production. The Henry Ford generation gave us the automobile, the telephone, electrical energy, canned foods, movies, radio, and the phonograph. For the Bob Hope generation some of the key inventions were the television, the jet engine, the mainframe computer, radar, and home appliances such as washers and dryers. These clusters came 40 to 50 years apart, and Dent says we are now due for another.

Steady Growth

No. 2: Stormy Weather to Clear Gradually, Occasional Sunshine. . . . Most of the forecasters *Fortune* spoke with take only a moderately bullish view. According to the plurality's outlook, the U.S. economy is likely to settle into a steady annual growth rate of slightly more than 2%, which will edge up to slightly under 3% in the decade's latter half.

The key reason these forecasters don't think we can hope for the sprightly expansion of the mid-Eighties is that two crucial elements of economic expansion, increases in population and productivity, have slowed in recent years. The U.S. population overall will probably grow around 1.8% annually through the 1990s, with no big increase in the working-age population either. So there simply won't be all that many more people entering the labor force to pump out goods and services. Productivity improvements . . . have been running less than 1% annually for the economy as a whole.

The only change that would significantly boost the work force—an enormous influx of immigrants—is unlikely. Productivity growth would probably have to double to produce GDP [gross domestic product] increases in the 4% range, and that too is improbable. As John Williamson, a senior fellow at the Institute of International Economics in Washington, D.C., puts it: "Unless you have a strong reason to think things are going to change, they usually stay the same."

To be sure, these modestly optimistic forecasters do find some signs of economic vigor, especially in the corporate sector. Widespread restructuring and downsizing may have wreaked havoc with people's lives, but they have produced thousands of far more efficient and flexible enterprises. Corporate profits should be strong because payroll costs are down and interest rates on short-term corporate debt have tumbled, providing up to a 10% lift to earnings. Says James Annable, chief economist at First National Bank of Chicago: "In response to tough global competition, we are coming out of recession with a much leaner, more productive corporate base."

The end of the Cold War remains a cause for comfort about the future. Even if no "Pax Americana" envelops the planet, new markets for U.S. exports will almost certainly be opening. The so-called peace dividend also provides an opportunity to trim the federal deficit and shift some manufacturing capacity to more economically productive pursuits. Reorienting big defense contractors and retraining workers will require formidable effort, but the more optimistic forecasters point to the past as evidence of American industry's capacity for change. . . .

National Wealth and Use of Income

For a country as rich as America is, getting richer faster is not a very important goal—or at least it is less important than it used to be and less important than it is in other countries. America's most important problems are not problems of the inadequacy of total national income but rather problems of inappropriate use of the national income the economy produces.

Herbert Stein, *The American Enterprise*, July/August 1990.

Nearly all forecasters who predict solid if unspectacular growth through the 1990s add a caveat or two. Most stress that a series of strong economic shocks, however unlikely, could upset their predictions. Commercial banking is a particular concern. New laws that would shut down institutions with insufficient funds have prompted warnings about a wave of bank closings and another raid on the Treasury, as the Federal Deposit Insurance Corp. pays off hordes of depositors. But the banking business has been reasonably good for some time now, and many balance sheets have improved markedly. . . .

The mildly optimistic scenario requires relatively stable financial markets, or at least no huge upset on the order of the 1987 stock market crash. The mere presence of Alan Greenspan as Federal Reserve chairman seems to have a calming effect on those markets, and this script for the Nineties depends in part on his serving out at least the remaining years of his term. . . .

With much new economic activity continuing to be driven by smaller businesses, forecasters believe the society will likely adjust in a number of subtle ways. Says Richard S. Belous, senior economist at the National Planning Association, a Washington research and policy group: "In the 1980s the flavor of the labor market continued to be set by large corporations. But in the Nineties, perception will finally adjust to realities." That will mean, says Belous, that national labor policies attuned to lifetime employment at a megacorporation will change. Workers will need to carry their own social-welfare system as they move from job to job. You, not your employer, will be responsible for amassing your retirement funds and providing your health coverage; when you switch jobs, your benefits will move with you.

In short, don't let the moderate-growth scenario lull you. The future may bring a measure of economic stability, but each of us will be increasingly under the gun to take control of our careers and make sure we share in the prosperity.

A Stagnant Economy

No. 3: The Beltway Blues. . . . A few of our seers, particularly those of a conservative political bent, take a dimmer view of the Nineties. They envision a decade of little if any economic growth and rising unemployment, punctuated by intermittent recessions. The cause of their moderately grim vision can be summed up in two words: the Democrats.

In this scenario, Bill Clinton unleashes a motley army of lobbyists, labor officials, blowhard Congressmen, and assorted special-interest groups ready for plunder after 12 years' absence from the public trough. Says Stephen Moore, director of fiscal policy studies at Washington's conservative Cato Institute: "There are people all over this town who are simply drooling as they dream about opening up the coffers.". . .

Clinton's conservative critics have grave doubts about his promise to keep a tight grip on spending in order to halve the budget deficit by the end of his first term; a failure on that front could be costly. The private sector, especially smaller businesses, would suffer from higher interest rates for precious capital while sectors crucial to the country's living standards—education, health research, and law enforcement among them—would be starved for funding. Why? Federal budgeting is heading quickly toward virtual paralysis. Within a few years, points out former Senator Warren Rudman, about 60% to 65% of the budget will be earmarked for entitlement programs, 13% or 14% will go to defense, and 17% will pay interest on the ever-mounting federal debt. A mere 5% to 6% will be left for everything else.

Taxes and Regulations

According to the skeptics who favor this scenario, even surprising restraint by Clinton on spending will matter little because his plans are so out of whack on the revenue side. For example, critics consider Clinton's promise to squeeze $45 billion in new taxes out of foreign companies doing business in the U.S. the height of folly at a time of high unemployment and a global scramble for investment dollars. Similarly, say the skep-

183

tics, soak-the-rich aspects of Clinton's program will have the opposite of the effect intended. Researchers at the conservative National Center for Policy Analysis in Dallas predict Clinton's proposed higher taxes on the wealthy will lead to a $413 billion drop in private-sector investment and the loss of 750,000 jobs by 1996. They add that reduced output will in turn generate less tax revenue and inflate the federal deficit by about $113 billion.

These pessimists are especially worked up about a cascade of costly new regulations that could flow out of Washington and stifle growth. The Dallas group estimates that Clinton's health insurance proposals could put 710,000 to 965,000 people out of work because of higher costs to employers, and that new mandatory worker-training programs could cost another 175,000 to 350,000 jobs.

Stephen Moore of the Cato Institute estimates that the Clean Air Act, passed during the Bush Administration, will cost an astounding $150 billion per year and lead to the loss of one million jobs when fully implemented. He contends, too, that a stack of legislation likely to be passed by Congress could be nearly as troublesome. . . .

Employers of all sizes are dreading the effects of these new laws—and the stiff penalties for noncompliance. The Better Business Bureau reports that the new Americans with Disabilities Act has spawned dozens of dubious enterprises that offer seminars and other services to small businesses struggling to figure out their potential liabilities under the statute.

On top of everything else, Clinton's critics fret about the possibility of a global trade war on his watch. . . . An all-out trade war could have terrible consequences for the U.S. economy and Americans' living standards in the Nineties. Not only would U.S. exports slump and Americans wind up paying more than in the past for imported goods, but the very industries supposedly being protected could lose their edge in the race to remain globally competitive.

An Economic Nightmare

No. 4: Apocalypse Then. . . . Another small minority of forecasters offer an even darker view of the near future. This crowd talks global depression, massive unemployment, widespread social unrest—a veritable nightmare. While they differ about the causes of this impending collapse, most seem to agree that an economic disaster could be touched off during the next few years by some momentous happening overseas. One of the more common doomsday fears: a violent civil war in what was the Soviet Union that sends oil prices skyward and threatens global stability. Kemper [Financial Services' chief economist] David Hale also keeps a wary eye on China, which boasts a 9% economic growth rate and could reach superpower status by the end of the decade. Should this giant become expansionist or belligerent, all bets on a new, more stable world order would be off.

Hale says the Middle East will likely remain a hot spot through the decade: Iran and Iraq will no doubt stay dangerous foes, and the region's poorer countries are in the throes of a population explosion. By 2010 the Mideast population will nearly double to 450 million or so, and the rich, sparsely settled oil states might seem inviting targets to poorer neighbors.

Some gloom-meisters insist a collapse is inevitable even without any new shock to the system from abroad. Barry Minkin, a California futurist, paints a particularly ugly scenario in his book, *Econoquake:* "Hundreds of companies will go bankrupt. Real estate markets, already down by 30% in some areas, will go into free fall. Unemployment will reach 15%, putting many middle-class families out on the streets. Retirees will find their investments and pensions turning to dust."

Minkin says that, unlike most economic seers, he has based his predictions on his years of experience as a senior management consultant with the Stanford Research Institute. He argues that nearly all the enterprises he has worked with—including Coca-Cola and IBM—share common failings, and these add up to economic "fault lines" that all but assure disaster.

The first problem, says Minkin, is America's poor international competitiveness. He contends that since we buy much more than we sell in world markets and borrow to make up the difference, we have become like some sorry debtor in hock to the neighborhood loan shark. He likens Treasury auctions to a kind of national debt consolidation loan. We have marched so far down the path to ruin, he argues, that even a complete overhaul of America's industrial base would probably be useless. Says Minkin: "There is very little we can do to stop the decline at this point."

The Income Gap

A subtext in the gloomy scenarios is the potential for a social upheaval that would thoroughly undermine what has come to be called the American way of life. What most concerns analysts is the widening social and economic gap between rich and poor in the U.S. The core of the problem, says George Peterson, a senior fellow at Washington's Urban Institute, is that the population is becoming increasingly segregated by income level. Inner cities and rural areas are more and more home only to the underclass, while the more affluent concentrate in suburban enclaves. As a result, the poor are completely shut off from good schools, good jobs, and all sorts of economic opportunities.

These researchers charge that short-term solutions such as enterprise zones will help little; Isabel Sawhill, another Urban Institute senior fellow, dismisses the schemes as "people taking in each other's laundry." Experts assert that pressure is building—"There's a lot of suppressed anger out there," says Peterson—and an explosion of social unrest may be inevitable. The Nineties, according to this troubling scenario, could be the decade when our cities burn.

Periodical Bibliography

The following articles have been selected to supplement the diverse views presented in this chapter.

Dollars & Sense	Special issue on the global economy, September/October 1994.
Leslie Eaton	"Cloudy Sunset: A Grim Surprise Awaits Future Retirees," *Barron's*, July 12, 1993. Available from Dow Jones and Co., 200 Liberty St., New York, NY 10281.
Robert Eisner	"Is the Deficit a Friendly Giant After All?" *Harvard Business Review*, July/August 1993.
James Fallows	"What Is an Economy For?" *The Atlantic Monthly*, January 1994.
Ralph Z. Hallow	"Is a Generational Conflict Coming?" *The World & I*, May 1993. Available from 2800 New York Ave. NE, Washington, DC 20002.
Neil Howe and Phillip Longman	"The Next New Deal," *The Atlantic Monthly*, April 1992.
Laurence J. Kotlikoff and Jagadeesh Gokhale	"Passing the Generational Buck," *The Public Interest*, Winter 1994.
Paul Krugman	"Competitiveness: Does It Matter?" *Fortune*, March 7, 1994.
Paul Krugman and Robert Z. Lawrence	"Trade, Jobs, and Wages," *Scientific American*, April 1994.
Robert B. Reich	"American Workers Must Face Reality," *USA Today*, March 1994.
Joan Edelman Spero	"The United States and the Global Economy," *U.S. Department of State Dispatch*, September 26, 1994.
Murray L. Weidenbaum	"How Domestic Regulation Handicaps U.S. Global Business," *Vital Speeches of the Day*, November 1, 1994.
Daniel Yankelovich, Faith Popcorn, and Theodore J. Gordon	"Business and the Future—A Round-Table Discussion," *The Futurist*, May/June 1992.
Steven Yates	"Rights Versus Entitlements," *The Freeman*, September 1994. Available from the Foundation for Economic Education, Irvington-on-Hudson, NY 10533.

The Ecological Environment: Sustainable or Not?

AMERICA
BEYOND
2001

Chapter Preface

In the United States, many government agencies, universities, and private firms conduct research to determine whether and where the environment is being damaged. Environmental Protection Agency experts, for example, process and scrutinize more than one hundred thousand field reports annually. Thus, many arguments about environmental harm are based on available scientific evidence.

One observer who contends that there is overwhelming proof of an ecological crisis now and in the future is U.S. vice president Al Gore, author of *Earth in the Balance*. Gore cites data showing dangerous levels of acid rain, global warming, and airborne and solid toxic wastes such as dioxin in North America and much of the world. He believes that nations must heed his and others' warnings to act quickly to avert long-term environmental damage.

Others, however, assert that Gore and many environmentalists are alarmists who are basing their conclusions on inaccurate scientific results. As economist John A. Baden writes in the anthology *Environmental Gore: A Constructive Response to "Earth in the Balance,"* "A large number of scientists do not feel comfortable with the extreme positions presented in *Earth in the Balance*." For example, Baden and scientists in the book contend that global data show no signs of unusual global warming. Others who disagree with Gore maintain that no solid evidence supports claims that acid rain damages forests and lakes or that dioxin causes cancer or otherwise seriously harms humans.

While scientists on each side of the environmental debate see clear evidence to support their positions, others argue that more and improved studies are needed to accurately determine the extent of environmental damage. In the following chapter, authors discuss the future of America's ecological environment.

1

"In the not too distant future, there will be a new 'sacred agenda' in international affairs: policies that enable the rescue of the global environment."

Sustainable Development Is Possible

Al Gore

Al Gore was elected the forty-fifth vice president of the United States in 1992. Author of *Earth in the Balance: Ecology of the Human Spirit*, which warns of an environmental crisis, Gore addressed the first United Nations "Earth Summit" in Rio de Janeiro in 1992. In Part I of the following viewpoint, Gore explores the relationship of people to the earth, arguing that the rapid pace of change on earth may irreparably harm the environment. Gore believes that America must join in a global partnership to foster economic development along with environmental protection, what he describes as "sustainable development." In Part II, Gore contends that the environment is the world issue of our time, and that it will become a "sacred agenda" in the near future.

As you read, consider the following questions:

1. According to Gore, what is the difference between an "exemptionalist" and an ecologist?
2. Why does Gore believe that population growth and water scarcity are creating an environmental crisis?
3. What does the author mean by "sacred agenda"?

Adapted from Al Gore, "In Pursuit of Sustainable Development," a speech made before the first session of the United Nations Commission for Sustainable Development, 1994. Al Gore, "Ecology: The New Sacred Agenda," *New Perspectives Quarterly*, Winter 1993. Reprinted with permission.

I

In 1992 in Rio the great riches of human creativity were on full display. Scientists displayed startlingly beautiful computer images of every square inch of the Earth—as seen from space. Artists crafted spectacular sculptures, paintings, music, graphics and films. And they all seemed more alike than different: the indigenous person and the artist, the scientist and the child, the tourist and the diplomat. All seemed to share a deeper understanding—a recognition that we are all part of something much larger than ourselves, a family related only distantly by blood but intimately by commitment to each other's common future.

Clear Dangers

And so it is today. We are from different parts of the globe. But we are united by a common premise: that human activities are needlessly causing grave and perhaps irreparable damage to the global environment. And the dangers are clear to all of us.

Degradation of land, forests and fresh water—individually and synergistically—plays critical roles in international instability. Huge quantities of carbon dioxide, methane, and other greenhouse gases dumped in the atmosphere trap heat, and raise global temperatures. Harvard Professor Edward Wilson, writing in the *New York Times*, summarized the notions of those who have a different view.

'Population growth? Good for the economy—so let it run. Land shortages? Try fusion energy to power the desalting of sea water, then reclaim the world's deserts . . . by towing icebergs to coastal pipelines. . . .

'Species going extinct? Not to worry,' the skeptics say. 'That is nature's way. Think of humankind as only the latest in a long line of exterminating agents in geological time. Resources? The planet has more than enough resources to last indefinitely.'

Wilson called this group the 'exemptionalists' because they hold that humans are so transcendent in intelligence and spirit that they have been exempted 'from the iron laws of ecology that bind all other species.'

The Human Race Is Not Exempt

The human race is not exempt. The laws of ecology bind us, too. We made a commitment at Rio to change our course. We made a commitment to reject the counsel of those who would continue along the road to extermination.

But of course, what we have done so far is only a beginning. We cannot overestimate the difficulties that lie ahead. In fact, from the vast array of problems about which it is possible to be pessimistic, let me mention two.

First, population growth. It is sobering to realize what is happening to the world's population in the course of our lifetimes. From the beginning of the human species until the end of World War II, when I was born, it took more than 10,000 generations to reach a world population of a little more than 2 billion. But in just the past 45 years, it has gone from a little over 2 billion to 5.5 billion. And if I live another 45 years, it will be 9 or 10 billion.

Immediate Effects

The changes brought about by this explosion are not for the distant future. This is not only a problem for our grandchildren. The problems are already here. Soil erosion. The loss of vegetative cover. Extinction. Desertification. Famine. The garbage crisis.

The population explosion, accompanied by wholesale changes in technology, affects every aspect of our lives, in every part of the globe.

Now, sometimes, developing countries feel the population argument is one made by wealthy countries who want to clamp down on their ability to grow.

Sometimes the developing countries are right. So I say this to citizens of the developed nations: we have a disproportionate impact on the global environment. We have less than a quarter of the world's population—but we use three quarters of the world's raw materials and create three quarters of all solid waste. One way to put it is this: a child born in the United States will have 30 times more impact on the Earth's environment during his or her lifetime than a child born in India.

The affluent of the world have a responsibility to deal with their disproportionate impact. But population growth affects everyone. By the year 2000, 31 low-income countries will be unable to feed their people using their own land.

Is population growth only a problem of birth control? Of course not. Paradoxically, reducing infant mortality is important as well. Several decades ago, Julius Nyerere put this matter cogently: 'The most powerful contraceptive is the confidence of parents that their children will survive.'

Slowing population growth is in the deepest self-interest of all governments. It is a responsibility for rich and poor countries alike.

Rapid population growth is only one of the causes of a profound transformation in the relationship between human civilization and the ecological system of the Earth. The emergence of extremely powerful new technologies that magnify the impact each of us can have on the global environment has also played an important role.

Most significant of all, many people now think about our relationship to the Earth in ways that assume we don't have to concern ourselves with the consequences of our actions—as if the global environment will forever be impervious to the rapidly mounting insults to its integrity and balance. But the evidence of deterioration is all around us.

Take, for example, the threat to our supply of fresh water.

There is a lot of water on Earth. But there isn't very much fresh water—only about 2.5% of all water on Earth is fresh and most of that is locked away as ice in Antarctica or Greenland, or other areas.

Furthermore, much of that water is used inefficiently. It may also be polluted by toxics and human waste. Meanwhile, by the year 2000, 18 of the 22 largest metropolitan areas in the world—those with more than 10 million people—will be in developing countries. By 2025, 60% of the world's population will live in cities—that's more than 5 billion people. They will urgently need fresh water and water sanitation.

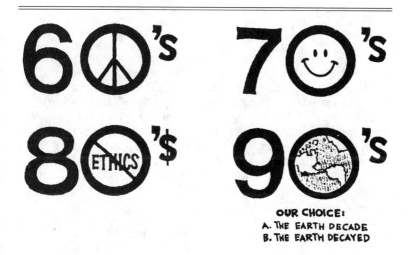

OUR CHOICE:
A. THE EARTH DECADE
B. THE EARTH DECAYED

ROTHCO
© THE SIGNAL
1990

Even though our worldwide civilization confronts an unprecedented global environmental crisis, we go from day to day without confronting the rapid change now under way. We must recognize the extent to which we are damaging the global environment, and we must develop new ways to work together to foster economic progress without environmental destruction.

193

How do we do it? Two principles must guide us as we set about the pursuit of sustainable development.

First, the principle of national responsibility. Will the United States show that sense of commitment? We can and we will.

But just as each nation must assume national responsibility, so must we all act together. If sustainable development is to become a reality, the second principle we must follow is that of partnership.

There are still those who think the wealthy countries on this planet have a monopoly on technology and insight. That's nonsense. We can all learn from each other. Over the last 20 years we have made some progress in creating the basis for a global partnership. The Earth Summit was a landmark in unifying 'environment' and 'development' in the term 'sustainable development'. Now this insight must be given life within the policies of every government. Trade, commerce, agriculture . . . all interests need to be part of the effort.

II

I fear we are on a downslope toward a future catastrophic event that will dim history. At a gut level, people throughout the world realize that the environment is the issue of our time. In the not too distant future, there will be a new "sacred agenda" in international affairs: policies that enable the rescue of the global environment. This task will one day join, and then perhaps supplant, efforts to prevent the world's incineration through nuclear war as the principal test of statecraft. . . .

Startling graphs showing the loss of forest land, topsoil, stratospheric ozone, and species all follow the same pattern of sudden, unprecedented acceleration in the latter half of the 20th century. And yet, so far, the pattern of our politics remains remarkably unchanged. To date, we have tolerated self-destructive behavior and environmental vandalism on a global scale.

Even with top-level political focus, the pervasive nature of all the activities that cumulatively create the greenhouse effect make the global solutions almost unimaginably difficult. Therefore, our first task is to expand the circumference of what is imaginable. It is not now imaginable, for example, to radically reduce CO_2 emissions. Even if all other elements of the problem are solved, a major threat is still posed by emissions of carbon dioxide, the exhaling breath of the industrial culture upon which our civilization rests. Yet, emissions must be curbed. We can make that task imaginable by building our confidence with successful assaults on more easily achievable targets, like elimination of CFCs [chlorofluorocarbons] and reversing the practice of deforesting the earth.

The cross-cut between the imperatives of growth and the imperatives of environmental management represents a supreme test for modern industrial civilization. Can we devise dynamic new strategies that will accommodate economic growth within a stabilized environmental framework?

The effort to solve the global environmental problem will be complicated not only by blind assertions that more and more environmental manipulation and more and more resource extraction are essential for economic growth. It will also be complicated by the emergence of simplistic demands that development, or technology itself, must be stopped. This is a crisis of confidence that must be addressed.

There is no assurance that a balance can be struck. Nevertheless, the effort must be made. And because of the urgency, scope, and even the improbability of complete success in such an endeavor, I will borrow from military terminology: To deal with the global environment, we will need the environmental equivalent of the Strategic Defense Initiative—a Strategic Environment Initiative. Even opponents of SDI, of which I am one, recognize that this effort has been remarkably successful in drawing together previously disconnected government programs, in stimulating development of new technologies, and in forcing a new wave of intense analysis of subjects previously thought to have been exhausted.

Stewards of the Earth

I have likened our newfound awareness of ozone depletion and the greenhouse effect to the Kristallnacht which forewarned the holocaust. The logic of this analogy can be extended, as [New Perspectives Quarterly] editor Nathan Gardels did in his foreword to the Spring 1989 issue on the ecology, to include Hannah Arendt's memorable notion of "the banality of evil" which emerged from her reflections on Hitler's lieutenants at the Adolf Eichmann trial.

My own religious faith teaches me that we are given dominion over the earth, but that we are also required to be good stewards. If, during our lifetimes, we witness the destruction of half the living species God put on this earth, we will have failed in our responsibility as stewards. Are those actions, because of their result, "evil"? The answer depends upon our knowledge of their consequences. The individual actions that collectively produce the world's environmental crisis are indeed banal when they are looked at one by one—the cutting of a tree, the air conditioning of a car. The willingness to trace the line of responsibility from individual action to collective effect is a challenge that we as a civilization have not yet learned to master.

"Evil" and "good" are terms not frequently used by politicians. And, yes, we know from historical experience the dangers of mixing public policy and religion. But, in my own view, while we must avoid zealotry, this ecological crisis cannot be met without reference to spiritual values.

In truth, as a civilization we don't have much faith left. The idea that we can totally abandon any but the secular values comes perilously close to saying that nothing has worth unless it can be consumed in our lifetimes.

The word "faith" need not be defined in conventional religious terms. Whether or not an individual has faith in life after death, they must have faith that life on earth continues after their death. If we are so far gone as a civilization that such a belief system cannot be put together, then nothing can save this species.

Ultimately, I believe that the ecological solution will be found in a new faith in the future of life on earth after our own, a faith in the future that justifies sacrifices in the present, a new moral courage to choose higher values in the conduct of human affairs, and a new reverence for absolute principles that can serve as guiding stars by which to map the future course of our species.

"There is remarkable consistency in the history of resource exploitation: resources are inevitably overexploited, often to the point of collapse or extinction."

Sustainable Development Is Unlikely

Donald Ludwig, Ray Hilborn, and Carl Walters

According to zoologists Donald Ludwig, Ray Hilborn, and Carl Walters, sustainable resource exploitation is unlikely. In the following viewpoint, the authors argue that the concept of "maximum sustained yield" (maximum sustained use of resources) is not feasible, largely because resources are inevitably overexploited. The authors include as causes of this phenomenon human prospects for wealth and a lack of scientific understanding. They believe that biological and political systems preclude optimum management of resources and that resource problems are human problems, not environmental problems. Ludwig and Walters are with the University of British Columbia Department of Zoology in Vancouver, Canada. Hilborn is at the University of Washington School of Fisheries in Seattle.

As you read, consider the following questions:

1. According to the authors, why is science incapable of predicting safe levels of resource exploitation?
2. Why do the authors believe that scientific certainty and consensus are insufficient to prevent the misuse of resources?
3. Why is decision making under uncertainty (using common sense) necessary for resource policies, according to the authors?

There are currently many plans for sustainable use or sustainable development that are founded upon scientific information and consensus. Such ideas reflect ignorance of the history of resource exploitation and misunderstanding of the possibility of achieving scientific consensus concerning resources and the environment. Although there is considerable variation in detail, there is remarkable consistency in the history of resource exploitation: resources are inevitably overexploited, often to the point of collapse or extinction. We suggest that such consistency is due to the following common features: (i) Wealth or the prospect of wealth generates political and social power that is used to promote unlimited exploitation of resources. (ii) Scientific understanding and consensus is hampered by the lack of controls and replicates, so that each new problem involves learning about a new system. (iii) The complexity of the underlying biological and physical systems precludes a reductionist approach to management. Optimum levels of exploitation must be determined by trial and error. (iv) Large levels of natural variability mask the effects of overexploitation. Initial overexploitation is not detectable until it is severe and often irreversible.

In such circumstances, assigning causes to past events is problematical, future events cannot be predicted, and even well-meaning attempts to exploit responsibly may lead to disastrous consequences. Legislation concerning the environment often requires environmental or economic impact assessment before action is taken. Such impact assessment is supposed to be based upon scientific consensus. For the reasons given above, such consensus is seldom achieved, even after collapse of the resource.

Maximum Sustained Yield

For some years the concept of maximum sustained yield (MSY) guided efforts at fisheries management. There is now widespread agreement that this concept was unfortunate. P. Larkin concluded that fisheries scientists have been unable to control the technique, distribution, and amount of fishing effort. The consequence has been the elimination of some substocks, such as herring, cod, ocean perch, salmon, and lake trout. He concluded that an MSY based upon the analysis of the historic statistics of a fishery is not attainable on a sustained basis. Support for Larkin's view is provided by a number of reviews of the history of fisheries. Few fisheries exhibit steady abundance.

It is more appropriate to think of resources as managing humans than the converse: the larger and the more immediate are prospects for gain, the greater the political power that is used to facilitate unlimited exploitation. The classic illustrations are gold rushes. Where large and immediate gains are in prospect, politicians and governments tend to ally themselves with special

198

interest groups in order to facilitate the exploitation. Forests throughout the world have been destroyed by wasteful and shortsighted forestry practices. In many cases, governments eventually subsidize the export of forest products in order to delay the unemployment that results when local timber supplies run out or become uneconomic to harvest and process. These practices lead to rapid mining of old-growth forests; they imply that timber supplies must inevitably decrease in the future.

Harvesting and the Ratchet Effect

Harvesting of irregular or fluctuating resources is subject to a ratchet effect: during relatively stable periods, harvesting rates tend to stabilize at positions predicted by steady-state bioeconomic theory. Such levels are often excessive. Then a sequence of good years encourages additional investment in vessels or processing capacity. When conditions return to normal or below normal, the industry appeals to the government for help; often substantial investments and many jobs are at stake. The governmental response typically is direct or indirect subsidies. These may be thought of initially as temporary, but their effect is to encourage overharvesting. The ratchet effect is caused by the lack of inhibition on investments during good periods, but strong pressure not to disinvest during poor periods. The long-term outcome is a heavily subsidized industry that overharvests the resource.

The history of harvests of Pacific salmon provides an interesting contrast to the usual bleak picture. Pacific salmon harvests rose rapidly in the first part of this century as markets were developed and technology improved, but most stocks were eventually overexploited, and many were lost as a result of overharvesting, dams, and habitat loss. However, in the past 30 years more fish have been allowed to spawn and high seas interception has been reduced, allowing for better stock management. Oceanographic conditions appear to have been favorable: Alaska has produced record catches of salmon and British Columbia has had record returns of its most valuable species.

We propose that we shall never attain scientific consensus concerning the systems that are being exploited. There have been a number of spectacular failures to exploit resources sustainably, but to date there is no agreement about the causes of these failures. J. Radovitch reviewed the case of the California sardine and pointed out that early in the history of exploitation scientists from the (then) California Division of Fish and Game issued warnings that the commercial exploitation of the fishery could not increase without limits and recommended that an annual sardine quota be established to keep the population from being overfished. This recommendation was opposed by the fishing industry, which was able to identify scientists who would state that it was virtually impossible to overfish a pelagic species. The debate persists today.

After the collapse of the Pacific sardine, the Peruvian anchoveta was targeted as a source of fish meal for cattle feed. The result was the most spectacular collapse in the history of fisheries exploitation: the yield decreased from a high of 10 million metric tons to near zero in a few years. The stock, the collapse, and the associated oceanographic events have been the subject of extensive study, both before and after the event. There remains no general agreement about the relative importance of El Niño events [oceanic conditions along the western coast of South America that prevent upwelling of nutrient-rich cold water] and continued exploitation as causes of collapse in this fishery.

Doubting Sustainable Development

Scientists are beginning to acknowledge that theories of sustainable use and development almost never work in practice. "What we are seeing is that conservation and development are not the same process," says the Wildlife Conservation Society's John Robinson, a leading revisionist on sustainable use. "If you are interested in development, you cannot get there by doing conservation, simply because the most diverse ecosystems are usually not the most productive in human terms." This means that development almost always brings losses of biological diversity. Instead of preserving the variety of a rain forest, for example, humans have the urge to chop down the trees and plant uniform crops.

What's good for society in the long run is of no immediate concern to people who use up natural resources. Given the high cost of modern fishing equipment, an individual fisherman is driven to catch every last fish rather than limit catches and ensure long-term supply. And no matter how good the plan to manage an ecosystem, some people will cheat.

Eugene Linden, *Time*, May 24, 1993.

The great difficulty in achieving consensus concerning past events and a fortiori [all the more] in prediction of future events is that controlled and replicated experiments are impossible to perform in large-scale systems. Therefore there is ample scope for differing interpretations. There are great obstacles to any sort of experimental approach to management because experiments involve reduction in yield (at least for the short term) without any guarantee of increased yields in the future. Even in the case of Pacific salmon stocks that have been extensively monitored for many years, one cannot assert with any confidence that present levels of exploitation are anywhere near optimal because the requisite experiments would involve short-term losses for the industry. The impossibility of estimating the sustained yield without reducing fishing effort can be demonstrated from statistical arguments. These results suggest that sustainable exploitation cannot be achieved without first overexploiting the resource.

The difficulties that have been experienced in understanding and prediction in fisheries are compounded for the even larger scales involved in understanding and predicting phenomena of major concern, such as global warming and other possible atmospheric changes. Some of the time scales involved are so long that observational studies are unlikely to provide timely indications of required actions or the consequences of failing to take remedial measures.

Scientific certainty and consensus in itself would not prevent overexploitation and destruction of resources. Many practices continue even in cases where there is abundant scientific evidence that they are ultimately destructive. An outstanding example is the use of irrigation in arid lands. Approximately 3000 years ago in Sumer, the once highly productive wheat crop had to be replaced by barley because barley was more salt-resistant. The salty soil was the result of irrigation. E. W. Hilgard pointed out in 1899 that the consequences of planned irrigation in California would be similar. His warnings were not heeded. Thus 3000 years of experience and a good scientific understanding of the phenomena, their causes, and the appropriate prophylactic measures are not sufficient to prevent the misuse and consequent destruction of resources.

Some Principles of Effective Management

Our lack of understanding and inability to predict mandate a much more cautious approach to resource exploitation than is the norm. Here are some suggestions for management.

1. Include human motivation and responses as part of the system to be studied and managed. The shortsightedness and greed of humans underlie difficulties in management of resources, although the difficulties may manifest themselves as biological problems of the stock under exploitation.

2. Act before scientific consensus is achieved. We do not require any additional scientific studies before taking action to curb human activities that effect global warming, ozone depletion, pollution, and depletion of fossil fuels. Calls for additional research may be mere delaying tactics.

3. Rely on scientists to recognize problems, but not to remedy them. The judgment of scientists is often heavily influenced by their training in their respective disciplines, but the most impor-

tant issues involving resources and the environment involve interactions whose understanding must involve many disciplines. Scientists and their judgments are subject to political pressure.

4. Distrust claims of sustainability. Because past resource exploitation has seldom been sustainable, any new plan that involves claims of sustainability should be suspect. One should inquire how the difficulties that have been encountered in past resource exploitation are to be overcome. The work of the Brundland Commission [World Commission on Environment and Development] suffers from continual references to sustainability that is to be achieved in an unspecified way. Recently some of the world's leading ecologists have claimed that the key to a sustainable biosphere is research on a long list of standard research topics in ecology. Such a claim that basic research will (in an unspecified way) lead to sustainable use of resources in the face of a growing human population may lead to a false complacency: instead of addressing the problems of population growth and excessive use of resources, we may avoid such difficult issues by spending money on basic ecological research.

5. Confront uncertainty. Once we free ourselves from the illusion that science or technology (if lavishly funded) can provide a solution to resource or conservation problems, appropriate action becomes possible. Effective policies are possible under conditions of uncertainty, but they must take uncertainty into account. There is a well-developed theory of decision-making under uncertainty. In the present context, theoretical niceties are not required. Most principles of decision-making under uncertainty are simply common sense. We must consider a variety of plausible hypotheses about the world; consider a variety of possible strategies; favor actions that are robust to uncertainties; hedge; favor actions that are informative; probe and experiment; monitor results; update assessments and modify policy accordingly; and favor actions that are reversible.

Political leaders at levels ranging from world summits to local communities base their policies upon a misguided view of the dynamics of resource exploitation. Scientists have been active in pointing out environmental degradation and consequent hazards to human life, and possibly to life as we know it on Earth. But by and large the scientific community has helped to perpetuate the illusion of sustainable development through scientific and technological progress. Resource problems are not really environmental problems: They are human problems that we have created at many times and in many places, under a variety of political, social, and economic systems.

"It's nice to know there are so many viable options to gasoline and that the majority of them could be made from renewable resources."

The Future Looks Bright for Alternative Fuels

Shawna Tracy and Roberta Stauffer

Both government and scientists increasingly urge the development and use of alternatives to gasoline. In the following viewpoint, Shawna Tracy and Roberta Stauffer provide evidence of America's improved technologies and increased use of alternative fuels, including natural gas, propane, and hydrogen. Tracy and Stauffer maintain that although these fuels are vital to America's future, no one option will satisfy our transportation needs, nor will gasoline be completely replaced in the short-term future. Tracy and Stauffer are former information specialist and technical writer, respectively, for the U.S. Department of Energy–sponsored National Center for Appropriate Technologies in Butte, Montana. Tracy now lives in North Carolina. Stauffer is a freelance writer and editor in Butte.

As you read, consider the following questions:

1. According to Tracy and Stauffer, how are fossil fuels polluting the atmosphere?
2. What drawbacks of alternative fuels do the authors cite?
3. How could using renewable alcohol fuels not add to atmospheric carbon dioxide, in the authors' opinion?

Shawna Tracy and Roberta Stauffer, "An Advance Look at the Future of Alternative Energy," Mother Earth News, February/March 1992. Copyright ©1992 (Sussex Publishers, Inc.). Reprinted with permission.

Right now, more than 500 million motor vehicles around the world are polluting the atmosphere—spewing emissions equivalent to their weight each year. They foul our air and poison our rain, and are also a major contributor to the global-warming effect which is dramatically altering the world's climate. Americans consume approximately 226 million gallons of gasoline each day. That's 82 billion gallons each year, 60% of the world's total oil consumption. And as crises—political and environmental—have shown us, we need new options.

Some answers will be found in a combination of alternative-fuel vehicles and more-efficient conventional cars. Technology already exists to power vehicles using alcohol fuels, electricity, natural gas, propane, and hydrogen. And vehicles using these propellants are beginning to show up on the road today in converted fleet vehicles such as buses, delivery vans, and utility trucks.

And as cities like Los Angeles, New York, Denver, Houston, and Phoenix scramble to comply with the Clean Air Act legislation, we'll see more fleets—as well as personal cars—converted in the next few years. Even more impetus will come from the 1988 Alternative Motor Fuels Act, intended to increase use of alcohol fuels and natural gas as energy sources and to spur the production of vehicles designed to run on them.

Alcohol Fuels

Perhaps the best news about alcohol fuels is that they can be made from renewable resources such as corn and wood waste. Researchers are also studying ways to convert municipal solid waste—especially paper—into an alcohol fuel.

The two most promising alcohol fuels are ethanol and methanol. Their increased use lessens our dependence on fossil fuels, and they emit less carbon dioxide and monoxide and fewer hydrocarbons. The downside is that their exhaust is not wholly benign: The aldehydes they emit, including formaldehyde from methanol (a probable human carcinogen), may require special catalytic converters to minimize environmental risk.

Ethanol is primarily made from corn, though it can be made from other sources of biomass or from natural gas and crude oil. The U.S. Department of Energy is focusing its research on identifying alternative biomass feedstocks for ethanol since corn is valuable for other uses (and even if the nation's entire corn harvest were devoted to fuel, it would supply only 20% of our motor-vehicle needs at current efficiency).

Ethanol might not be a new name to some people, since about 8% of the automobile fuel pumped at service stations is "gasohol"—a gasoline blend containing 10% ethanol. Between 800 and 850 million gallons of ethanol are produced in the United States each year, and most of it is blended with gasoline, though it can be used as a "neat" fuel, which means "at full strength."

Gasohol is available mainly in the Midwest. You could fill your car's tank now with the mixture without having to make any alterations. And only up to $500 worth of adjustments would have to be made to your car's engine for it to run on pure ethanol.

Methanol, nicknamed "wood alcohol," is most commonly made from natural gas, though it can be produced from biomass or coal as well. Approximately 1.4 billion gallons are produced each year, but only about 530 million gallons, or 38%, are used in fuel applications. (It's primarily used as a chemical feedstock, extractant, or solvent.)

In fuel applications, methanol is used either as a gasoline-octane enhancer or blended with 15% gasoline to form a fuel called M85. This fuel is most available in California and Hawaii—states currently testing methanol-powered fleets. Converting the rest of the country to pure methanol would require replacing parts of a car's fuel tank and distribution system with materials that can withstand the highly solvent fuel. (Chevron performed tests on methanol-fueled conventional vehicles and found decomposing fuel systems and clogged filters.)

Practically speaking, the development of alcohol fuels as alternatives to gasoline is still in its infancy. For them to make sense environmentally, they should be mass-produced from a cheap, abundant source of biomass or waste product, and this segment of the technology remains at the research stages. Corn is not the ideal feedstock for ethanol, and large-scale methanol production from fossil fuels would either mean the eventual importation of natural gas (continued energy dependence) or increased pollution from coal production.

While research progresses to find economical biomass feedstocks, we can continue to blend alcohol fuels with gasoline to reduce emissions and at least lessen our demand for imported oil. And by the way, it's technically feasible, if not economical, to produce ethanol or methanol on a small scale for personal use.

Electric Vehicles

In this design, a simple, battery-powered electric motor replaces the complex internal-combustion engine. No exhaust system pollutes the air. Electric vehicles are on the market today, and more choices are coming in the next few years.

The future looks bright for electric vehicles. Practically every major automaker, both foreign and domestic, has some sort of electric vehicle in the works. The one getting the most attention is General Motors's Impact—a flashy two-seater which GM says can go from 0 to 60 mph in eight seconds and travel 120 miles between charges.

GM is also developing an electric van, as are Ford and Chrysler.

Why this seemingly sudden interest in a century-old technology? California. The country's most populous state has passed air-quality targets for 1998 that only the electric vehicle should be able to meet. By that year, 2% of all new vehicles sold in the state must emit no air pollutants; by 2003, 10% of all new vehicles sold, or about 200,000 cars, must meet that standard.

Most northeastern states are also expected to pass similar regulations. As a result, car manufacturers will be striving to increase the average speed and driving range of electric vehicles. Cars on the market today can only go an average of 60 miles at about 35 mph between charges. Higher speeds and stop-and-go traffic sacrifice driving range, and recharging (at a standard wall outlet) can take up to eight hours.

Competition Among Promising Fuels

To comply with the 1990 Clean Air Act Amendments, fleet owners across the country are converting their buses, trucks, and autos to cleaner burning fuels. And while compressed natural gas (CNG), methanol, ethanol, and electricity show some promise, propane is leading the pack. . . .

As more fleet owners begin converting vehicles, the competition between the two most promising fuels, natural gas and propane, has intensified. Both fuels could help reduce America's dependence on foreign oil. American oil companies currently produce more than 7 billion gallons of propane a year. The domestic natural gas supply, at current rates of consumption, will last more than 50 years. Both fuels are cheaper than gasoline, can extend engine life, and can reduce maintenance costs. But thus far, propane is winning more converts than CNG.

Robert Bryce, *The Christian Science Monitor*, July 26, 1993.

The key to making electric cars practical is improved battery technology. Conventional lead-acid batteries are the only commercially available ones right now, but new types such as nickel-iron, nickel-cadmium, sodium-sulfur, lithium-sulfide, and zinc-air are being developed to increase the range to 200 miles at a top speed of 70 mph.

These new batteries are lighter and can store more energy. They may also last up to 100,000 miles, whereas lead-acid batteries must be replaced every 20,000 miles at a cost of $1,500. Each type has its drawbacks, however: Nickel-iron batteries emit potentially explosive hydrogen gas when recharging (recharging area must be well-ventilated), and sodium-sulfur batteries must be kept at extremely high temperatures (car must be run at least every four days).

Another potential solution for short driving ranges is the electric hybrid vehicle. These contain a small gas engine that powers a generator to recharge the batteries while the car is cruising. Such cars could also run on electricity alone during short trips and to help meet zero-emissions standards.

New cars such as the Impact are expected to cost between $20,000 and $30,000. A few small companies are now selling converted electric cars for about $17,000. And you can purchase do-it-yourself conversion kits for about $7,000.

Electric cars seem to be a viable solution for metropolitan areas battling smog. But this technology isn't totally pollution-free: Electricity production, especially from coal, is a major polluter and carbon-dioxide generator. Renewable energy sources, solar in particular, could at least augment conventional power production, especially in sunbelt states like California. Parking lots could be equipped with solar electric (photovoltaic) battery-recharging stations, and the cars themselves could utilize solar panels. Some car ventilation systems are solar-powered now, but only experimental racing cars are actually powered by the sun.

Other issues needing further attention are crash safety and the disposal or recycling of spent batteries. Since batteries contain hazardous materials, both of these issues are extremely important.

Natural-Gas Vehicles

Natural gas has become a key contender in the search for alternative fuels because of its many advantages over gasoline, including 90% less carbon monoxide and hydrocarbon emissions, no lead emissions, good cold-start capability, and smoother operation.

Perhaps its greatest advantage is cost. Refueling stations are selling natural gas for 57¢ per therm, or the gasoline equivalent of 70¢ per gallon.

Utilities service most of the 30,000 natural-gas vehicles operating in the United States today. Most of them are fleet vehicles supported by their own private refueling stations. City bus systems, utility company fleets, Postal Service trucks, and United Parcel Service vans are big users of natural gas.

Of the 308 natural-gas pumps in the United States today, only a few are open to the public, so there aren't many personal cars making the switch yet. If your home has natural gas, you can spend about $3,000 for a unit that will allow you to refuel in your own backyard. And in California, Chevron and Pacific Gas & Electric installed at least 40 public-refueling stations during 1992.

Natural gas is most commonly dispensed in compressed form (CNG), though it can also be turned into a liquid fuel (LNG) using high pressure and extreme cold. We'll probably see more LNG stations in the future because research has shown that it's more efficient that CNG.

Conversion to CNG is relatively simple: It takes less than a day and costs about $2,000. An aluminum tank is added to hold the gas, and modifications are made to the fuel delivery and carburetion systems. Once converted, the car can run on either gasoline or CNG. Maintenance costs, however, are lower with CNG use because the fuel doesn't form sludge, thus keeping the oil, spark plugs, and exhaust system cleaner.

GM trucks [including Sierra pickups] built specifically to run on CNG [came] on the market in 1992. . . . Most sales [have been] to utilities in California, Texas, and Colorado, but the trucks will also be available to the general public. They initially cost between $2,500 and $3,500 more than their gasoline counterparts.

Cars designed to run on CNG will be slower in coming, mainly because new designs are needed to accommodate the bulky fuel tank. In converted automobiles, the CNG tank eats up about half the trunk space. A big tank is needed because CNG has a lower energy density than gasoline. And even with the oversize tanks, driving range is only about 150 miles between refills.

Natural gas is making inroads into America's transportation scene mainly because it is cleaner-burning and less expensive than gasoline. It *is* still a fossil fuel, however, so burning it produces carbon dioxide, which contributes to global warming. And though the United States has an abundance of natural gas right now, we'd have to import if it became our main transportation fuel.

Propane

Another fossil fuel–based alternative to gasoline is liquefied petroleum gas, commonly known as propane. It is a by-product of natural-gas processing and crude-oil refining, and like natural gas, it emits less carbon monoxide and fewer hydrocarbons. It also shares a similar cost advantage and has a comparable energy density.

Propane is more established as an alternative fuel than natural gas—it's been used this way for 60 years. Because of its clean-burning properties, it often propels forklifts, stationary engines, and other equipment operating in enclosed areas. About 350,000 vehicles in the United States are using it—again, most of them fleet vehicles. Ten thousand propane retail outlets offer vehicle-refueling stations, mainly at truckstops, RV centers, and campgrounds, but not often at regular service stations. Conoco is the first oil company to begin offering propane at its service stations, primarily in the Denver area. The vast majority of propane-powered vehicles are converted and can also operate on gasoline. The conversion process is similar to that for natural gas and costs about as much.

Although the United States is one of the world's largest producers of propane—making about 20 billion gallons a year—only 2% is used for transportation. The remainder is used for home heating and to make products such as pesticides, synthetic fiber, rubber, antifreeze, and solvents. The demand for it in these non-transportation areas is probably the major reason it's not getting as much attention as the other alternative fuels. Also, available quantities of propane are limited by natural gas and oil production, since it's a by-product of these processes.

Hydrogen

In the 1930s, scientists in England and Germany converted over 1,000 test vehicles to operate on hydrogen and hydrogen/gasoline mixtures. Today, NASA uses hydrogen to fuel space shuttles and rockets.

Hydrogen fuel seems ideal because the only by-products of combustion are water and a manageable amount of nitrogen oxide. It can be burned in standard internal-combustion engines, and we appear to have a limitless supply from a renewable source—water.

But if only it were that simple! Since pure hydrogen does not exist in a natural state, it must be extracted from other materials. Hydrogen is now produced most economically from natural gas, and, in the process, as much carbon dioxide is released as if the natural gas were burned. Another extraction option is electrolysis, or using an electric current to split water into hydrogen and oxygen. This option, while technically sound, isn't economically feasible at current electricity rates. (And it raises the question: Why use electricity to create hydrogen when electricity itself is an emissionless alternative fuel?)

Once extracted, hydrogen storage poses further difficulties because it's a dangerous gas with a low energy density. It's most commonly stored in metal cylinders in highly compressed form, but this method isn't practical for vehicles because the tanks are too heavy and bulky. Bavarian Motor Works (BMW) has developed a working prototype using liquid storage: The gas is liquefied at −423°F and placed in superinsulated vacuum tanks.

Perhaps the safest method of storage uses metal-hydride technology. The tank contains combinations of metals (in powder form) that have a strong attraction to the hydrogen, actually trapping it in their crystalline structures. Mercedes-Benz has been researching this technique. However, an 800-pound tank holds only the equivalent of four gallons of gasoline. Hydrides using superactivated carbon may double the storage capacity of this method, but it still won't provide driving ranges comparable to gasoline.

Another option for hydrogen as a transportation fuel is to use a hydrogen-powered fuel cell to generate electricity to power the car. A New Jersey company is developing a prototype of this option, which would make the driving range of electric cars comparable to that of conventional vehicles.

Large-scale hydrogen use probably won't commence until the fuel can be produced economically using renewable energy (solar or wind). A prototype solar-powered hydrogen plant using water electrolysis has been built in Riverside, California, and another has been completed in Germany.

What the Future Holds

It's nice to know there are so many viable options to gasoline and that the majority of them could be made from renewable resources. Renewable fuels are important not only for energy sustainability, but also to slow global warming. There's no escaping carbon-dioxide emissions when burning fossil fuels—oil, natural gas, and coal—no matter how efficient they burn. Carbon dioxide is also created when methanol and ethanol are produced and burned, but if they are made from grain or woody materials, the next crop reabsorbs an equal amount of carbon dioxide, so there is no net increase to the atmosphere.

Though vital to our future, none of these alternatives will *totally* replace gasoline, at least not in our lifetime. The massive infrastructural changes necessary to totally switch are mind-boggling, and we probably couldn't make enough of any one option to satisfy our needs.

"The best alternative to gasoline is probably no alternative at all—it's gasoline."

The Future Looks Dim for Alternative Fuels

Len Frank and Dan McCosh

In the following viewpoint, Len Frank and Dan McCosh report on U.S. Department of Energy studies of alternatives to gasoline. Frank and McCosh contend that problems with such fuels as ethanol, methanol, and electric power involve major cost increases for vehicles and their fuel delivery systems. The authors argue that comparisons of exhaust emissions, engine performance, and infrastructure costs of alternative fuels and reformulated gasoline support the latter as the most viable fuel. Frank is a freelance writer and McCosh is the senior editor of *Popular Science* magazine.

As you read, consider the following questions:

1. How is California addressing vehicle emissions, according to Frank and McCosh?
2. According to the authors, which alternative fuels are the most attractive? Why?
3. What effect would alternative fuels have on smog, in the authors' opinion?

Excerpted from Len Frank and Dan McCosh, "Power to the People: The Alternative Fuel Follies—Part Two," *Popular Science*, August 1992. Reprinted with permission from *Popular Science* Magazine, ©1992, Times Mirror Magazines Inc. Distributed by Los Angeles Times Syndicate.

The year is 2006, and California commuters have come a long way toward weaning themselves from gasoline dependency. Huge oceangoing methanol tankers are anchored off San Diego; compressors run in neighborhood garages pressurizing cylinders storing compressed natural gas (CNG); and on a quiet night you can hear the steady buzz of batteries recharging in the distance. A quarter of the cars in California are running on something other than gasoline, still the most popular motor fuel. In fact, the main reason you bought your alternative-fuel commuter car was to get past the checkpoints into the clean-air zone at the center of town. Still, it can be tough to see Los Angeles, and sometimes you wonder if things have improved all that much, if the smog will ever actually go away. . . .

This should be a simple story—the issues seem so clear-cut: The use of gasoline in internal combustion engines causes air pollution, photochemical smog, increases the greenhouse effect, punches holes in the ozone layer, and will bring mankind to its collective knees. And besides, we're running out of oil.

The solutions presented thus far seem equally clear: Cut back on the use of oil until we can stop using it altogether and, until the magic-bullet batteries are found, bum clean fuels like natural gas, propane, ethanol, methanol, and hydrogen. But under closer scrutiny, the issues become murky. . . .

California's Air Resources Board's (CARB) . . . emissions standards present a timetable that starts in 1996, and by 2003 calls for 15 percent of all new vehicles sold to be so-called ultralow-emissions vehicles, likely burning alternative fuels, and another 10 percent to be zero-emissions vehicles, which means electric cars. So far, about 15 states have voted to adopt the California standards, making a broad-based shift to alternative fuels seem inevitable. Auto companies already are producing a handful of cars that run on alternative fuels, and electric cars are expected to be on the road in a few years. But getting a genuine alternative-fuel infrastructure in place could take a lot longer.

The Methanol Alternative

The U.S. Department of Energy (DOE) has been studying alternatives to crude oil since as far back as the energy crisis of the mid-1970s—long before the current concern about ultralow emissions standards. The most attractive fuels—methanol and compressed natural gas—are genuine alternatives mainly because they are in plentiful supply. Methanol is now produced in abundance primarily from natural gas, or methane, after the flurry of worldwide oil exploration sparked by two oil embargoes.

The California methanol program started in 1979, after the second gasoline shortage. By 1986, California had a test fleet of methanol-powered vehicles that had logged 12 million miles of service.

Methanol's chief advantages, aside from the convenience of a liquid fuel, are slightly improved performance compared with gasoline and increased range compared with CNG, due to the difficulty of storing CNG in cylinders. A car originally designed to be powered by methanol could be lighter, from savings in the size and weight of the cooling system, and could have slightly more power.

A mixture of 15 percent gasoline, 85 percent methanol—called M85—will corrode or dissolve many normal fuel-system materials, however. M85 has less energy content per gallon than gasoline, which cuts range with the same size tank to slightly more than half that of a gasoline car (about 1.6 gallons of M85 to 1 gallon of gasoline).

The Fuel of Choice

The power that propels family cars and a variety of other vehicles in the United States might be gasoline, steam, electricity, alcohol, natural gas, compressed air or—for the sake of fancy—giant rubber bands. Consumers appear to care little about what turns the crank so long as the power source provides the expected performance and is safe, environmentally sound, affordable and readily available.

Those characteristics explain why gasoline long ago became the motor vehicle fuel of choice in the competitive marketplace. Gasoline is a convenient and efficient energy package that, for most needs, yields the best value for the money among fuel choices.

Downs Matthews, *The Lamp*, Summer 1994.

Exhaust emissions from M85 are claimed to be less reactive—that is, less likely to form photochemical smog. About 75 percent of the hydrocarbons formed when it burns have low reactivity. In contrast, exhaust from gasoline cars is about 75 percent moderately reactive. M85, however, has double the highly reactive emissions compared with gasoline (10 percent versus 5 percent). Further, an M85-powered vehicle with any tuning problem (a bad spark plug wire, bad dioxide [O_2] sensor, for example) will have vastly increased production of carcinogenic aldehydes.

Costs vs. Benefits

A DOE report on the cost versus benefits of alternative fuels assumes that most methanol consumed as a motor fuel will be produced overseas, where natural gas is virtually free and huge methanol production plants are already built. It can be shipped, stored, and distributed more or less like gasoline, but the sheer increase in bulk due to the lost energy content per gallon translates into some impressive numbers. Storage tank farms would have to double in size and be specially constructed to eliminate water contamination. Likewise, the number of tank trucks on the road would dramatically increase. Methanol can be handled in gas stations, but the chemical properties attack some hoses and even dissolve some fiberglass underground tanks—which would have to be doubled in size in any case.

To distribute enough methanol to displace about 10 percent of the petroleum now consumed in the United States would take some heavy new construction. The DOE lists 116 new marine terminals for unloading tankers, 91,000 new service stations equipped (or re-equipped) to dispense methanol, and about 1,500 new tank trucks added to the existing fleet—about 50 percent more trucks on the road. Some $16.2 billion of the estimated $21 billion for a full-blown methanol program is the cost of the methanol-burning vehicles themselves—which presumably would be paid for by consumers as a premium when they buy the flexible-fuel cars.

Yet with all its drawbacks, methanol remains one of the easiest fuels to adapt to today's fuel distribution system. Vehicles can be switched from methanol to gasoline simply by putting it in the tank. Methanol forms a kind of chemical null point at the intersection of many different potential feedstocks: It can be synthesized from natural gas, coal, or even wood. (The DOE has actually studied the potential of converting trees to methanol, at about $1.25 per gallon.)

Natural Gas

Natural gas, the other leading alternative fuel, likewise has several potential sources, including recovery from decomposing dumps. But most of it is recovered from fossil gas trapped underground. It is already widely distributed in the United States, and the DOE estimates no new reserves or storage systems would be needed, even to supply enough to account for the same 10 percent petroleum substitution.

Currently more than 750,000 vehicles worldwide use CNG, many in plants and warehouses. CNG is low in tailpipe emissions, but the picture is confused by "nonreactive hydrocarbons," which are counted differently than those with greater volatility. Methane gas is a greenhouse gas, as is carbon dioxide. Presumably, methane helps the smog problem but contributes to global warming. According to one emissions engineer, the cleanest running nonelectric production vehicle available today is the dedicated CNG-fueled full-size Dodge van.

The downside of CNG is lack of range. Fueled at about 3,500

pounds per square inch (psi), a full-size car has a range of only about 100 cruising miles, which translates into a need for significantly more fueling stations. Higher pressures for quicker fill-ups require far more energy to compress. Refueling stations must raise the pressure to the required 3,500 psi for fast fill, about five minutes. Slow fill, requiring about eight hours, is more efficient because it heats the gas less and cooler CNG is denser. CNG engines require less maintenance than gasoline- or alcohol-fueled engines.

The compressors are the major cost of a CNG infrastructure, according to the DOE. A typical service station capable of quickly refueling passenger cars costs more than $300,000 to build, and a truck stop with special pipelines and heavy compressors could exceed $1 million (there are about 2,000 truck stops in the United States). Most CNG fueling stations are currently in local gas companies or fleet garages. Filling nozzles are not yet as standardized as those for gasoline, but are not much more difficult to use. Some oil companies have installed CNG stations along with their gasoline pumps.

Other alternative fuels less favored than methanol or CNG are still under scrutiny.

Ethanol and Other Fuels

Ethanol (ethyl alcohol or grain alcohol) is as familiar as your favorite beer. Ethanol was used as a motor fuel as long ago as any petroleum distillate—the 1870s at least. Considerably more benign than M85, E85 (15 percent gasoline, 85 percent ethanol) otherwise has similar characteristics. Brazil launched an ambitious ethanol fuel program in the mid-1970s, and major car manufacturers, such as Ford, Volkswagen, and General Motors, have produced millions of ethanol-burning vehicles for that market.

Because ethanol is generally distilled from crops, the "30 percent to 50 percent lower emissions" claim made for ethanol (the same as that made for methanol) must be tempered with the knowledge that the growing, fertilizing, harvesting, drying, and transporting of those crops produces considerable carbon monoxide (CO), carbon dioxide (CO_2), and even some nitrogen compounds—the EPA [Environmental Protection Agency] estimates six times as much as producing and burning a gallon of gasoline. Burning ethanol, however, does not produce dangerous aldehydes.

Liquefied petroleum gas (LPG or propane) has been used as a vehicle fuel since 1913. More than 3.5 million propane-powered vehicles are running worldwide, 350,000 in the United States. There are 10,000 propane refueling sources in this country— more infrastructure for the transportation and distribution of

LPG than for any other alternative fuel.

Hydrogen as a vehicle fuel is a wild card. Every other fuel available today has big business behind it, with concurrent lobbying pressures and with, or without, government proponents pushing for its use. In the United States, though, only the American Hydrogen Association (AHA), well-intentioned enthusiasts, supports hydrogen.

There is, of course, a limitless supply of hydrogen—if it can be separated from water economically. Separating the "hydrogen" from its companion "O" requires large amounts of electricity. . . .

DOE projections reveal the magnitude of converting a significant number of the nation's vehicles to alternative fuels. The scenarios for each type of fuel vary, but according to the DOE it would take between 30 and 40 million alternative-fuel vehicles on the road to displace the fuel consumption of 10 percent of the current petroleum-powered fleet nationwide. It would take about ten years of steady production, starting in 2006, to sell that many cars and trucks—assuming the full number mandated by the CARB scenario is actually built and sold.

Unfortunately, the net gain in air quality that comes from substituting alternative fuels in internal-combustion engines is much less than the savings in gasoline. Only half the smog in the United States is blamed on the nation's vehicles to begin with. The improvement anticipated with the "clean" fuels could make them about twice as clean as gasoline. But with just 15 percent of these cars and trucks burning "clean" fuel, the best case for overall improvement is only about 7 percent of the total smog-producing emissions from mobile sources—a meager 3.5 percent reduction overall. Zero-emissions electric cars, if they eventually reached the anticipated 10 percent goal of the vehicle fleet, would have a much higher impact on air quality. But clearly, improvements in emissions control of the much larger fleet of conventional gasoline cars will be even more meaningful, particularly the new mandate that cars must meet emissions standards for 100,000 miles, rather than the current 50,000 miles. . . .

Is Gasoline Best?

A few points to remember: Burning any of the fuels, fossil or renewable, produces oxides of nitrogen—this includes burning fuels to produce electricity. Burning any of them except hydrogen produces carbon dioxide—increasingly thought to be a contributor to the greenhouse effect and the formation of ozone. At this point it becomes a matter of pessimism versus optimism—which side do you believe?

According to an engineer who studies emissions for a major manufacturer, the best alternative to gasoline is probably no alternative at all—it's gasoline.

Reformulated gasoline has a reduced benzine content, additional oxygen-containing additives, and is reconstituted to reduce the volatile organic compounds. The performance and emissions benefits are still being evaluated, but gasoline companies are hopeful that it could produce similar benefits to alternative fuels.

Reformulated gasoline is gaining momentum: It has the performance, it has the infrastructure for refining and distribution, and it is the devil that we all know.

"*Nowhere is the greenhouse effect in the United States likely to be felt earlier or more severely than on the Great Plains and in the Midwest— America's breadbasket.*"

Greenhouse America: A Twenty-First-Century "Wild Card"

Harold W. Bernard Jr.

The greenhouse effect—an atmospheric warming phenomenon— is a real and looming threat, according to many experts and scientists. In the following viewpoint, Harold W. Bernard Jr. predicts that greenhouse warming in America will be felt first and most seriously in the Midwest, the nation's primary grain-producing region. Bernard is concerned that increasing temperature and decreasing precipitation will cause severe agricultural and livestock losses annually. Bernard is a meteorologist with DBS Associates, meteorological consultants in Atlanta.

As you read, consider the following questions:

1. According to NASA, as cited by Bernard, what are the probabilities of hot summers in future decades?
2. Why is the author concerned about groundwater in the Midwest?
3. What does Bernard believe the economic consequences of greenhouse warming will be in the Great Plains?

Excerpted from Harold W. Bernard Jr., *Global Warming Unchecked: Signs to Watch For.* Bloomington: Indiana University Press, 1993. Copyright ©1993 by Harold W. Bernard Jr. Reprinted by permission of Indiana University Press.

Nowhere is the greenhouse effect in the United States likely to be felt earlier or more severely than on the Great Plains and in the Midwest—America's breadbasket. It was here that the legendary Dust Bowl of the 1930s caused wheat and corn yields to plummet by up to 50 percent. It was here where, despite modern technology, the heat and drought of 1988 triggered a 40 percent reduction in midwestern corn yields. And it is here where the first major battle of our new greenhouse world will likely be joined: the Great Drought of the 1990s.

Increasing Temperatures

Based on the climatic analog of the 1930s, the northern and central Plains and western portions of the Midwest may well experience the largest annual greenhouse warming of any place in the United States during the latter part of the 1990s. The analog suggests yearly means [mean, or average, temperatures] will climb as much as 3° F (1.7° C). July is likely to manifest the greatest hike in temperatures, especially from Kansas City northward along the Missouri Valley into North Dakota. Those regions could bake under July readings averaging 4° to 5° F (around 2.5° C) higher than current means. In the hottest summers, monthly temperature departures could reach a withering 12° F (6.5° C) or more.

The NASA climate model, under scenario A ("business as usual"), also depicts hotter summers during the late 1990s for much of middle America. [The National Aeronautics and Space Administration monitors global climate from the ground, air, and outer space.] The model suggests that summer (the combined months of June, July, and August) will average 2° to 3° F or more (1° to 2° C) hotter than recently over a broad area of the country centered on southeastern Missouri. Even under the more moderate scenario B ("limited [greenhouse gas] emissions"), the NASA model predicts that by the 2010s, all of the Midwest and Great Plains will be averaging 2° to 3° F or more warmer *on an annual basis*.

As the greenhouse effect figures more and more prominently in our climate, each successive decade will grow warmer. By midcentury the GFDL [global climate] model foresees summers averaging an astounding 14° to 16° F (8° to 9° C) hotter over the northern Great Plains, northern Great Lakes, and southern plains of Canada. Summers in Fargo, North Dakota, would feel like summers do now in Dallas–Fort Worth, Texas.

Hot Summers and Corn

James Hansen and his co-workers at NASA came up with a good way of describing what the trend toward more torrid summers will mean in terms of the probability of any *one* summer's being "hot." For Omaha, Nebraska, they arbitrarily defined the ten warmest summers (June, July, and August) in the period 1950 through 1979 as "hot," the ten coolest as "cold," and the middle ten as "normal." In other words, for that period there was a 33 percent (one out of three) chance of any one summer's being "hot." Under scenario A the probability of a "hot" summer for Omaha rises sharply to 80 percent (eight out of ten) for the late 1990s, drops back a bit in the first decade of the new century, rises to 85 percent for the 2010s and 2020s, then locks in at 100 percent for the remainder of the century!

Meyer, for the *San Francisco Chronicle*. Reprinted with permission.

Things aren't much better with scenario B. The probability of a "hot" summer under that scenario is over 50 percent after 1995. From there it increases each decade, reaching 85 percent for the 2020s, the same as under scenario A. (No scenario B calculations were made for decades beyond the 2020s.) Even given the unlikely, relatively benign scenario C ("Draconian emission cuts"), the chances of a "hot" Omaha summer exceed 50 percent each decade after the turn of the century.

In terms of what farmers are more concerned about, consider the likelihood—as NASA researchers did—of five consecutive days with maximum temperatures over 95° F (35° C) in Omaha. Such conditions are thought to represent a threshold above which the productivity of corn suffers. During the period 1950 through 1979, at least one five-day heat wave with maxima exceeding 95° F occurred in three out of every ten years. Under scenario A this becomes five out of every ten years by the late 1990s and seven out of every ten years in the 2020s. Even if scenario A doesn't hold up into early next century, the outlook isn't a whole lot better given scenario B: by the 2020s six out of every ten years would suffer corn-killing hot spells.

The NASA calculations warn that for doubled CO_2 [carbon dioxide], nine years per decade will experience such runs of fiery temperatures. In other words, near the middle of next century or shortly thereafter, virtually every summer around Omaha would be blistered by one or more severe heat waves.

Greenhouse Summers

By midcentury, give or take a decade, all parts of the Plains and Midwest most likely will have undergone a significant climatic change. The sweaty grip of greenhouse summers should be unmistakable. Chicago, Illinois, may experience the frequency of days over 90° F (32° C) that parts of the lower Mississippi Valley currently do. (The Chicago figure is expected to soar from sixteen to fifty-six such days per year.) In Dallas, Texas, the number of days over 90° F could approach that which Phoenix, Arizona, now has (the Dallas figure is forecast to escalate from 100 to 162 per year). And in Dallas it wouldn't be a dry heat.

On the meltdown side of the thermometer scale, consider the frequency of days over 100° F (38° C) in a world with doubled CO_2. In Omaha the number of days per year exceeding 100° F is predicted to be seven times greater than now (twenty-one versus three). In Chicago, which rarely suffers readings over 100° F currently, such sweltering weather is forecast to come along about half-a-dozen times each year by midcentury. In Dallas, where reaching the century mark is not uncommon even today, it will be even more common with twice as much CO_2 in the air (the annual tally of 100° F–plus days is expected to soar from nineteen to seventy-eight).

Greenhouse Winters

Don't get the idea, however, that even though summer heat will likely be more widespread and oppressive than ever by midcentury, cold weather will have disappeared. Certainly cold

221

waves will be fewer and further between, and what frigid weather does occur will be less intense; but freezes and frosts won't be a thing of the past. In Omaha, for instance, the number of days with mimina below 32° F (0° C) is predicted to drop from 139 days annually to 75. In Chicago, the yearly frequency is forecast to plunge from 132 to 71 days; in Dallas, from 40 to just 11. Keep in mind, too, that in the near term, the 1930s analog suggests that frigid winters will still plague us through the 1990s. Remember, the coldest month ever in the United States, February 1936, directly preceded the hottest summer on record. (The lesson here is that a cold winter does not mean the greenhouse threat has lessened, any more than a single hot summer—such as 1988—is incontrovertible evidence that the greenhouse effect has taken complete control of our weather.)

Precipitation

The thirties analog implies that during the latter half of the 1990s, the state likely to be hardest hit by a *combination* of reduced precipitation and higher temperatures is Kansas, the leader in U.S. wheat production. Also likely to suffer a blend of significant drying and warming are large parts of Nebraska, Iowa, and the Dakotas. Other areas may endure it to a lesser extent: portions of Oklahoma, Missouri, and Wisconsin. Any amalgam of diminished rainfall and enhanced heat leads to drier soils, of course, and it is dry soils that most worry the farmers of America's heartland.

If any region of the Plains and Midwest is likely to escape the initial onslaught of the greenhouse effect, it is probably Texas. There the thirties analog suggests slightly greater precipitation through the 1990s. Even that is likely to change by midcentury, though. The GFDL model indicates that within another sixty years or so all of middle America—with the possible exception of the Texas coast—will find drier soils a recurrent feature, at least in summer.

Extreme summertime drying—soil moisture reductions exceeding 50 percent—is suggested by the GFDL model for the far northern Plains and northwestern Great Lakes. Soils at least 30 percent drier are foreseen for the remainder of the northern Plains, across the central Plains, and throughout the Midwest.

Different Answers, Same Results

The three models examined by the EPA [Environmental Protection Agency] come up with different answers regarding the magnitude and seasonal patterns of midcentury precipitation changes likely for the Great Plains. When considered on an annual basis, however, there is no disagreement relative to end results: all three models point toward diminished soil moisture.

Two of the models foresee less annual rainfall and snowfall on the Plains, while one predicts a tiny increase. But given the sharp warming likely, such a slight increase would be quickly gobbled up by enhanced evaporation. Result: drier soils. . . .

Consequences

Across the Great Plains and in the Midwest, agriculture will suffer the most in a full greenhouse environment. (That's an ironic way to state it I suppose.) The bad news for the latter part of the 1990s: tens of billions of dollars in crop and livestock losses due to heat and drought. Don't expect it to get any better after that.

For example, although the GFDL-modeled precipitation decreases for midcentury in Kansas and Nebraska are no greater than those of the worst Dust Bowl years (1934 and 1936), temperatures are forecast to be substantially higher than during the Dust Bowl. And higher temperatures appear to be the primary culprits in expected crop yield declines. High temperatures shorten the period during which crops can mature.

One researcher, using a crop-yield model tuned to 1975 technology, determined that a recurrence of 1934 and 1936 climate conditions would more than halve wheat yields on the Great Plains. And this result did not even consider the hotter weather in the offing. Other researchers, looking at corn and soybean production in the Midwest and Great Lakes states, suggest that dryland (nonirrigated) crop yields could tumble by as much as 60 to 65 percent under the GFDL climate scenario for doubled CO_2. But under some of the wetter scenarios as foreseen by different climate models, crop yields in some northern areas—around Duluth, Minnesota, for example—could actually increase.

Mitigation?

Admittedly, a couple of things could help mitigate the extensive crop losses feared for the Great Plains and Midwest. One is CO_2 itself. An increase in carbon dioxide should enhance the growth of crops, but the jury may still be out on that. (Researchers found that although soybeans grew more prolifically in a high-CO_2 environment, pests ate more of their leaves because the leaves were less nutritious.) The other mitigating factor is irrigation.

First, carbon dioxide. Although atmospheric CO_2 may well provide a fertilizing effect to crop growth, the EPA cautions that "experimental results from controlled environments may show more positive effects of CO_2 than will actually occur in variable, windy, and pest-infected (e.g., weeds, insects, and diseases) field conditions." The EPA also warns: "The more severe the climate change scenario, the less compensation provided by direct effects of CO_2." In other words, there is a threshold beyond which carbon dioxide won't help. If it's too hot and too dry for crops to grow, crops won't grow . . . no matter how rich in carbon dioxide the atmosphere is.

Now, irrigation. In many parts of the Great Plains, irrigated farming of corn, rice, and cotton has replaced dryland wheat production, especially in western Kansas and the Texas Panhandle. Overall, around 12 percent of Great Plains cropland is irrigated. In Nebraska, Kansas, and Oklahoma, about three-quarters of the water for irrigation is supplied by groundwater, most of it coming from a vast underground reservoir known as the Ogallala Aquifer. This aquifer, extending from Nebraska through the Texas Panhandle, supplies irrigation to approximately fourteen million acres (5.7 million hectares) of land in Nebraska, Kansas, Oklahoma, Texas, Colorado, and New Mexico.

A Threat to the Gulf Stream

Assuming the accepted annual carbon dioxide growth rate of 1%, [Princeton University scientists] Syukuro Manage and Ronald J. Stouffer calculated [in *Nature* magazine in 1993] that the level of the greenhouse gas would double in 70 years and quadruple in 140 years.

Using a computer model to simulate the effect of the resulting increased temperature, they predicted an eventual collapse of the Gulf Stream, a conveyor belt of warm ocean water from the Gulf of Mexico to the north Atlantic Ocean.

Mark A. Stein, *Los Angeles Times*, July 15, 1993.

But forty years of heavy use has taken its toll on the aquifer, and it is being depleted of its water far faster than it can be replenished. Part of the reason for the rapid depletion is the switch by farmers to corn to satisfy the nation's appetite for corn-fed beef. Corn requires a 50 percent supplement of water relative to normal rainfall, while wheat and sorghum need only a 10 to 20 percent augmentation. In some parts of Kansas, Oklahoma, and Texas, the Ogallala is dropping three feet (one meter) per year. It is recharged in those areas at the rate of one-half inch (slightly more than a centimeter) per year.

Conservation efforts, along with hard times that have forced some farmers off their lands, have cut the drawdown rate of the Ogallala in half over the past decade. Still, the long-term outlook, even without a greenhouse effect, is sobering. Donald Reddell of Texas A & M University explains that although the aquifer will never be pumped dry, "what is going to happen is that the water yield, in gallons per minute, is going to drop, and because of energy costs it will reach a point where the farmer cannot afford to pump water to irrigate his crops . . . and [he] will stop farming."

Economic Impacts

The EPA studied the economic consequences likely to result from changes in crop yields and water availability fostered by the greenhouse effect. The conclusion: "The results of the . . . study imply that wheat and corn production may shift away from the southern Great Plains, causing dislocations of rural populations. For many rural communities in the region, this may further weaken an economic base already under pressure from long-term structural changes in U.S. agriculture." The report goes on to warn of potential risks to financial institutions supporting farmers and to emergency relief resources.

In the Midwest and around the Great Lakes, because of the differing climate change scenarios foreseen by the models, it is difficult to predict whether crop yields would decline or rise. . . .

Livestock and Forests

Not only crops but also livestock will suffer in a greenhouse world. Texas, for instance, raises nearly 40 percent of the beef cattle in the United States. Heat stress for these and other farm animals will increase markedly as the greenhouse effect becomes more pronounced. . . . Livestock reproduction dwindles with increasing heat, and hotter weather may allow tropical diseases to extend their ranges into the Great Plains.

Livestock problems of a different sort might plague the northern Plains. Dried-up duck-nesting ponds could cause the populations of mallards and canvasbacks to plummet. Of course, indigenous wildlife in general will suffer in a hotter and drier climate.

Around the Great Lakes the distribution and abundance of forests will change as the climate grows steadily warmer. The range of spruce trees will gradually shift northward out of the region, while in Minnesota—within thirty to sixty years—the number of balsam firs will start to decline. Both of these tree species have commercial importance to the pulp and paper industry. Hardwood trees, such as oak, sugar maple, and yellow birch, will likely slowly replace the softwood evergreens as well as the white birch and quaking aspens. . . .

Energy Demand

Throughout the Great Plains and Midwest, hotter summers will lead to ever-greater demands for cooling, and thus for electricity. By 2055, electric generating capacity to meet peak demand during the hottest weather could be as much as 30 percent greater than currently foreseen (i.e., no climate warming considered).

The largest jumps in peak demand would occur over the central and southern Plains (Nebraska, Kansas, Oklahoma, and Texas) and in Missouri. In those states, 20 to 30 percent more new capacity is likely to be needed by midcentury. In Illinois, a 10 to 20 percent increase in generating capacity—relative to what is currently expected—is probable.

In the more northern states of the region, winter heating requirements could dip sharply. But since the greatest summertime warming will likely be here, even these northern states would need additional electric generating facilities to meet peak demand (for cooling). Across the northern Plains and through the Great Lakes, up to 10 percent more new capacity would need to come on line by midcentury.

Michigan or Bust

Maybe everyone will just forget the whole thing and move to Michigan. The Great Lakes states, with milder winters and warmer summers, may well prove to have a more temperate climate than regions to the south come midcentury. And even though Great Lakes levels may well be dropping, the lakes will still contain vast amounts of freshwater. That in itself could be a big draw by the middle of the next century. "Consequently," the EPA concludes, "the Great Lakes may be relatively more attractive than other regions." Like the Pacific Northwest, the Great Lakes states could become part of America's new Sun Belt in the twenty-first century.

Think of it. Spring break on the shores of Lake Michigan.

"Small amounts of warming during the coldest time of day during the coldest months hardly make for a great disaster in the United States!"

Normal Weather: A Twenty-First-Century Trend

Robert C. Balling Jr.

In the following viewpoint, climatologist Robert C. Balling Jr. presents his research of national weather and climate records to dispute the "popular vision" of an impending greenhouse warming crisis in America. The author compares forecasts of global climate models with historical records and patterns of change in temperature, precipitation, and hurricanes, and concludes that there is no concrete evidence that greenhouse warming is occurring. Balling is the director of Arizona State University's Office of Climatology in Tempe.

As you read, consider the following questions:

1. According to Balling, what are the components of the "popular vision" of greenhouse warming?
2. In Balling's opinion, what appears to be the trend in precipitation?
3. What evidence does the author offer to challenge drought predictions?

Americans have been told that their temperatures will increase, droughts will plague the agricultural heartland, extreme high temperatures will occur much more frequently, hurricane and severe storm activity will increase, streams and rivers will dry up, sea level will rise and inundate low-lying coastal areas, wildfires will become more common, and on and on. And the culprit for this apocalypse is, as always, the buildup of the greenhouse gases. However, the climate patterns in the United States observed over the past century have not been particularly supportive of this apocalyptic view. . . .

From the outset, it is critical to realize that the area of the conterminous [continental] United States (excluding the U.S. portion of the Great Lakes) covers only 1.53 percent of the surface of the globe; the conterminous United States accounts for slightly more than 5 percent of the total landmass of the planet. What happens to the climate of the United States may seem vitally important within the country, but in terms of global climate change, what happens in the continental United States has little effect on the planetary trends.

Nonetheless, a substantial portion of the scientific literature on the greenhouse effect has focused on potential changes in the climate patterns of the United States. Given the number of climatologists in the country, the number of professional journals published within its borders, and the number of decision-makers concerned about climate changes in the United States, the importance of climate trends in this 1.53 percent of the planet has been inflated with respect to the greenhouse debate. However, the "popular vision" is full of predictions that are highly specified for this area.

Patterns in U.S. Temperatures

One of the many reasons scientific investigators are drawn to the analysis of climate change in the United States is the availability of long-term, reasonably homogeneous weather and climate records. One outstanding data base is the United States Historical Climatology Network (HCN) developed by climatologists at the National Climatic Data Center in Asheville, North Carolina. The HCN was developed to detect regional changes in climate as opposed to station-specific changes that may have occurred over the past century. The network consists of 1,219 stations rather evenly distributed through the conterminous United States. . . .

An extremely complex set of quality control measures was applied to the temperature and precipitation records from the 1,219 stations. The history of each station was carefully examined, and the records were statistically adjusted for changes in the time of observation, the actual instruments used in the measurements, the location of the instruments, and the location of the station. Homogeneity tests were run on the temperature and precipitation data, and ultimately a time series of mean monthly temperatures (including mean maximum, mean minimum, and average temperature) and monthly precipitation totals was established for the past century. . . .

Figure 1. United States mean annual temperatures for the period 1901–1987.

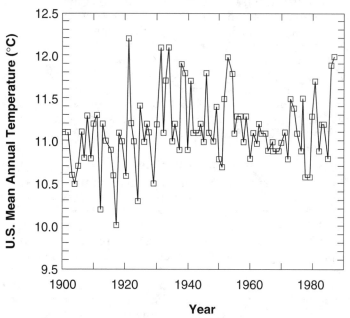

Robert C. Balling Jr., *The Heated Debate*, 1992.

Figure 1 presents the mean annual temperatures for the continental United States during the twentieth century. Much like the temperatures for the Northern Hemisphere and for the globe, the U.S. temperatures show no trend from 1901 to 1920, warming from the early 1920s to the late 1930s, cooling through the 1970s, followed by a return to relatively warm years in the 1980s. Overall, the linear trend in annual temperatures is 0.29°C (0.52°F) over the 1901 to 1987 time period; however, the trend is not statistically significantly different from zero. In other words, we cannot say with confidence that there has been *any* trend in U.S. mean annual temperatures in this century! And although not statistically significant, the period from 1920 to 1987 has been dominated by a *cooling* of 0.13°C (0.24°F). Here we have possibly the best temperature data set for any area of the planet, and during a time (1920–1987) when equivalent CO_2 [carbon dioxide] increased by over 30 percent (from approximately 325 to 425 ppm), the temperatures cooled slightly. [According to greenhouse effect theory, CO_2 is one of several gases that trap heat and warm the lower atmosphere.] . . .

The models strongly suggest that continental areas in the mid-latitudes of the Northern Hemisphere should experience most of their warming in the winter season. To test this hypothesis, the trends in season mean temperatures were computed for the HCN data. As seen in Table 1, during the summer (June–August) season, temperatures for the United States increased by 0.31°C (0.56°F) while during the winter (December–February) months, the temperatures increased by 0.47°C (0.85°F). However, these trends are not statistically significant at the 0.95 level of confidence. In addition, since 1920, summer temperatures have shown no change, but the winter temperatures have actually cooled by 0.73°C (1.32°F).

Temperature Trends

The trends in annual and seasonal temperature have shown distinctive spatial patterns across the United States. Generally, the New England area and western United States (west of the Rocky Mountains) have been warming while the central and southeastern United States have been dominated by cooling. This pattern appears in all seasons and is most pronounced in the winter season. . . .

Basically, the bulk of the warming seen in the United States over the past century has occurred at night and during the winter season. Small amounts of warming during the coldest time of day during the coldest months hardly make for a great disaster in the United States! . . .

These analyses lead to several generalizations regarding temperature changes in the United States during the twentieth century. First, temperatures are increasing, but in general, the temperature increases are not statistically significant. Minimum temperatures have increased more than maximum temperatures, and the diurnal [daily] temperature range has been declining over the past 50 years. Winter is consistently the season of greatest warming while autumn tends to have the least amount of warming. Finally, warming tends to occur in the West and Northeast and cooling is the tendency in the Midwest and Southeast. The temperature record from the United States since the turn of the century is not particularly consistent with the predictions of the greenhouse models. The seasonality of the trends is broadly consistent with the models, but the magnitude of the trends is far less than what should have been observed given the buildup in the greenhouse gases.

Increases in Extreme High Temperatures?

One component of the "popular vision" is the notion that the high temperatures of the summer season will increase in magnitude and in frequency. We are told that greenhouse warming will add heat to all air masses at all times of the day, and therefore, we will see substantial increases in the frequency of record-breaking high temperatures. This prediction is not just an exaggeration of the global warming issue; it is well-founded in the professional literature. In particular, published work by Linda Mearns et al. (1984) and James Hansen et al. (1988) leads directly to the conclusion that global warming will increase the frequency of extreme high temperatures. This issue becomes especially important and threatening given the linkage between extreme high temperatures and human health, agricultural productivity, and water and energy demand.

Several empirical studies have used data from the United States to investigate the prediction of increasing extreme high temperatures. In one research effort, Sherwood Idso and I used the HCN temperature record to define areas in the United States that have had statistically significant warming or cooling over the past 40 years. In general, we found that the summer mean maximum temperatures across the United States had *cooled* during the 1948 to 1987 study period. However, using mean summer temperatures, we identified stations in the western United States that had been warming at a significant rate and stations in New York and Texas that had been cooling at a significant rate. The daily maximum temperatures from these stations were collected for the 40-year period, and trends were established in the frequency of extremely high summer temperatures. For the stations that had experienced significant summertime warming, a 25 percent increase had occurred in the frequency of extreme events. At first glance, the prediction of increasing extreme highs with overall warming appeared to be supported. However, for the stations that had *cooled* significantly, a 38 percent *increase* in extreme high temperatures was identified. After noting that the relationships between overall warming or cooling and the frequency of extreme maximum temperatures were not statistically significant, we concluded that "there is no sound observational basis for predicting an increase in the frequency of occurrence of extreme high summer temperatures in response to greenhouse warming.". . .

Patterns in U.S. Precipitation

As equivalent CO_2 is doubled, the climate models tend to predict, for the conterminous United States as a whole, increases in temperature of between 2.0°C (3.6°F) and 4.0°C (7.2°F), slight increases in annual precipitation, rather substantial increases in winter precipitation, and general decreases in summer precipitation. Given the record of the twentieth century, the empirical evidence does not strongly support the predicted increases in U.S. temperatures. Just as the HCN record allowed fairly detailed analyses of the temperature patterns, the HCN also allows careful analyses of the precipitation record. . . .

Between 1901 and the early 1950s, the precipitation levels varied considerably, but the average value remained stationary. In the early 1950s, a sharp drop occurred in the values, and since that time, precipitation totals have been rising at a statistically significant rate. Over the entire time period (1901–1987), the precipitation levels showed a linear increase of 29.73 mm (1.17 inches) or approximately 4 percent (the global precipitation 100-year increase was near 6 percent), but this increase is not statistically significant.

As seen in Table 1, the increase in precipitation from 1901 to 1987 occurs in spring and autumn while summer and winter have both shown slight decreases in precipitation. Recognizing that the numerical models predict an increase in winter precipitation (which has not occurred) and a decrease in summer rainfall (which has occurred), one would expect the ratio between winter and summer precipitation to be increasing. The ratio of winter to summer precipitation shows no trend over the entire 1901 to 1987 period, and a slight decrease since the early 1950s. Again, an expectation from the models is not seen in the empirical data. . . .

The precipitation patterns of the United States are inconclusive in resolving any part of the greenhouse debate. The observed trend appears to be toward more rainfall on an annual basis, and this observation is largely consistent with the models. Seasonal and regional trends are not particularly consistent with predictions of the models. . . .

We should be very cautious in accepting the predictions of significant rainfall changes in America, particularly about the reduction of precipitation in the agricultural heartland of the country. At the present time, there appears to be little change in U.S. precipitation associated with the observed 40 percent increase in equivalent CO_2 over the past century.

Patterns in U.S. Droughts

Another of the many predictions associated with the "popular vision" is the increase in the frequency, magnitude, and duration of droughts in the United States, and in particular, an increase in droughts in the agricultural heartland. Like the other apocalyptic predictions, this vision of increased droughtiness is well-founded in the professional literature. . . .

This drought-related prediction is undoubtedly one of the most serious consequences of the greenhouse effect, and the seriousness of the prediction demands careful analysis. It is noteworthy that the predictions of increased droughtiness are far more strongly related to the increasing temperature than to any reduction in rainfall. Projected increases in temperature would raise the rate of evapotranspiration [loss of water from soil both by evaporation and by transpiration from the plants growing on it], particularly during the summer season. This increase in evapotranspiration would overwhelm any small changes in precipitation (and in addition, the precipitation totals may become more variable), and a soil moisture deficit could develop. And if a decrease in summer rainfall would occur as projected by many of the models, a significant increase in drought frequency, magnitude, and duration would certainly be realized.

Table 1. Linear Changes in United States Temperature, Precipitation, and Palmer Drought Severity Index.

Season	Temperature (°C)			Precipitation (mm)	PDSI
	Min	Max	Mean		
Winter	+0.47	+0.54	+0.47	−2.24	+0.46
Spring	+0.28	+0.46	+0.37	+11.14	+0.36
Summer	+0.38	+0.21	+0.31	−8.40	+0.23
Autumn	+0.31	−0.19	+0.17	+29.24	+0.55
Annual	+0.35	+0.26	+0.29	+29.73	+0.40

Note: Precipitation and temperature changes are for the period 1901–1987; PDSI changes are for the period 1895–1989.

Source: Robert C. Balling Jr., *The Heated Debate*, 1992.

Although the models generally predict this increase in drought conditions, there are many signals in the climate record that would cast doubt on the prediction. First, we have seen that the temperatures of the United States are not rising as quickly as they should to be consistent with the more apocalyptic view of the greenhouse effect. Without a large increase in temperature, the needed rise in evapotranspiration does not occur, and the droughts do not increase in magnitude, frequency, or duration. Second, we have seen a tendency for temperatures to increase at night, and not during the day. Increasing temperatures at night would have a much smaller effect on evapotranspiration than would temperature increases during the day. Third, precipitation totals are increasing on an annual basis, with largest increases in spring and autumn and only small decreases in summer rainfall. From these observed patterns in temperature and precipitation over the past century, one does not see much observational evidence to support the prediction of increased drought frequency and intensity for the United States.

An excellent drought record has been maintained for the United States throughout this century. The Palmer Drought Severity Index (PDSI) is available for some 344 climate divisions of the United States on a monthly basis. . . .

The PDSI is based on an estimate of the relative amount of soil moisture resulting from moisture inputs via precipitation and moisture outputs via evapotranspiration. The index is standardized for each division to account for climatic differences across the country. For example, a low soil moisture level for Louisiana may be an extraordinarily high amount of soil moisture in Arizona. So the PDSI is standardized to account for "normal" patterns in some area. Values for the PDSI range from above 4.0 for extreme wetness to near 0 for near normal conditions to below -4 for extreme drought. Many climatologists have used the PDSI in their studies of historical droughts in the United States.

A plot of the annual PDSI for the United States shows a highly variable pattern dominated by droughts in the early 1930s and early 1950s and relatively high moisture levels from 1970 to the mid-1980s. Over the entire 1895 to 1989 period, the trend in PDSI has been upward, but the linear increase is not statistically significant. In fact, the PDSI values have trended upward in all seasons, but the rates of increase cannot be judged significant. Nonetheless, there is no evidence of any trend toward increasing drought as suggested by the models. . . .

One may fairly argue that the models are suggesting increased drought over the central United States, and not over the United States as a whole. In a 1991 study of drought patterns on a state-by-state basis, Idso and I showed that the entire United States had seen a decline in PDSI values (a trend toward drought) from 1895 to the early 1950s. However, since that time, the country had seen a reversal with a trend away from drought and toward increasing soil moisture. Of the nine states with the largest change toward increasing soil moisture, six—Colorado, Iowa, Kansas, Missouri, Nebraska, and Oklahoma—are located in this agricultural heartland. Of all 48 states investigated, Nebraska showed the largest shift toward greater soil moisture availability! Once again, the predictions of the greenhouse modeling experiments are not consistent with the observations of the past century. . . .

Greenhouse Hurricanes in the United States

The appearance of Hurricane Gilbert in the summer of 1988 fueled the notion that greenhouse warming would be associated with an increase in the frequency and intensity of hurricanes striking the United States. If Gilbert was not sufficiently convincing, Hurricane Hugo's devastation in 1989 seemed to be further proof of a connection between the greenhouse effect and hurricane activity. As with many other components of the "popular vision," the greenhouse-hurricane connection is not without solid scientific basis. . . .

However, not all scientists agree with the prediction of increasing hurricane activity in a greenhouse world. Sherwood Idso and his colleagues suggested that greenhouse warming may actually decrease the frequency and intensity of hurricanes. Their argument is based on two fundamental predictions from the greenhouse models. First, the models tend to predict only a small change in the temperature of the oceans in the tropical area, but the upper portion of the tropical troposphere [the lowest part of the earth's atmosphere] is expected to warm much more than the underlying ocean surface. The result is less instability in the tropical atmosphere, and the greater stability would tend to retard convection and reduce the intensity of tropical cyclones. Also, the models predict greatest warming in the high latitudes and least warming in the tropics. The reduced equator-to-pole gradient in temperature would also tend to reduce the intensity and frequencies of the hurricane systems. . . .

The True Greenhouse Effect

The conterminous United States covers only 1.5 percent of the earth's surface, and therefore, what happens to the climate of the United States may seem unimportant to the debate about global climate change. And yet, the United States is a relatively large continental land mass, models make predictions for the grid points falling across the United States, an excellent set of climate records is available for the area, and some lessons can be learned when model predictions are compared to the climate patterns of the past century. Three rather important summary points stem from the analyses of the United States climate patterns:

1. Temperatures in the United States have increased over the past century, but the increase is not statistically significant from zero. We cannot say with any statistical confidence that there has been warming in the United States in the twentieth century. Most of the warming occurred prior to 1920, and in fact, from 1920 to 1987, the linear trend depicts cooling. Greatest warming has occurred in winter, and in general, more warming has occurred in the minimum temperature than the maximum temperature. The diurnal

temperature range is decreasing, and there is little evidence to support any claims of increasing frequencies in extreme maximum temperatures. The seasonal and diurnal temperature patterns are broadly consistent with the model predictions given the observed increase in equivalent CO_2, but the magnitude of the warming is far below what the models suggest should have been observed.

2. The trends in precipitation for the United States are marginally consistent with the model predictions. Much like the globe as a whole, the precipitation totals have increased over the twentieth century by about 4 percent. All of the increase occurred in spring and autumn while summer and winter have shown a linear decrease in precipitation totals. The models predict an increase in the winter-to-summer precipitation ratio, but no trend in the ratio could be found in this century.

3. Virtually all of the models are predicting an increase in drought intensity, duration, and frequency in the central United States as a consequence of the buildup in the greenhouse gases. Yet, in all seasons, the trend is away from aridity and toward increasing soil moisture; the trend away from aridity is most pronounced in the central United States. Along with the observed increases in precipitation and soil moisture, cloudiness in the United States is increasing through this century.

Over the past century, and during a time when equivalent CO_2 levels rose by almost 40 percent, several signals appear which seem to be related to the exponential increase in the greenhouse gases. The conterminous United States is receiving more precipitation, cloud cover is increasing, soil moisture levels are rising, and the diurnal temperature range is decreasing. These changes have been observed throughout much of the hemisphere and globe, and these changes are largely consistent with the predictions of the models. These climate signals are not apocalyptic, but they represent what is more likely to become recognized as the true greenhouse effect.

Periodical Bibliography

The following articles have been selected to supplement the diverse views presented in this chapter.

Virginia Abernathy   "Changing the USA's Population Signals for a Sustainable Future," *Futures*, March 1994.

Bruce Bartlett   "The High Cost of Turning Green," *The Wall Street Journal*, September 14, 1994.

Wallace S. Broecker   "Global Warming on Trial," *Natural History*, April 1992.

Kenneth A. Dahlberg   "A Transition from Agriculture to Regenerative Food Systems," *Futures*, March 1994.

Herman E. Daly and Jagdish Bhagwati   "Debate: Does Free Trade Harm the Environment?" *Scientific American*, November 1993.

The Economist   "Biology Meets the Dismal Science," December 25, 1993–January 7, 1994.

Walter Goldstein and Volker A. Mohnen   "Global Warming Debate in the USA," *Futures*, January/February 1992.

Robert Goodland, Herman E. Daly, and John Kellenberg   "Burden Sharing in the Transition to Environmental Sustainability," *Futures*, March 1994.

Paul Hawken   "A Declaration of Sustainability," *Utne Reader*, September/October 1993.

Robert William Kates   "Sustaining Life on the Earth," *Scientific American*, October 1994.

Richard D. Lamm   "The Future of the Environment," *The Annals of the American Academy of Political and Social Science*, July 1992.

Joseph L. Ling   "Design for the Environment," *Vital Speeches of the Day*, August 1, 1993.

Dan McCosh and Stuart F. Brown   "The Alternative Fuel Follies," *Popular Science*, July 1992.

Linda Stuntz   "The Environmentally Ugly American," *Vital Speeches of the Day*, June 15, 1992.

Malcolm Wells   "Pollution . . . or Property?" *The Futurist*, September/October 1992.

America's Political Status: What Does the Future Hold?

**AMERICA
BEYOND
2001**

Chapter Preface

Many Americans are skeptical that politicians and the federal government are willing or able to function in their best interest. According to pollster Louis Harris, many people believe there exist "two tiers of justice and opportunities, one for those with access to power . . . and another for the rank and file of people." It is clear to many politicians that Americans are growing intolerant of what they view as the "politics-as-usual" status quo. Explaining one possible cause of this public mood, U.S. vice president Al Gore writes, "Cynicism can arise when political leaders cavalierly promise to do things and then fail to deliver."

What America needs to remedy this cynicism, argue economist Richard Carlson and journalist Bruce Goldman, authors of *Fast Forward: Where Technology, Demographics, and History Will Take America and the World in the Next Thirty Years*, is politicians who will accomplish "the swift formulation of non-ideological policies that work" without "promising the impossible." Among those confident that this reform can be achieved are Gore and U.S. president Bill Clinton, elected in 1992 with what they recognized as a public mandate to reinvent government.

But others, including Malcolm Wallop, a retired senator from Wyoming, argue that government should be limited, not reinvented, in order to strengthen citizens' voices regarding their own affairs. Wallop wrote in 1994, "The people who elected a new [Republican] Congress firmly believe in the observation of Thomas Jefferson that, 'Here, sir, the people govern.'"

The effect on America of such fundamental reform is one aspect of political change debated in the following chapter.

"All the relevant numbers . . . suggest a chilling forecast: the descent of the United States into the Third World."

America Is Becoming a Third World Country

Edward N. Luttwak

America could be a Third World country by the year 2020, Edward N. Luttwak predicts in the following viewpoint, adapted from his book *The Endangered American Dream*. Luttwak maintains that a linear forecast of gross national product per person by that year shows German and Japanese productivity surpassing that of America by a wide margin. The author presents statistics and analysis of what he calls the "Third-Worldization" of America—the gap between rich and poor that is characteristic of Third World nations. Luttwak, the author of numerous works on America and international politics, is director of Geo-Economics at the Center for Strategic and International Studies, a foreign policy think tank in Washington, D.C.

As you read, consider the following questions:

1. How seriously impoverished could America become, in Luttwak's opinion?
2. What indicators of decline does the author present?
3. According to Luttwak, why is the upper class of the Third World opposed to taxes?

Abridged from Edward N. Luttwak, "2010," *Across the Board*, January 1994. Reprinted by permission of the author.

When Buenos Aires was still a leading world metropolis, when the people of Argentina still enjoyed their famous steak-for-every-meal abundance that lasted into the 1950s, they would never have believed that the immediate future of their country would be a 40-year slide into poverty. Similarly, the people of the United States, still today by far the richest country in the world, have been slow to recognize the economic decline that has been happening over the past 20 or more years, and what future is in store for them if present trends simply continue. Yet all the relevant numbers confirm the slide and suggest a chilling forecast: the descent of the United States into the Third World.

That economic statistics can easily mislead is not in doubt ("There are lies, damned lies, and statistics," goes the jibe), especially when it comes to international comparisons. But everyday life provides telling evidences of Third-Worldization, even if no statistics can measure them. Americans living in solidly middle-class city districts, in pleasant suburbs, and in untroubled small towns still have to confront a pervasive and increasingly *accepted* lack of skill in shops, banks, garages, and their own workplaces—for there, too, the more recent products of American high schools daily demonstrate that it is possible to graduate with little reading, scarcely any writing, and no mathematics at all. . . .

Yearning Helplessly

So when will the United States become a Third World country? It depends on how we define that unhappy condition. But going by some estimates, the date might be as close as the year 2020. That is hardly much time when it comes to the agonizingly slow timetable of reforms powerful enough to change the country's future. More optimistic projections might add another 10 or 15 years. Either way, if present trends simply continue, all but a small minority of Americans will be impoverished soon enough, left to yearn hopelessly for the lost golden age of American prosperity. . . .

A "Straight-Line" Projection

In 1970, the United States was still by far the most productive of countries in the world, with a gross national product (GNP) of $1,014,750,000,000, which worked out to $4,950 per man, woman, and child in the total population of some 205 million at that time. In the same year, the equivalent figure for Japan was only $1,950 per person, while for the European Community (EC) as a whole it was $2,360 per person. By that *very* rough measure of total output, Americans were therefore still more than twice as productive on average as the EC countries in 1970, and their edge over the Japanese was greater still. But within 10 years the pattern of decline had already set in. With a GNP per person of $12,000, the United States in 1980 was still well ahead of the European Community average of $9,760 and Japan's of $9,870, but its margin of superiority had been cut in half.

At that point, the simplest "straight-line" projection—it requires only a pencil, a ruler, and a bit of graph paper—would have shown that given another 10 years, the United States would be overtaken by both Japan and the richer European countries. Professional economists make fun of such crude oversimplifications (they are fond of recalling the pre-motorcar predictions that the manure of horse-cabs and wagons would submerge cities), but that is exactly what happened: The 1989 figure for the United States was $21,000, while Japan's GNP per person had soared to $23,810. Distorted by the entry of three poor countries—Greece, Portugal, and Spain—the EC average was only $15,980, or 76 percent of the American level, but Germany at $20,750 was practically even, and Switzerland, a non-EC country, well outpaced the United States at $30,270.

Because those numbers clearly show a 20-year trend of relative decline and not just some brief downturn, it is not utterly foolish to calculate what the future numbers will be if the United States remains on its present path. Already in the year 2000, now just around the corner in the time-scale of significant action to overcome serious national problems, Japan's GNP per person would be almost twice as large, while the richest European countries would have a 50 percent edge. In 10 more years after that, Japan would be more than three times as productive as the United States, while the northern European countries would be almost twice as productive. They are certainly investing enough to achieve that result.

Finally, in 2020, when the children of today's middle-aged Americans will themselves be middle-aged, the leading European countries would be more than twice as productive on a per-person basis, while the gap between Japanese and Americans—at almost 5-to-1—would be just about the same as the 1980 gap between Americans and Brazilians. At that point, the United States would definitely become a Third World country—at least by Japanese standards. Certainly, nonelite Americans would no longer be in the same class as *average* Western Europeans. . . .

Heading "South"

Of course, to show by whatever numbers that other advanced countries are catching up is not the end of the world, and certainly does not begin to prove that the United States is becoming a Third World country. On the contrary, even a pathetically slow growth rate is still growth, all set to make the United States—by far the richest country in the world—even richer a country. In what follows, therefore, nothing more will be said of GNP and gross domestic product (GDP) figures, except to poke fun at attempts to compare them as if they were exact measures.

Unfortunately, the slow-growing American economy also happens to be an increasingly fractured economy, in which the top 1 percent have been becoming rapidly much richer, the top 20 percent as a whole are also increasing their share of all income, and the remaining 80 percent of all Americans have absorbed *all* the slow growth, and more than that—with a large fraction actually impoverished.

A National Debate Is Overdue

The obvious hazards of straight-line projections aside, Edward Luttwak's observations about the direction of our present course are on target. For 20 years, conventional wisdom has denied and then rationalized the steady erosion in the level and quality of life in America. For a long time we were assured that the initial fall of real wages wasn't happening. Then we were told that it was a function of the baby-boomer blip on the demographic screen. Then that it was happening only to high school dropouts. Then only to high school graduates who didn't go on to college (one-half of the labor force). Then to college dropouts. Data show that real wages of college graduates have been falling since 1987.

Not only do we lack a national strategy to address this decline, we don't even have a national debate. Politicians wring their hands and complain that the people are not patient. Tenured professors lecture their fellow citizens on the virtues of austerity. And the nation's editorial pages chide us for our short-term horizons, while the business news is obsessed with the hour-by-hour replay of today's Dow Jones average. . . .

Isn't it time we started talking about this?

Jeff Faux, *Across the Board,* January 1994.

The United States therefore remains a First World country and the richest, too, but a distinct majority of all Americans have long been headed "south" in stock-market parlance. For them, Third-Worldization is an ongoing reality manifest in that novel American phenomenon: the son who cannot afford a house like his father's when he matures into employment, nor his vacations and leisure, as more hours are worked in the attempt to offset the lower wages. As of now, the average of 1,847 hours per year of American industrial workers greatly exceeds the German, Swedish, French, Italian, and British averages, being exceeded in turn only by the Japanese—who work more hours even though

243

their wages keep increasing. The month-long summer vacations of their European counterparts are out of the question for American workers. Many can no longer find industrial employment at all and must instead poach traditional underclass jobs as janitors, warehouse loaders, cleaners, groundsmen, and security guards—the jobs that used to provide a first toehold on the lowest rung of the economic ladder for the black underclass especially. It is hard to rise when pressed down from above.

Third-Worldization

The underclass, urban or rural, perhaps 6 percent of the population at most, already lives in full Third World conditions, but without the solace of tropical sunsets or the heartening family stability that can be retained even in extreme poverty within well-rooted traditional cultures. Instead, their often-disordered lives are bereft of hope, as many of their children start out on careers of atrocious schooling, unemployment, crime, addiction, imprisonment, and violence. That accounts for some 15 million Americans who would have been better off morally, if not materially, if they had been born in Nepal or Thailand. Another 28 million Americans are already listed as poor or near-poor by official reckoning. By world standards, they are not poor at all, but they *are* becoming poorer rapidly enough to be undergoing Third-Worldization toward Brazilian, if not Indian, levels. And that fate will be shared in turn, if more slowly, by many more Americans if present trends continue. How could it be otherwise when the real hourly pay of 8 out of 10 Americans in all forms of nongovernment employment is now smaller than it was 20 years ago?

That poverty should mark Third-Worldization is obvious enough. But as any visitors to those countries can readily see, a special kind of wealth is also one of the traits of Third-Worldization. At the end of a dirt road lined with shacks along which barefoot children play, there is a fenced mansion with manicured gardens, illegally dug antiques, private zoos (a Latin American fad), modern art, satellite dish, and all the latest Japanese entertainment machines—although garden, house, and kitchen need no labor-saving appliances given the abundance of gardeners, servants, cooks, and maids.

The charming host and hostess, recently back from their latest shopping trip to Paris or Miami, well-educated or at least magazine-sophisticated, are happy to entertain at length, often offering to escort the visitor to local attractions in gratitude for the diversion that can occupy their ample time. Naturally they are nationalistic, if only politely, readily protesting their intense love of their country.

But do not ask them why the children along the way are not

in school, or why the road is unpaved, as most of the country's roads still are. Usually that special kind of wealth is disconnected from any real work, and your hosts are thus profoundly uninterested in improving public education, for that would require "new" taxes, while they employ only gardeners, servants, cooks, and maids, the less educated and more pliant the better. Paved roads would be convenient, sparing the Mercedes or Range Rover, but are not worth "new" taxes either, because there is no daily commute to the office, and no factory or depot with trucks to send off and receive.

Actually there is almost no public investment at all that your hosts are willing to pay for with their taxes. For they actually live on their land on urban rents, stocks and bonds, trusts, and bank deposits safely overseas. Such "rentiers" are very different creatures from the *working* rich, whether professionals or businesspeople, who do need well-educated people and good roads, among other public services.

At the last count, and by the best estimate, the richest 1 percent of all families in the United States owned $1.25 trillion of rental real estate, $1.12 trillion of stocks and bonds, $221.9 billion in trusts, and $524.6 billion in bank and other accounts, for a total of some $3.1 trillion, as compared to only $2.5 trillion invested in their own business enterprises. As a group, these Americans' "rentier" income was roughly half their total income of $503 billion, and even though they must make do with few servants, to that extent they resemble the rich of the Third World. Of such wealth, poverty is made.

Undignified Pleadings

The United States' economic decline, even if it is only relative, cannot remain only economic. The arts, scientific research, and all culture cannot flower and grow in poverty. Only an increasing prosperity can maintain the world lead of American universities, research centers, libraries, museums, theaters, orchestras, ballet companies, and artists of all sorts. It was the ample earnings of Italian traders and bankers that fed the scholars, painters, sculptors, architects, and poets who gave us the Renaissance. When Italy was bypassed by the new flows of ocean trade, its impoverished merchants and bankrupt financiers could no longer commission artists nor keep scholars at work. Many emigrated to embellish Paris, St. Petersburg, and half the towns in Europe, and to adorn the courts of foreign princes. Thus, commercial decline was soon followed by the bleak downfall of Italian art and scholarship.

As it is, many American academic and cultural institutions are shrinking rather than growing as their funding diminishes, while some of the most celebrated eagerly solicit foreign donations in pathetic competition with Third World hunger campaigns. In September 1991, Arima Tatsuo, the chief cabinet councilor for external affairs in Japan's prime minister's office, complained of the dozens of begging letters from American universities and research centers that were stacked on his desk. He had been a student in the rich and confident United States of the 1950s, and was now plainly embarrassed by the undignified pleadings of once-eminent institutions.

Democracy, too, must become fragile when better hopes are worn away by bitter disappointment, opening the way for the strong, false remedies of demagogues. Once the politics of affluence for all—the politics of the American dream—become too blatantly unrealistic for most Americans, the politics of racist, xenophobic, or class resentment can more honestly gain votes; all they promise to people are emotional satisfactions that even an impoverished government can provide readily.

To hope is human, but to expect a fair share in an ever-increasing prosperity is distinctly American. If that ambition is relentlessly denied, the political consequences can hardly fail to be catastrophic. After all, Americans have no shared national culture to unite them as the French or Italians have—there are many different cultures in our pluralist society. Nor can citizens of the United States rely on ethnic solidarity alone, as the Japanese say they can—we have many different ethnic origins.

What Americans have in common are their shared beliefs, above all in equality of opportunity in the pursuit of affluence. It would be too much to expect that democratic governance would long survive the impoverishment of all Americans except for a minority of fortunate inheritors, talented professionals, brilliant or merely lucky businesspeople, 700,000 often-rapacious lawyers, and a few cunning financial manipulators.

"Far from sinking into decline, America is now at the center of one of the great, exciting moments in mankind's economic history."

America Is Not Becoming a Third World Country

Robert L. Bartley

America has emerged victorious from the Cold War and is increasing its influence worldwide, Robert L. Bartley argues in the following viewpoint. Bartley maintains that American ideals of democratic pluralism and market economics will continue to spread to other nations. He asserts that those who believe America is in decline are wrong. Rather than decline, according to the author, the nation is experiencing a second Industrial Revolution—the shift from an industrial to an information economy. He foresees a future of "rich opportunity" for America. Bartley, editor of the *Wall Street Journal*, is the author of *The Seven Fat Years: And How to Do It Again*, on which this viewpoint is based.

As you read, consider the following questions:

1. According to Bartley, what fears did foreign investment in America in the 1980s stir?
2. What previous eras of economic progress were regarded pessimistically, according to Bartley?
3. Whom does the second Industrial Revolution empower, in the author's opinion?

From Robert L. Bartley, "Is America on the Way Down? No." Reprinted from *Commentary* (March 1992), by permission; all rights reserved.

To the ordinary, everyday senses of mankind, America has not declined, it has prevailed. Its foe of two generations has collapsed and now even seeks to adopt American institutions of democracy and market economics.

Though to people who use their eyes and ears it is obvious that American influence in the world is on the rise, we have not been able to put the notion of decline behind us. For a segment of American opinion refuses to use its eyes and ears. Instead, proponents of decline confuse themselves with statistics they do not understand, or in some cases willingly distort. They invoke jingoism by turning international trade into some kind of combat, instead of a series of mutually beneficial arrangements among consenting adults.

The Theme of Decline

The notion of decline has recently been a fad of the Left, in alliance with a coterie of nonideological special interests. It is instructive to remember, though, that as the 1980's opened decline was a theme of the Right. Conservatives, notably but far from solely Jean-François Revel, warned that the West was falling behind in the military competition with the Soviet Sparta. It found itself manipulated by Soviet campaigns like the one that stopped the neutron bomb. The United States, the natural leader of the alliance, was wracked by inflation and stagnant productivity at home, preoccupied with hostages held by a primitive cleric, and unable even to fly six helicopters across the desert [Iran hostage crisis and rescue attempt, 1980].

In those days, conservatives worried that the West lacked the will to use its superior economic resources even to defend itself. They can take heart that their warnings were heeded, that free peoples found the will to resist, that fear of Communist arms did not stunt them into self-doubt and inaction. But American will is now being tested in a more subtle way by the theme of decline, another recipe for confusion and self-destruction. If America generally falls prey to this delusion, it may throw away its birthright as the hub of a new and progressive world civilization. . . .

The containment policy the West had patiently pursued for two generations predicted that under steady pressure the Soviet empire would mellow or crack. Then it happened at a stroke. In 1989 the Berlin Wall was breached, and by 1991 the Communist remnants proved themselves inept even at coup-making. Meanwhile, an American-led attack [against Iraq] decimated the world's fourth-largest army in six weeks of combat and at the cost of 148 Americans lost in action. . . .

Nor is American predominance merely or even primarily a matter of military power. American ideals of democratic pluralism and market economics were spreading not only in the former

Soviet Union but throughout South America, Eastern Europe, and even Africa. America remains the favored destination of the world's refugees and immigrants. Its university system (despite the political-correctness plague) is unparalleled: it graduates many foreign nationals in science and engineering, of course, but many of them choose to stay in the United States. For all the accomplishments of the industrious Japanese, America still dominates scientific innovation. Many transnational corporations, even if based in Germany or Switzerland, locate their research divisions in New Jersey or North Carolina. Japanese auto companies open design labs in Los Angeles. Above all, the United States utterly dominates the single capstone technology of our era, which in every language is called "software."

Wealthiest Society in History

Whatever the momentary economic ups and downs, too, the plain fact is that the United States is the wealthiest society in the history of mankind. Or at least this is plain to the economically literate, who understand that no meaningful comparison can be based on momentary exchange rates among different national currencies. In translating among currencies to make international comparisons, the only meaningful basis is purchasing-power parity (PPP), the exchange rate at which two currencies would each buy the same basket of goods. . . .

Current comparisons built on current exchange rates show America falling behind, but properly adjusting the comparisons to PPP makes the picture entirely different. *The Economist Book of Vital World Statistics*, for example, found that at 1988 figures and exchange rates, the United States ranked only ninth in the world in gross domestic product per capita—behind Switzerland, Japan, and the Scandinavian countries. But it also reported that at PPP exchange rates, the American standard of living was far above other advanced nations. . . .

In short, the American standard of living is substantially above that of Japan and most of Europe. . . .

Trade and Foreign Investment in America

The most remarkable feature of the 1980's was economic globalization. The 24-hour trading markets were stitched together; dollars circled the world at electronic speed. . . .

A great source of the confusion about the American economy, and a great source of the current poor-mouthing, is that the United States has still not come to terms with its integration into the world economy. Thus America's sages gazed on [soaring foreign investment in the United States in the 1980's] and decided the sky was falling. In sending their money here, those perfidious foreigners expected to get paid back. Indeed, the whole reason they were sending their money here was that they anticipated a higher return here than they could get at home. Their eagerness to invest in America instead of at home was turning us into—shame!—a debtor nation. And, of course, the American purchases that stimulated the European revival were reflected in—horrors!—a trade deficit. . . .

Grotesque Distortion, Alarmist Fulminations

Not to worry! At least not to the point of despair. The two catastrophes Edward Luttwak sees befalling the United States [see viewpoint 1] are only fraudulent inventions of a charlatan and muckraker. Well, to be fair, Luttwak isn't *completely* wrong. Only one of his two catastrophes is entirely phony. The second is merely a grotesque distortion of reality.

The phony disaster is the idea put forth by Luttwak that class warfare is imminent. It's true that income inequality has risen over the past couple of decades. But the change has been limited, and Luttwak is dead wrong to imply that four-fifths of American families are worse off and that the typical factory worker has entered the underclass. . . .

Luttwak's grotesque distortion is the idea that the United States is moving quickly to Third World status. In fact, after . . . feeding us statistical drivel such as "all but a small minority of Americans will be impoverished soon enough," and that by 2020 Japan's per-capita income will be five times as large as America's, Luttwak finally gets around to pointing out that U.S. living conditions still are advancing, and to identifying the problem correctly: The United States, although still at the top economically, is gradually losing ground *relative* to other major nations. That's a serious matter, but much different than "the descent of the United States into the Third World."

Edgar Fiedler, *Across the Board*, January 1994.

In the normal investment-trade seesaw, though, a zero trade balance is not normal or even desirable. The United States ran a trade deficit for nearly all of its first 100 years, and generated trade surpluses under the Smoot-Hawley Tariff in the midst of the Great Depression. Normally, a rapidly growing economy will demand more of the world's supply of real resources and run a trade deficit. It will also provide attractive investment opportunities and attract capital inflows. In a healthy world, the two will offset each other, for periods of perhaps a century.

Yet somehow we have come to measure our nationhood by the one statistic of the trade balance. The real mystery is why we even collect it; if we kept similar statistics for Manhattan island, Park Avenue would lie awake at night worrying about its trade deficit. We have even come to view trade as some kind of nationalistic competition. Winning, apparently, is selling more to the rest of the world than we buy from it. Leaving aside the fact that this is ultimately impossible, why? If we could do it, what would we do with the proceeds, bury them in Fort Knox?

The Rhetoric of Decline

In the midst of this burgeoning prosperity and creativity, the Left decided that America was declining, and undertook to prove it by peering into the international statistics. While there were earlier precursors, the theme came to its fruition with Paul Kennedy's *The Rise and Fall of the Great Powers*. In 1988, as voters were rewarding a platform of "read my lips" and Willie Horton, book-buyers were handsomely rewarding Professor Kennedy's thesis of "imperial overstretch." In this view, the filling of the spare-parts bins and the reassertion of American military power abroad was not the cure for decline, it was the cause of decline. Indeed, it was decline itself.

Though it topped the lists for 24 weeks, *The Rise and Fall of the Great Powers* was no doubt an example of the contemporary phenomenon of the unread best-seller. Few could have been interested in Kennedy's account of the Hapsburgs or Ming China, and he did not get to the predicament of the United States until pages 514–35. But on op-ed pages and in seminar rooms these pages triggered a national debate. It very much centered on the economy. Excessive military spending undermined the economy, the critique went, and the slackening economy could not support the military commitments. To be sure, the United States was still only in "relative decline," still first in importance, but its lead was shrinking. For

> the only way the United States can pay its way in the world is by importing ever-larger sums of capital, which has transformed it from being the world's largest creditor to the world's largest debtor nation *in the space of a few years*.

The Left naturally found great appeal in this double-barreled critique of the Reagan administration: the evident economic prosperity was marred by hidden flaws, and the root of the flaws lay in the military build-up. . . .

The liberal declinists did find some allies on the presumed Right. . . . There was a species of financial conservative who found debt worse than taxes. Bond traders and central bankers have a natural tendency to focus on the supply of and demand for credit (to whatever extent they can be measured). And though growing corporations add debt every year as a matter of course, the executives running them were taught in their childhood to judge government finance solely by whether current income matches current outgo. And finally, there is a jingoistic conservatism casting about for a new foe to fight after the decline of Communism; it has settled on the Japanese trading companies.

Given these various roots of support, it is perhaps not surprising that the notion of decline proved so resilient in the face of both self-evident prosperity and intellectual refutation. I thought the matter had been laid to rest in the *Wall Street Journal* by May 1988, when Charles Wolf of the RAND Corporation took his usual beady aim. Yes, said Wolf, the U.S. share of world product had declined from 45 percent in 1950, "a manifestly atypical year." But against the mid-1960's or 1938, the U.S. share remained at 22 percent to 24 percent. "Japan's central-government debt is a larger fraction of its GNP [gross national product] than is that of the U.S., while the foreign indebtedness of the U.S. has been grossly overestimated in the official statistics." Somehow statist politics and economics had spread internationally in the 1960's and 1970's, while market economics and democracy had advanced in the 1980's. "The rhetoric of decline is wrong because it portrays a past that wasn't, a present that isn't, and a future that probably won't be.". . .

The Information Age

Far from sinking into decline, America is now at the center of one of the great, exciting moments in mankind's economic history. A second industrial revolution is remaking world society. Not since the industrial revolution itself has technological advance been so breathtaking, or more pregnant with changes in the way mankind lives and thinks of itself.

More breathtaking now, probably, than even then. James Watt's steam engine pales beside what our generation has already seen: the splitting of the atom, the decoding of the gene, and the invention of the transistor and the computers it spawned. These are not only magnificent leaps of the technological imagination, they are potential precursors of currently unimaginable economic advance. Atomic power, unless cold fusion turns out to be real after all, has perhaps not realized what we once thought of as its potential. The first fruits of biotechnology are just now entering the markets. But already the transistor and the rest are changing the world.

Indeed, we live every day with the electronic revolution. As the first industrial revolution changed an agricultural economy into an industrial economy, a second industrial revolution is changing an industrial economy into a service economy. More specifically, into an information economy, in which the predominant activity is collecting, processing, and communicating information. We are headed toward a world in which everyone on the globe is in instant communication with everyone else.

It is this web of instant communication that has stitched the world into increasing interdependence. In fact, throughout this century the world economy has been more interdependent than anyone realized: the Great Depression, for example, was preeminently a world event, and its origins lay in disturbances in the international economy. But with today's 24-hour financial markets and transnational corporations, economic interdependence is hard to miss. . . .

Naturally our time and our nation have their problems. Americans should take education more seriously, instead of subordinating it to goals like racial balance and asbestos removal. Our legal system should let police enforce the law against vagrants, and should stop inflicting a parasitic tort-bar industry upon us. Our political system is so frozen it seems unable to address these everyday problems.

More broadly, there is such a thing as being too liberated, having too many options. We are still learning to live with our new freedoms. The onslaught of modernity has not been good for institutions such as the family. We are overly susceptible to fads—health scares, for example—and for that matter the fad of declinism.

Change Is Unsettling

For all these problems, what mostly needs to be explained is not what is wrong with America, but how so much of our articulate elite can so completely mistake reality. A great part of the answer is that progress is unsettling, as rapid change always is. Looking back over history, indeed, we see that ages of economic advance have often been ages of pessimism.

In particular, history's all-time champion economic pessimist, Thomas Malthus, published his first essay on population in 1798; this was 29 years after James Watt's first patent in connection with the steam engine. The first industrial revolution, in other words, was the venue for Malthus's gloomy theorizing. He was explaining why economic progress was impossible just as mankind was taking the greatest economic leap in history. . . .

If, then, we are currently experiencing a second industrial revolution, it is not surprising to hear such Malthusian themes as overpopulation and the exhaustion of resources echoing through our public discourse. From the primitive technology of a wooden sailing ship, the earth's forces look overwhelming. Now that we have the technological prowess to put men on the moon, the earth looks like a fragile flower, puny beside our own powers.

The rapid change of the second industrial revolution, moreover, upsets established institutions and established elites. As instant information and instant markets erode the power of governments, so too they erode the power of corporate chieftains and labor bosses. . . .

So too with intellectual elites, who find their skills fading in relevance and their positions endangered. Perhaps political correctness in the academy is best seen as a brand of Luddism. And surely much of our articulate class feels threatened in a deeply personal way by the notion that a historic corner was turned under a simpleminded movie actor.

This mixture of neurosis, special pleading, ideological hostility, ignorance, and confusion is obviously a phenomenon to be reckoned with. Indeed, even an unbridled optimist has to admit that there is after all one way America actually could decline. To wit, if this neurotic pessimism becomes a self-realizing prophecy.

This would be a historic tragedy, for the confluence of the second industrial revolution and the collapse of totalitarianism presents the human race with an unparalleled opportunity. The decade of the 1990's is not a time for pessimism, but a time for large thoughts and large ambitions. The tide in the affairs of men is running, and we must take the current when it serves. The brightest hope for mankind today is that the breaching of the Berlin Wall on November 9, 1989 marked the end of a beastly era that started with the assassination of Archduke Francis Ferdinand in Sarajevo on June 28, 1914 [which sparked World War I].

The consciousness of everyone alive today was forged in an abnormal era, a century of world war, revolution, and totalitarianism. While mankind has always suffered wars and other miseries, our century ranks with the most wretched in history. Technology turned battle from a contest of knights into an assault on whole civilian populations. A Great Depression sank the world economy. With the rise of Adolf Hitler and Joseph Stalin, the human soul was under siege. World War II dissolved into a worldwide confrontation between the West and Communism.

At issue was the nature of man—a cog in the great dialectical machine of history, or an autonomous individual capable of free will and self-government? If reform succeeds in Russia, or even survives, all this will be history. We will have a new era to define. . . .

The Challenge of Decline

Today we are in a position to build a new version of the institutions of the Belle Epoque [the period of peace and cultural productivity in western Europe before the outbreak of World War I] and rekindle its spirit. We can hope, too, to avoid another Sarajevo, for the technology of the second industrial revolution is less threatening than that of the first. The Eiffel Tower [Paris,

France; 1889] was the product of a master engineer, in its way a monument to central planning. The smelting of steel and the building of railroads were enterprises that demanded central planning and the mobilization of massive capital. Napoleon had demonstrated how to conscript whole societies for war, and in the ensuing century the experience of mankind taught it efficient logistics and bureaucratic order. The very advance of science led philosophers like Karl Marx to think of "laws of history." In 1914 this technology, combined of course with the recurrent follies of mankind, marched the world into war.

Ever since, we have been struggling to tame the impact of technology and the mindset it engenders. As the assembly line turned men into interchangeable cogs, the centralized, bureaucratic state became a breeding ground of totalitarianism. But the technology of the second industrial revolution empowers the governed rather than the governors. In its constant churning today's technology has a dark side to be conquered, but its bright side offers the hope of a liberating era.

Certainly technology is not everything. Its opportunities must be exploited by the human spirit. Our dilemma is that all of us living in the 1990's have been taught from the cradle not to believe in dreams. We are cynical about politicians, and they live down to our expectations. Instead of a century of science and democracy [as invoked by 19-century French novelist Emile Zola], we have Andy Warhol proclaiming that everyone will be famous for fifteen minutes. Instead of Toulouse-Lautrec we have Robert Mapplethorpe.

And instead of the promise of world cooperation led by the United States, we have the gloomy apostles of decline, alarmed because goods and capital move across lines someone drew on maps, trying to manufacture conflict out of the peaceful and mutually beneficial intercourse among peoples.

The last time the will of the West was tested, it rose to the challenge. In particular, the American electorate understood that the threat was Soviet Communism, not the military-industrial complex. With the more subtle test of a litany of decline coming out of Cambridge, Detroit, and Washington, there will again be confusion and apparent close calls, but in the end the delusion will not sell. Indeed, given any sort of intellectual and political leadership to frame the challenge, the American nation will rise to the rich opportunity before it.

3 VIEWPOINT

"Our long-range forecast for [America] is good."

From Cold War to American Renaissance

Marvin Cetron

Marvin Cetron is a noted futurist who has been a consultant to several U.S. presidents, including John F. Kennedy and Bill Clinton. He is the founder and president of Forecasting International, a consulting firm in Arlington, Virginia. In the following viewpoint, extracted from a 1994 article, Cetron presents a list of trends he believes are highly probable for America by the year 2000 and beyond. Cetron predicts that by the year 2000, an American renaissance will have begun, setting the stage for an optimistic future after the millennium. Cetron contends that the nation will thrive in the twenty-first century in such areas as the economy, education, technology, and work.

As you read, consider the following questions:

1. What changes will take place among the rich, poor, and middle classes, according to Cetron?
2. How will the educational system change, in the author's opinion?
3. According to Cetron, what will become of the women's movement?

Excerpted from Marvin Cetron, "An American Renaissance in the Year 2000," *The Futurist*, March/April 1994. Reproduced with permission from *The Futurist*, published by the World Future Society, 7910 Woodmont Ave., Suite 450, Bethesda, MD 20814.

1. Economic prosperity—affluence, low interest rates, low inflation rate—will continue through the foreseeable future.

• There may be minor recessions during the 1990s, but they will only be perturbations. Our long-range forecast for the economy is good: Through the year 2000, the U.S. economy should be the best in the world.

• [Federal Reserve Board] monetary policies instituted by chairman Paul Volker and continued by his successor, Alan Greenspan, will keep interest and inflation rates in check. Housing starts will continue to grow, and building construction will increase.

2. The growth of the information industries is creating an extremely knowledge-dependent society.

• The computer industry will continue to offer vast opportunities for creative entrepreneurs. Though hardware remains promising, software developers will reap the greatest rewards.

• Expert systems will issue reports and recommend actions based on data gathered electronically, without human intervention.

3. The very poor and very wealthy will decline in American society.

• The very rich will still own a disproportionately large fraction of the nation's wealth; yet they will make up a smaller percentage of the population.

• Statistics overstate the number of very poor in the United States, because they omit income-equivalents such as food stamps, housing allowances, and free medical care. When these are included, the poverty rate falls sharply. Official figures show that 10.5% have incomes under $10,000 per year, but the effective percentage is closer to 6%–7%.

4. Rural land is being colonized by suburbs and cities.

• Suburbs are developing more rapidly than cities, largely because land there is cheaper and road systems provide easy access. Three-fourths of the U.S. population live in cities and their suburbs, while only one-fourth live in rural areas.

• "Superburbs" will increasingly connect cities, especially in the South and West, where most of the population growth through the 1990s and beyond is expected to occur.

5. The middle-class society will prevail.

• The middle 60% of families have received 52%–54% of income since 1950. This proportion will grow slightly through the 1990s.

6. Growing acceptance of cultural diversity will promote the growth of a truly integrated national society.

• Information technologies are promoting long-distance communication as people hook up with the same commercial databases and computer networks. Two-way cable television will accelerate this process.

257

- Minorities will exert more influence over the national agenda as the population of African Americans, Latinos, and Asian Americans increases from 17% in 1990 to 33% by 2000.

7. The permanent military establishment will continue to shrink.

- By 2000, young men and women will probably spend two years in compulsory national service. They will have three options: military service; VISTA [Volunteers in Service to America]-type work with poor and disabled; or duty with the Peace Corps.

8. Americans will grow increasingly mobile in key areas: personal life, location, occupations.

- Job mobility—changing location or firm, but doing the same work—will increase. People soon will expect to change jobs four to five times during their lifetimes.

- The new information-based model for the organization—a nonhierarchical, organic system able to respond quickly to environmental changes—fosters greater occupational flexibility and autonomy.

9. International affairs and national security are becoming major factors within U.S. society.

- Observation/verification activity [for arms-reduction treaties] between the East and the West has grown since the end of the Cold War.

- East-West television and radio satellite hookups will increase.

Technology Trends

10. Technology will increasingly dominate both the economy and society.

- Personal robots will appear in the home by 2000. Robots will also work at mundane commercial and service jobs, environmentally dangerous jobs, and assembly and repair of space station components in orbit.

- Computers will become part of our environment, rather than just tools we use for specific tasks. Portable computers will give us wireless access to networked data wherever we go.

11. Technological advances in transportation will dispel the specter of national gridlock in the air and on land.

- [Traditional railroad tracks] are on the way out, but trains are not. Late in the 1990s, high-speed trains [using advanced tracks] will begin to replace the spokes of the airline industry's existing hub-and-spoke system for journeys of 100 to 150 miles.

- Advances in automobile technology will give us the smart car, equipped with sensors, antilock brakes, computer-orchestrated fuel-injection systems, continuously variable transmission, active suspension, and many other innovations.

12. The U.S. economy is growing more integrated.

- New industrial standards—for building materials, fasteners, even factory machinery—allow both civilian and government buyers to order from any supplier, rather than only from those with whom they have established relationships. The acceptance of global standards is one of the most important industrial trends now operating.

• To aid "just-in-time" purchasing, many suppliers are giving customers direct, on-line access to their computerized ordering and inventory systems. The order may go directly from the customer to the shop floor, and even into the supplier's automated production equipment. Many manufacturers will no longer deal with suppliers who cannot provide this access.

America in the Early Twenty-First Century

What should America be like ten or twenty years from now? . . . If all goes well, America will be a country where housing, health, jobs, and transportation are a part of every citizen's life; citizens are safe, the aged are respected, and the young are nourished; business flourishes, backed by careful money management and creative scientific developments; the environment is protected, energy is abundant, and agriculture thrives; arts and humanities are in partnership with business, equally supported by education and advances in scientific knowledge; American defense is built on worldwide leadership and contributions to foreign nation development; and opportunity, freedom, and brotherhood prevail among all.

James T. Ziegenfuss Jr., *USA Today*, November 1994.

---

13. The U.S. economy is becoming integrated with the international economy.

• Imports continue to increase, international capital markets are merging, and buying patterns around the world coalesce. All these factors promote the interdependence of business and government decisions worldwide.

• Nationalistic self-interest will continue to yield to international trade cooperation. Both developing and developed countries will focus less on dominating economic competitors and, instead, will put efforts into liberalizing trade cooperation.

14. The international economy will gain importance throughout the 1990s.

• Privatization is a growing trend, with governments around the world selling off public services. In the United States, this could mean an end to the U.S. Postal Service's monopoly on regular mail service. Globally, this means a transition from governmental to private ownership of airlines, railroads, water, and electricity.

15. Research and development (R&D) will play a growing role in the economy.

- R&D outlays as a percentage of GNP [gross national product] rose steadily in the decade after 1978, then stabilized in 1988. The increase in R&D outlays will likely resume as the effects of the recent recession are left behind.

16. Technology is turning over faster every year.

- The design and marketing cycle—idea, invention, innovation, imitation—is shrinking steadily. Successful products must be marketed quickly, before the competition can copy them.
- All the technological knowledge we work with today will represent only 1% of the knowledge that will be available in 2050.

17. Mass telecommunications and printing are continuing to unite the nations of the world.

- Telecommunications removes geographic barriers. In the Caribbean and other low-wage regions, it costs only 50¢ per hour to have two people type data into a computer and reconcile their mistakes. The total cost, including two-way satellite transmission to the United States, is less than $1.50. In the United States, it costs $5 per hour to have one person enter data.
- The "integrated information appliance" will combine a computer, a fax, a picture phone, and a duplicator in one unit for less than $2,500 by the year 2000. The picture will appear on a flat screen of 20 inches by 30 inches.

18. Major medical advances will continue to appear almost daily. [See also Trends 51 and 52.]

- Genetic engineering will do $100 billion worth of business by 2000. Artificial blood will be on the market by 2000; it could eventually replace blood banks. Memory-enhancing drugs should arrive in the 1990s. Newborn babies will be artificially endowed with particular disease immunities.
- The ethical issues raised by technologies such as organ transplants, artificial organs, genetic engineering, and DNA mapping will cause a growing public debate. Among the key problems: surrogate motherhood, when to terminate extraordinary life-support efforts, and whether fetal tissues should be transplanted into adults in order to combat disease.
- Brain cell and tissue transplants will enter clinical trials by 2001 to aid victims of mental retardation and head trauma. Transplanted animal organs will find their way into common use until doctors begin to grow new organs from the patient's own tissue, around 2015. Laboratory-grown bone, muscle, and blood cells also will be used in transplants.

Educational Trends

19. Demand for lifelong education and training services will heat up throughout society.

- Fundamental changes in the economy are destroying the few

remaining well-paying jobs that do not require advanced training.

• Schools will train both children and adults around the clock: The academic day will stretch to 7 hours for children; adults will work a 32-hour week and prepare for their next job in the remaining time.

20. New technologies will greatly improve education and training.

• Job-simulation stations—modules that combine computers, videodiscs, and instrumentation to duplicate work environments—will be used in training.

21. Business is taking on a greater role in training and education.

• More businesses will form partnerships with schools and offer job-training programs.

22. Education costs will continue to rise.

• Communities will put heavy pressure on school systems to control costs.

• Costs may reach the point where they threaten to reduce the pool of college graduates over the next decade.

23. School districts throughout the United States are reinventing the educational system.

• Policy changes designed to improve students' performance in the U.S. school system may include lengthening the school year to 210 seven-hour days and cutting class size from an average of about 18 students to 10.

24. Educational institutions will pay more attention to the outcomes and effectiveness of their programs.

• Faculty will support (reluctantly) efforts to assess their classroom performance and effectiveness.

• Academic departments will also support evaluation of their academic programs' results and effectiveness.

25. Improved pedagogy—the science of learning—will revolutionize education.

• Individuals will learn more on their own, so the "places" of learning will be more dispersed, and the age at which things are learned will depend on individual ability, not tradition.

26. Universities will stress development of the whole student. They will redesign the total university environment to promote that development.

• Individual students will receive more support from faculty and advisers in deciding about academic programs and career paths.

• By 2001, nearly all college textbooks will come with computer disks to aid in learning.

27. Institutions of higher education are shrinking.

• By 2001 there will not be enough adolescents to sustain the current number of colleges and universities. Colleges will close their doors, merge with other schools in a federation, reduce faculty size and class offerings, and seek more adult students.

Trends in Labor Force and Work

28. Specialization is spreading throughout industry and the professions.

• Globalization of the economy calls for more independent specialists. For hundreds of tasks, corporations will turn to teams of consultants and independent contractors who specialize more and more narrowly as markets globalize and technologies differentiate. (See Trends 44 and 45.)

29. Services are the fastest-growing sector of the American economy.

• Half of service workers in information industries will opt for flextime, flexplace, or work-at-home arrangements, communicating with the office via computer terminals.

30. The agricultural and manufacturing sectors will continue to shrink.

• By 2001, manufacturing will employ less than 10% of the labor force, down from 18% in 1987. However, productivity will rise 500% in industries that become more automated, add robots, and remain flexible in their production.

• With the evolution of new materials and production technology—CAD [and] CAM [computer-aided design and manufacturing], robotics, and semiconductors—the few remaining unskilled and semiskilled jobs in manufacturing will disappear.

31. The information industries are growing rapidly, creating an information society in the process. (This is an outgrowth of Trend 2.)

• Information is the primary commodity in more and more industries today.

• Seventy percent of U.S. homes will have computers in 2001, compared with 30% now. More than three-fourths will be equipped to permit communication with computers elsewhere.

• People will use their personal computers to vote, file income tax returns, apply for auto license plates, and take college entrance exams and professional accreditation tests.

32. More women will continue to enter the labor force.

• Businesses will seek to fill labor shortages with stay-at-home mothers by offering childcare programs and job sharing.

33. Women's salaries will slowly approach men's.

• Women's salaries have grown from 61% of men's in 1960 to 74% in 1991. The figure will be 83% or more by the year 2000.

34. More African Americans and other minority groups are entering the labor force.

• One out of six workers belonged to an ethnic minority in 1990. By 2000, they will be one out of three.

35. Workers are retiring later.

• As life expectancy increases, the standard retirement age will climb to 70 by the year 2000. Social Security may even delay eligibility for benefits. Workers can now retire as young as 62.

36. Unions will continue to lose power.

• Unions enrolled 29% of employed wage and salary workers in 1975, but only 23% in 1980. By 1985, union membership had declined to only 18%. Union members are expected to drop to 11% by 1995 and to less than 10% by 2000, according to the United Auto Workers.

37. Pensions and pension funds continue to grow.
• Private pension and government retirement funds held only 4% of total institutional assets in 1970. By 1991, they held 6.5% of institutional funds.
• There will be more people in the labor force for longer periods, adding to pension-fund holdings.

38. Second and third careers are becoming common, as more people make mid-life changes in occupation.
• People change careers every 10 years, on average.

39. The work ethic is vanishing from American society.
• Tardiness is increasing. Sick-leave abuse is common.
• In a 1992 poll of the under-30 population, 38% said that being corrupt was "essential" in getting ahead.

40. Two-income couples are becoming the norm.
• They made up 38% of all married couples in 1980 and 47% in 1991. The figure will reach 75% by 2000.

41. Entry-level and low-wage-rate workers will soon be in short supply.
• The declining birthrate in the 1960s and early 1970s means that fewer young people are entering the job market today. The number of jobs is increasing, creating entry-level labor shortages. This problem will grow in the late 1990s, especially in the service sector.

Management Trends

42. More entrepreneurs start new businesses every year.
• More mid-career professionals will become entrepreneurs as they are squeezed out of the narrowing managerial pyramid in large companies. By 2001, only 1 person for every 50 will be promoted; in 1987, it was one person for every 20. (See Trend 46.)
• More women are starting small businesses. Many are leaving traditional jobs to go home, open businesses, and have children.

43. Information-based organizations are quickly displacing the old command-and-control model of management. Information technology is the driving force.
• Expect managers to rely increasingly on consultants rather than full-time workers.

44. Work will increasingly be done by task-focused teams of specialists.
• Research, development, manufacturing, and marketing specialists will work together as a team on all stages of product de-

velopment rather than keeping each stage separate and distinct.

45. The typical large business will be information-based, composed of specialists who rely on information from colleagues, customers, and headquarters to guide their actions.

• Decision processes, management structure, and modes of work are being transformed as businesses take the first steps from using unprocessed data to using data that have been converted into information that is analyzed, synthesized, and organized in a useful way.

46. A typical large business in 2010 will have fewer than half the management levels of its counterpart today and about one-third the number of managers.

• Middle management will all but disappear as information flows directly up to higher management for analysis.

• Downsizing, restructuring, reorganizations, and cutbacks of white-collar workers will continue until the late 1990s.

Trends in Values and Concerns

47. Societal values are changing rapidly.

• Family issues will dominate the 1990s: long-term health care, day care, early childhood education, anti-drug campaigns, and drug-free environments.

• Middle age will be "in" by 2000; the "youth culture" will be "out."

48. Diversity is become a growing, explicit value.

• The old idea was to conform, blend in with the group. This is giving way, especially among minorities, to pride in cultural heritage and a general acceptance of differences in all aspects of society. One example is the tolerance, still contested but growing, for atypical sexual preferences.

• The United States is not a melting pot, but a mosaic. People have different roots, and increasingly they cling to them.

49. Americans place growing importance on economic success, which they have come to expect.

• The emphasis on economic success will remain powerful. However, the means to achieve aspirations may not be there. Only one in three high-school graduates goes on to receive a college degree, and without higher education, expectations may never be met.

• More young people report earning no money at all.

50. Tourism, vacationing, and travel (especially international) will grow throughout the 1990s.

• By 2000, 1 of every 10 people in the United States will work for the hospitality industry.

• Multiple, shorter vacations spread throughout the year will continue to replace the traditional two-week vacation.

51. A high level of medical care is increasingly taken for granted.

- Medical knowledge is doubling every eight years.
- There will be a surplus of 100,000 physicians by 2001, even if health-care reform brings new patients into the medical system. The result: Doctors will pay closer attention to individual patient care and extend their office hours to evenings and weekends.

52. *The physical-fitness culture and personal-health movements will remain strong.*

- Emphasis on preventive medicine is growing. By 2001, some 90% of insurance carriers will expand coverage or reduce premiums for policyholders with healthy lifestyles.
- Personal wellness, prevention, and self-help will be the watchwords for a more health-conscious population. Interest in participant sports, exercise equipment, home gyms, and employee fitness programs will create mini-boom industries.

53. *Americans increasingly expect a high level of social service.*

- More services and accommodations have catered to the deaf, blind, disabled, poor, infirm, and aged since the 1992 disability act was signed.

54. *Concern for environmental issues is growing.*

- Zoos will serve as "Noah's Archives," collecting not only species but genetic materials in an effort to slow the increasing extinction rate of animals.
- Fusion reactors producing "clean" nuclear energy will appear after 2010; by 2030 they will be a major source of power.

55. *Consumerism is still growing rapidly.*

- With a wealth of information, consumers will become smarter buyers.
- Discount stores such as factory outlets and food clubs will continue to grow.

56. *The women's equality movement will become less strident, but more effective.*

- "Old girl" networks will become increasingly effective as women fill more positions in middle and upper management.
- An infrastructure is evolving that allows women to make more decisions and to exercise political power, especially where both spouses work. The effects will include more childcare services, greater employment opportunities, and rapidly closing pay gaps between men and women.

"As we enter the twenty-first century, life looks more like the turbulent 1920s and 1930s—when order broke down, and there was no nation to take the lead."

From Cold War to Cold Peace

Jeffrey E. Garten

Jeffrey E. Garten is the undersecretary for commerce for international trade. He also held senior posts in the White House and U.S. Department of State in the Nixon, Ford, and Carter administrations. In the following viewpoint, Garten argues that in the new world order, the replacement for the Cold War is likely to be a "cold peace." His projected scenario of world relations in the late 1990s illustrates how America's former allies in the Cold War—Japan and Germany—could become America's new enemies. The author predicts that conflicts over trade and international crisis management will result in a breakdown in cooperation among the "Big Three"—Germany, Japan, and America—and contribute to a turbulent twenty-first century.

As you read, consider the following questions:

1. What threats could a future U.S. president make against other countries, in Garten's opinion?
2. According to Garten, what assumptions did Americans make about the world after the Cold War?
3. What path will former communist nations of Eastern Europe likely take, according to the author?

Excerpted from Jeffrey E. Garten, *A Cold Peace: America, Japan, Germany, and the Struggle for Supremacy*, ©1993 by The Twentieth Century Fund. Reprinted by permission of the Twentieth Century Fund, New York.

Looking back, historians in the early twenty-first century are unlikely to have settled on any one explanation of how conflict among America, Japan, and Germany caused the new world order of the mid-to-late 1990s to become a nightmare. "Economic warfare" will not precisely describe what happened, because even though protectionism increased, business dealings, flows of money, and volumes of trade steadily increased among the major nations. "Military clashes" will not be accurate because Washington, Berlin, and Tokyo will certainly not have taken up arms against one another. Something else will have come about between the Big Three, not willfully, not spitefully. It will have happened simply because these powerful nations, driven by the force of their differing histories, institutions, and cultural preferences, weighed down by new sets of responsibilities and constraints, and exhausted by having had to respond to one crisis after another, simply couldn't find a way to overcome their narrowly defined interests. Although the breakdown of order will have had no precise starting date, it might have evolved like this:

Wielding a Big Stick

It is 20 January 1997. A newly elected U.S. president is delivering his or her inaugural speech. He or she points to all the failed promises of the previous administration to improve schools, to deal with drugs and crime, to rebuild America's crumbling road and rail networks, and to strengthen its tottering banking system. He/she calls for a crash program of internal rebuilding—a domestic Marshall Plan. He/she pledges his/her administration's total efforts to find the money to do these things, including, for the first time, truly radical cuts in the defense budget and drastic reductions in financial contributions to the UN, the World Bank, and other international organizations. He/she threatens other nations whose markets are not fully open to American exports with substantial trade retaliation. To show that he/she means business, he/she announces a tripling of tariffs on imports of Japanese telecommunications gear and German machine tools, and he/she promises a wide-ranging investigation by the Justice Department of potential antitrust violations by Japanese and European firms—many of the latter now dominated by German interests—whose U.S.-based facilities are part of a concentrated global network. Referring to the large military establishment that America has maintained for more than half a century, and to the American blood that was shed to protect the West and Japan, and vowing that enough is enough, the president announces the withdrawal of all America's remaining forces from abroad. As the applause builds, he/she says he/she will use the North American trade bloc, consisting of the new common market of the U.S., Canada, and Mexico, as a big stick against those who don't play fair.

The events in Washington have little impact on Europe. Gathering in Potsdam, Germany, in the winter of 1997, the European heads of state have other problems to worry about. Their decision to create a European bloc of nations, stretching from Lisbon to Moscow, had been taken years before and has created enough political and administrative headaches to preoccupy them for the next quarter of a century. Europe was dismayed, for example, when the dream of a European Community of co-equal nations faded as Germany began to dominate the new European Central Bank, the new political institutions, and the new European defense organization. More aggravation came when Berlin demanded the incorporation of several Eastern European countries into the EC and then proceeded to create a Teutonic coalition composed of Croatia, Hungary, and the Baltics within the enlarged EC. Next, one crisis has cascaded over another, taking up the time and attention of German leaders more than any of the whining from Washington. There was, for example, persistent rioting in the eastern portion of Germany as widespread inequalities mounted and market reforms produced intolerable strains. Then came the large-scale debt defaults of the Eastern European countries, Russia, Ukraine, and other newly independent republics, followed by waves of refugees, which stretched Germany's public finances and social tolerance to the breaking point. There was no single event, no single meeting in which it was said, "We've got to look after ourselves, above all; the Americans are no longer very relevant." They never said it exactly that way, but somehow it happened.

Japan Is Well Prepared

None of these events come as a great surprise to Japanese officials. For them, the omens were clear for a long time. They had long ago discounted the U.S. security umbrella. They knew that the long recession in the United States, which began in 1990 and lingered for years, would force them to lay off workers in their American-based factories, and they were prepared for the congressional outcry. As General Motors gave pink slips to more than 70,000 employees, they expected increased harassment not just of Toyota, Nissan, and other auto companies, but also of Hitachi, Matsushita, and other Japanese firms operating in America by the IRS, the Department of Labor, the Civil Rights Commission, the White House Office of Equal Economic Opportunity, the Environmental Protection Agency, and countless congressional committees. They knew their decision to draw closer to China in economics and politics would upset Washington, whose policy was increasingly antagonistic toward Beijing. They were not surprised that the United States resented Japan's accelerated efforts to build a tighter East Asian community with

Japan at the center. But there is no panic in the Japanese cabinet. The era of the Cold War, Tokyo reminds itself, is over. The Asian nation has its own problems to worry about, including its aging population, chronic labor shortages, and its growing class divisions. Washington's new economic aggressiveness, however, has annoyed the Japanese, who have become tired of being the whipping boy for America's homegrown deficiencies. Two can play America's game, they conclude, and Tokyo's Ministry of Finance instructs Japanese lenders to slow up loans to America; its Defense Agency quietly blocks the technology transfers that the Pentagon had been expecting; Japan's space agency gives orders to accelerate "Project Independence" for its aerospace industry, one of the few sectors in which the United States was still supreme; and U.S. investors with operations from Osaka to Sapporo find out how uncomfortable life can become under the refocused glare of Japan's regulators.

The Future: Subordination to Japan?

The United States will, initially, have difficulty swallowing its new subordination to Japan. The first seizures of Japanese-owned property in the United States in the name of national security cannot be far off. Yet, the United States cannot long resist because it hasn't the means to finance the Pacific Rim on its own. Sooner rather than later, the proud but fading superpower will discover that all paths lead to the source of provisions. Japan already supplies most of the key technologies for America's arsenal.

Jacques Attali, *New Perspectives Quarterly*, Spring 1990.

Both Berlin and Tokyo are unimpressed with the American president's lament that the United States has shouldered disproportionate military burdens. What about the German-dominated European intervention force stretching from Poland to Russia that is trying to maintain some semblance of order as one nation after another has eyed its neighbors' borders and as economic and ethnic tensions have brought widespread civil disorder in their wake? What about the Japanese naval fleet now patrolling some of Asia's contested territorial borders? What's America's complaint?

The Breakdown of Order

Tokyo and Berlin have also stopped listening to American harangues about free-market economics. Yes, they say, we all love Adam Smith, but life has become more complicated than that.

The new industrial order requires big firms, big banks, harmonious labor relations, a proactive government, they say. The instability and fragility of the former Communist nations require extensive support by governmental intervention. America should worry a little more about its own competitiveness than about ideology, more about its saving and investment, or its schools, than about our antitrust policies or our financial regulations. Washington wants to threaten us with its protectionist club? Let it try. No one wants a trade war, but if there has to be one, we are in a stronger position than America is to fight one.

By the late 1990s, moreover, Washington, Berlin, and Tokyo have had their fill of crisis management. The initial anxieties over the collapse of the old order in Eastern Europe, followed by worries about whether a unified Germany would again upset international politics, followed by the Gulf War, followed by civil war in Russia, followed by a dramatic economic slowdown in the industrial world—all this in the first half of the 1990s—was simply too much for political leaders to deal with. But this was not all. The Big Three were also constantly bickering over which factions and leaders in the unstable former Soviet republics to support and how. When millions of refugees began pouring into Western Europe both from the East and from North Africa, another clash took place over how to respond. When political instability began to rock the Asian mainland, including turmoil in China as the old leadership died off, each of the Big Three defined a different set of primary interests. When monetary instability and protectionism increased, all hopes for close cooperation among the Big Three were dashed.

A Cold Peace

And so after the round of congratulations following the collapse of the Berlin Wall, the Cold War evolved into a Cold Peace. In its postinaugural editorial *The New York Times* wrote,

> Looking back these past few years, no one should have been surprised by the sharp erosion of relationships between America, Japan, and Germany. Most of our resentments are problems of our own making, but we needed an enemy to replace the old Soviet Union and we turned quickly on our former allies. There is more than enough blame to go around, however, for both Tokyo and Berlin seem to have fallen into their pre–World War II pattern of dominating their immediate neighborhoods and thinking very little about the welfare of the world outside their narrow concerns. The growth of global trade and investment—the borderless economy, as some call it—has been a great disappointment from the standpoint of world politics. We thought that when communism collapsed the great political and ideological rivalries of the twentieth century were over. We thought that the main chal-

lenge was to consolidate the movement for freely elected governments that embraced American-style capitalism. As we enter the twenty-first century, life looks more like the turbulent 1920s and 1930s—when order broke down, and there was no nation to take the lead—than like the era of peace we spent the last half century fighting for. It is not clear how we will extricate ourselves from this mess.

A wild fantasy? Hardly. In fact, it is almost impossible to make a completely crazy projection of events these days. Whether or not you believe we're headed for trouble does not depend very much on assumptions about the kinds of problems that will arise, because the nature of those problems is pretty clear. We can expect more ethnic and regional strife outside the United States, Western Europe, and Japan. We can expect economic convulsions as national economies interact with one another with ever-more-competitive ferocity. We can expect that the pressure for the major industrial democracies to work as a team will be reduced in the absence of a military threat from a monolithic enemy. The really contentious issue is not whether all this will happen but whether it is within the ability of the key countries to deal with these problems in an effective way—whether the Big Three are up to the unprecedented degree of sustained cooperation that will be required. The issue is not what is the most *desirable* outcome but what is the *likely* one. Forget the lofty speeches of today's leaders, filled as they are with references to new world orders and the like. The critical questions are all variations on a single theme: *Where are we really heading?*

Questions to Consider

There are some big questions that need to be asked:

How will America deal with a changing domestic and international setting? The United States is no longer in the kingpin position it once was. Whether or not we are in decline can be debated, but no one can deny that America's relative power vis-à-vis Germany and Japan has slipped. Moreover, the United States faces at least two challenges that it has not faced in half a century. Never before has it been so plagued by domestic economic and social problems that require new programs and massive resources at every turn. And not since much earlier in its history has it so needed the assistance of other nations to achieve its goals at home and abroad.

The American dream is of a constant and steady improvement in lifestyle, an upward and unending spiral of individual satisfaction. But what if the dream is no longer real? Will the United States turn inward in an attempt to deal with its internal challenges, and if so, will its stance toward the outside world become increasingly distant and protectionist, mixing military withdrawal with an overly aggressive trade policy? Or will it

271

adopt a more internationalist stance, regaining its confidence by attending to its homegrown problems and trying to create new sets of global arrangements within which it will exercise a new kind of influence, based not on single-handed domination but on more traditional diplomatic give-and-take?

What kinds of countries will Germany and Japan become? During the Cold War, these two countries were living in unique circumstances. They may have been sovereign in a legal sense, but in fact they were half-nations, riddled with inhibitions and restrictions stemming from their defeat in World War II. This was partly the case because their neighbors still viewed their actions with suspicion, especially when either appeared to be too assertive. Partly it was because they derived substantial advantages from being able to concentrate on building their economies while America took responsibility for their defense.

In the mid-1990s the environment for Germany and Japan will be changing. Each nation will be less constrained in telling the world what it wants and in pursuing its national interests; consequently, each will be acting more independently of America than it did for the previous forty-five years. Americans will need to pose the most fundamental questions regarding these two countries. Before 1945 they were unstable mavericks, resisting integration into the global community except on their own terms. Are all such drives behind them now? Will they remain close allies of the United States despite the withering of a common security threat and the passing of the generation that remembers World War II and its aftermath? Can German energy and ambition be channeled in such a way as not to alarm and dominate its neighbors? Will Japan continue its unprecedented climb up the global economic ladder without doing more to accommodate the interests and concerns of other nations? Will either nation continue to be an economic powerhouse without projecting a military capability beyond its borders, or will the two types of power inevitably come together?

Burden-Sharing

How will military and economic burdens be distributed among the Big Three? From 1945 to the mid-1960s, America shouldered most of the military and economic burdens for the free world— from fighting wars to maintaining open markets. In the ensuing decades, German and Japanese contributions increased—from helping to offset the costs of U.S. troops to providing large loans to the U.S. government. But the issues of burden-sharing among the Big Three have not yet been resolved. After the Gulf War, America's growing dilemma was starkly revealed: Washington can be the world's policeman as long as others help pay the way. Few Americans find this role appealing, but what are the alternatives? How to share military leadership and how to divide up economic responsibilities—these are the first questions. But a tough American view will have to take into account not just spreading the costs but also the degree to which the United States is willing for others to have an equal voice in the actual decision-making. In other words, how much power does America *really* want Japan and Germany to have?

Assumptions About the World

There are no definitive answers to these questions, but we must begin to think about them and form some general judgments. A starting point is a second look at the assumptions Americans generally make about the world.

We thought that after the Cold War, America, Japan, and Germany would be close partners in all endeavors. . . .

We assumed that in the post–Cold War era, Japan and Germany would naturally take on more responsibility for global peace and global economic management. . . .

We believed that America would continue to be the leader and Japan and Germany, while contributing more to the common effort, would remain followers. . . .

We assumed that the military alliances between Washington and Europe and between Washington and Tokyo would remain intact. . . .

We assumed that the energy and the aggressive tendencies of Germany and Japan, which were evident in the early part of this century, would be submerged and contained within multilateral frameworks. . . .

We thought that after the Cold War, the liberated Communist nations would follow an American model of politics and economics, as would most of the third world. . . .

None of these assumptions are more likely to hold than not hold true. Let us take a look at just this last assumption.

For forty-five years there were really two competing systems in our minds—democratic capitalism and communism. The first was championed by the United States, inculcated in the two other most powerful and dynamic nations of the free world—Japan and Germany—and more or less embraced by many third-world nations. On the other hand, communism, in both its political and economic dimensions, was totally discredited. What we did not envision was that there could arise another form of competition, this time among different kinds of capitalist systems. When the world was divided in two, these distinctions did not seem so important, nor were they so pronounced, as they may become. But the differences may go to the heart of what countries will be looking for in the future.

The capitalist systems of America, Germany, and Japan differ significantly in certain crucial respects: in the priority given to individual freedom versus the cohesion of their societies and in the relationship between government and business. Although most of the nations struggling to shake off the yoke of communism are enamored of the American dream, it is by no means clear that they will want or be able to use the freewheeling American system. The more tightly woven and highly organized societies of Germany and Japan, both of which have so clearly demonstrated the ability to revive their nations from total collapse, may prove much more relevant and attractive once the immediate euphoria of newfound freedom wears off.

Americans have assumed, moreover, that in an interdependent world there would be economic convergence on the American model. But this might not be the case. The formerly Communist nations behind the iron curtain are more likely to emulate the mixed capitalism of Western Europe, the most successful case being Germany's. The Asian tigers, Taiwan, Singapore, South Korea, Thailand, Malaysia, are already following the path of Japan. America's market system once produced unprecedented prosperity, to be sure. But for nations struggling to get on their feet, for those worried about explosive pressures of unemployment, for those trying to foster investment rather than consumption, for those looking for proven manpower-training programs, for those desperate for stable banking systems that can provide long-term capital, for those wanting the best way to develop technology for commercial application, is the United States likely to be the most practical model?

Why does it matter that the old assumptions cannot be trusted? It means that we have to go back to basics. We have to accept the facts that the Cold War era was a unique period and that the changes that will now occur will go well beyond what America has been willing to consider. It's not simply that there is no such common enemy as the former Soviet Union; not simply that Japan and Germany will be more assertive; not simply that we're in for tougher economic competition. The roots of the world as we have known it are being pulled up. The definitions of interests, friends, and foes are all changing. There is a pervasive sense that the world is on the threshold of a new era, wrote Zbigniew Brzezinski in late 1991. And so we are. But as the old framework shatters, the forces of divisiveness, not of cooperation, are gaining momentum. The events of the past years are enough to focus our minds, but more telling evidence is to be found in the underlying pressures that will drive the societies of the Big Three in different directions. These include not only historical events but also how we have interpreted them, in particular, how America has viewed Germany and Japan over time and what it means for the future.

5

"*The coming of the Third Wave is creating . . . two basic political camps. . . . One seeks to restore the smokestack past, the other to move us beyond it.*"

The Coming of the Information Revolution

Alvin Toffler and Heidi Toffler

In the following viewpoint, adapted from their 1994 book, *Creating a New Civilization: The Politics of the Third Wave*, futurists Alvin Toffler and Heidi Toffler assert that America's politicians and government must change in order to adapt to the "Third Wave" of historical change, which they believe promises to transform society. The Tofflers argue that this wave, giving rise to information-based economies and societies, conflicts with the Second Wave, consisting of Industrial Revolution manufacturing and industry that has dominated America for decades. Influential politicians and others continue to cling to Second Wave practices, the authors contend, but they cannot prevent the Third Wave from emerging on the national scene.

As you read, consider the following questions:

1. According to the Tofflers, why was the "infrastructure bill" of 1991 an example of Second Wave politics?
2. What obstacles prevent Democrats and Republicans from embracing the Third Wave, in the authors' opinion?
3. What industries does the Third Wave sector include, according to the Tofflers?

Alvin Toffler and Heidi Toffler, "Catch the (Political) Wave," *The Wall Street Journal*, October 13, 1994. Reprinted with permission of *The Wall Street Journal*, ©1994 Dow Jones & Company, Inc. All rights reserved.

Before election day 1994, political pundits predicted a major power shift in Congress and in state capitals across America as a new generation of political leaders arrived on the scene.

Yet Americans remain pessimistic and disengaged from the political process. Americans are increasingly alienated, bored and angry at both the media and politicians. Party politics seem to most people a kind of shadow play—insincere, costly and corrupt. Increasingly, they ask: Does it matter who wins?

The answer is Yes—but not for the reason we are told.

Ten thousand years or so ago the First Wave of historical change, the agrarian revolution, began to spread peasant-centered societies across the planet. Three hundred or so years ago a Second Wave, launched by the Industrial Revolution, burst upon the world and gave rise to a factory-centered way of life. What the United States and other countries are experiencing today is a Third Wave of change giving rise to information-centered economies and societies.

But that enormous change, which is reshaping business, has not yet penetrated our political system. It will, soon, with striking consequences.

The Third Wave

The coming of the Third Wave is creating in our midst two basic political camps that cross party lines, one dedicated to the Second Wave status quo and the other to Third Wave change. One seeks to restore the smokestack past, the other to move us beyond it.

The reason the public does not, even now, recognize the crucial importance of this cleavage is that much of what the press reports is, in fact, the politics-as-usual conflict between different Second Wave groups over the spoils of the old system. But despite their differences, these groups quickly coalesce to oppose Third Wave initiatives.

This is why, when Congress passed an "infrastructure bill" in 1991, $150 billion was allocated to roads, highways and bridges—providing profits to Second Wave companies and jobs for Second Wave unions—while a trivial $1 billion was allocated to help build the much-touted electronic superhighway. Necessary as they may be, roads and highways are part of the Second Wave infrastructure; digital networks are the heart of the Third Wave infrastructure.

This is why, more recently, Second Wave Naderites and Second Wave Buchananites [after consumer advocate Ralph Nader and conservative commentator Pat Buchanan] found common cause against the North American Free Trade Agreement [NAFTA], which will, over the long run, destroy Second Wave jobs in the United States and replace them with Third Wave jobs.

This is why Vice President Al Gore—with one toe wet in the Third Wave—has been unable, despite his efforts, to "reinvent" the government along Third Wave lines. Even as advanced corporations, driven by competition, are desperately trying to dismantle their bureaucracies and invent new Third Wave forms of management, government agencies, blocked by Second Wave civil service unions, have managed to stay largely unreformed, unre-engineered, unreinvented.

Congress-on-the-Internet

Computer and political enthusiasts alike agree that Congress-on-the-Internet has undeniable appeal. Thomas, [a computer system of] the Library of Congress, will give cyberspace travelers the text of all versions of House and Senate bills, accessible by bill number or key-word search and unfiltered by newspapers or television. "This is just the beginning," says Bill Pierce, spokesman for Rep. Bob Thomas, the California Republican who is overseeing the Thomas project. "There is way more to come."

Eventually, Thomas will carry the *Congressional Record*, the transcript of daily proceedings on the House and Senate floors. In addition, it will provide a House "gopher" or a directory of members and committees as well as their yearly calendars and weekly floor schedules; a primer on House rules and the legislative process; a C-Span directory; and a congressional bill tracker. "As more and more people know about it and more and more members know about it, more [of both] are going to be hooking into it," says Pierce.

Sean Piccoli, *Insight on the News*, February 20, 1995.

Second Wave elites in both business and the unions fight to retain or reinstate an unsustainable past because they gained wealth and power from applying Second Wave principles, and the shift to a new way of life challenges their wealth and power. But it isn't only the elites. Millions of middle-class and poor Americans also resist the transition to the Third Wave out of an often justified fear that they will be left behind and slide further down the economic and social slope.

The Second Wave sector is backed by those elements of Wall Street that service it. It is further supported by intellectuals and academics, often tenured, who live off grants from the foundations, trade associations and lobbies that serve it.

Their task is to collect supportive data and hammer out the ideological arguments and slogans used by Second Wave forces— for example, the idea that information-intensive service industries are "unproductive" or that service workers are doomed to "sling hamburgers" or that the economy must revolve around traditional manufacturing.

With all this firepower continually battering them, it is hardly surprising that both political parties reflect Second Wave thinking. The Democrats' reflexive reliance on bureaucratic and centralist solutions to problems like the health crisis is drawn straight from Second Wave theories of efficiency. The failure of the Democrats to make themselves the party of the future (as, indeed, they once were) throws the door wide open for their adversaries. The Republicans, less rooted in the industrial Northeast, thus have an opportunity to position themselves as the party of the Third Wave.

The Republicans are basically right when they urge us to take maximum advantage of the dynamism and creativity that market economics make possible. But they, too, remain prisoners of Second Wave economics. For example, even the free-market economists on whom Republicans rely have failed, as yet, to come to terms with the new role and inexhaustibility of knowledge. Republicans also are still beholden to some of the corporate dinosaurs of the Second Wave past, and to their trade associations, lobbies and policy-formulating "round tables."

The difference between the parties, however, is that while the Second Wave nostalgia-pushers in the Democratic Party are concentrated in its core constituencies, their counterparts in the Republican Party tend to be found on its frenetic fringe—leaving room for the center of the party, if it is inclusive and open to change, to seize the future, lock, stock and barrel.

Third Wave Industries

However powerful Second Wave forces may seem, their future is diminishing. Today the overwhelming majority of Americans are neither farmers nor factory workers. They are, instead, engaged in one form or another of knowledge work. America's fastest growing and most important industries are information-intensive. The Third Wave sector includes not only high-flying computer and electronics firms and biotech start-ups. It embraces advanced, information-driven manufacturing. It includes the increasingly data-drenched services, such as finance, software, entertainment, the media, advanced communications, medical services, consulting, training and education—in short, all the industries based on mind-work rather than muscle-work. The people in this sector—knowledge workers—will soon be the biggest constituency in U.S. politics.

Unlike the "masses" during the industrial age, the rising Third Wave constituency is highly diverse. Its very heterogeneity contributes to its lack of political awareness. It is far harder to unify than the masses of the past.

Thus the Third Wave constituency has yet to develop its own think tanks and unifying political ideology. It has not systematically marshaled support from academia. Its various associations and lobbies in Washington are still comparatively new and less well-connected. And except for one issue—NAFTA—in which the Second Wavers were defeated, the new constituency has few notches on its legislative guns.

Liberation

Yet there are key issues on which this broad constituency-to-come can agree. To start with: liberation from all the rules, regulations, taxes and laws laid in place to serve the smokestack barons and bureaucrats of the past. These arrangements, no doubt sensible when Second Wave industry was the heart of the American economy, today obstruct Third Wave development.

For example, depreciation tax schedules, lobbied into being by the old manufacturing interests, presuppose that machines and products last for many years. Yet in the fast-changing high-tech industries, and particularly the computer industry, the usefulness of products is measured in months or weeks. The result is a tax bias against high tech. Research-and-development deductions, too, favor big, old, Second Wave companies over the dynamic start-ups on which the Third Wave sector depends. The tax treatment of intangibles means that a company with a lot of obsolete sewing machines may well be favored over a software firm that has very little in the way of physical assets. Yet changing such rules will take a bitter political fight against the Second Wave firms that benefit from them.

Much of the Third Wave sector is engaged in providing a dazzling, ever-changing array of services. Instead of decrying the rise of the service sector, shouldn't it be expressly supported and expanded—or at least freed of old shackles? Yet no political party as yet has even begun to think this way.

Despite this political lag, the Third Wave constituency is growing in power every day. It increasingly expresses itself outside the conventional political parties because neither party has so far noticed its existence. Thus it is Third Wavers who fill the ranks of the ever more numerous and potent grass-roots organizations. It is Third Wavers who dominate the electronic communities proliferating around the Internet. And it is the same people who are busy "demassifying" the Second Wave media and creating an interactive alternative to it. Traditional party politicians who ignore these new realities will be swept aside like the MPs [Members of Parliament] in 19th-century England who, even as the Second Wave of change washed over them, imagined that their First Wave, "rotten borough" seats in Parliament were permanently secure.

6 VIEWPOINT

"*The curious tapestry of military authoritarianism and combat ineffectiveness that we see [in 2012] was not yet woven in 1992. But the threads were there.*"

The Potential Military Takeover of America

Charles J. Dunlap Jr.

America's military could conceivably overthrow the government in the next century, Charles J. Dunlap Jr. argues in the following viewpoint. Dunlap employs a fictional narrator—a retired, imprisoned military officer—to describe the events leading up to a military coup in the year 2012, focusing on the drift of the U.S. military into civilian affairs. Dunlap's narrator describes a military that is considered the only effective institution in what has become a problem-plagued society, with the inevitable result being a military takeover. Dunlap is a colonel in the U.S. Air Force and staff judge advocate for the U.S. Strategic Command at Offutt Air Force Base in Nebraska.

As you read, consider the following questions:

1. What are examples of America's social malaise, according to Dunlap's narrator?
2. How did the growth of the military undermine democracy, in Dunlap's narrative?
3. According to the narrative, why did the U.S. military fail in the Second Gulf War?

Abridged from Charles J. Dunlap Jr., "The Origins of the American Military Coup of 2012," *Parameters*, Winter 1992-93. Reprinted with permission.

The letter that follows takes us on a darkly imagined excursion into the future. A military coup has taken place in the United States—the year is 2012—and General Thomas E. T. Brutus, Commander-in-Chief of the Unified Armed Forces of the United States, now occupies the White House as permanent Military Plenipotentiary. His position has been ratified by a national referendum, though scattered disorders still prevail and arrests for acts of sedition are under way. A senior retired officer of the Unified Armed Forces, known here simply as Prisoner 222305759, is one of those arrested, having been convicted by court-martial for opposing the coup. Prior to his execution, he is able to smuggle out of prison a letter to an old [National] War College classmate discussing the "Origins of the American Military Coup of 2012." In it, he argues that the coup was the outgrowth of trends visible as far back as 1992. These trends were the massive diversion of military forces to civilian uses, the monolithic unification of the armed forces, and the insularity of the military community. . . .

It goes without saying (I hope) that the coup scenario above is purely a literary device intended to dramatize my concern over certain contemporary developments affecting the armed forces, and is emphatically *not* a prediction.

A Letter from Prison

Dear Old Friend,

It's hard to believe that 20 years have passed since we graduated from the War College! Remember the great discussions, the trips, the parties, the people? Those were the days!!! I'm not having quite as much fun anymore. You've heard about the Sedition Trials? Yeah, I was one of those arrested—convicted of "disloyal statements," and "using contemptuous language towards officials." Disloyal? No. Contemptuous? You bet! With General Brutus in charge it's not hard to be contemptuous.

I've got to hand it to Brutus, he's ingenious. After the President died he somehow "persuaded" the Vice President not to take the oath of office. Did we then have a President or not? A real "Constitutional Conundrum," the papers called it. Brutus created just enough ambiguity to convince everyone that as the senior military officer, he could—and should—declare himself Commander-in-Chief of the Unified Armed Forces. Remember what he said? "Had to fill the power vacuum." And Brutus showed he really knew how to use power: he declared martial law, "postponed" the elections, got the Vice President to "retire," and even moved into the White House! "More efficient to work from there," he said. Remember that?

When Congress convened that last time and managed to pass the Referendum Act, I really got my hopes up. But when the Referendum approved Brutus's takeover, I knew we were in serious trouble. I caused a ruckus, you know, trying to organize a protest. Then the Security Forces picked me up. My quickie "trial" was a joke. The sentence? Well, let's just say you won't have to save any beer for me at next year's reunion. Since it doesn't look like I'll be seeing you again, I thought I'd write everything down and try to get it to you.

I am calling my paper the "Origins of the American Military Coup of 2012." I think it's important to get the truth recorded before they rewrite history. If we're ever going to get our freedom back, we've got to understand how we got into this mess. People need to understand that the armed forces exist to support and defend government, not to *be* the government. Faced with intractable national problems on one hand, and an energetic and capable military on the other, it can be all too seductive to start viewing the military as a cost-effective solution. We made a terrible mistake when we allowed the armed forces to be diverted from their original purpose.

I found a box of my notes and clippings from our War College days—told my keepers I needed them to write the confession they want. It's amazing; looking through these old papers makes me realize that even back in 1992 we should have seen this coming. The seeds of this outrage were all there; we just didn't realize how they would grow. But isn't that always the way with things like this? Author Daniel J. Boorstin once said that "the true watersheds in human affairs are seldom spotted amid the tumult of headlines broadcast on the hour." And we had a lot of headlines back in the '90s to distract us: The economy was in the dumps, crime was rising, schools were deteriorating, drug use was rampant, the environment was in trouble, and political scandals were occurring almost daily. Still, there was some good news: the end of the Cold War as well as America's recent victory over Iraq.

Military Government Replaces Democracy

All of this and more contributed to the situation in which we find ourselves today: a military that controls government and one that, ironically, can't fight. It wasn't any single cause that led us to this point. Instead, it was a combination of several different developments, the beginnings of which were evident in 1992. Here's what I think happened:

Americans became exasperated with democracy. We were disillusioned with the apparent inability of elected government to solve the nation's dilemmas. We were looking for someone or something that could produce workable answers. The one institution of government in which the people retained faith was the military. Buoyed by the military's obvious competence in the First Gulf War, the public increasingly turned to it for solutions to the country's problems. Americans called for an acceleration of trends begun in the 1980s: tasking the military with a variety of new, nontraditional missions, and vastly escalating its commitment to formerly ancillary duties.

Though not obvious at the time, the cumulative effect of these new responsibilities was to incorporate the military into the political process to an unprecedented degree. These additional assignments also had the perverse effect of diverting focus and resources from the military's central mission of combat training and warfighting. Finally, organizational, political, and societal changes served to alter the American military's culture. Today's military is not the one we knew when we graduated from the War College.

Something to Take Seriously

Is "The Origins of the American Military Coup of 2012" something to be taken seriously? Yes, it is, even if one may be skeptical about just how likely to occur the developments that Charles Dunlap points to really are.

In his book *The Soldier and the State: The Theory and Politics of Civil-Military Relations*, the Harvard political scientist Samuel P. Huntington identifies a strong streak of antimilitarism in American politics. It has typically manifested itself through one of two impulses: the impulse to cut military budgets and the impulse to use the military "to further other socially desirable objectives." That is to say, the historical tendency in America has been to attempt either to reduce the military or to transform it. Obscured somewhat by the fifty years of the Cold War, this pattern is now reasserting itself.

Thomas E. Ricks, *The Atlantic Monthly*, January 1993.

Let me explain how I came to these conclusions. . . .

America's societal malaise was readily apparent in 1992. Seventy-eight percent of Americans believed the country was on the "wrong track.". . .

America wanted solutions and democratically elected government wasn't providing them. The country suffered from what magazine and newspaper owner Mortimer B. Zuckerman called a "deep pessimism about politicians and government after years of broken promises.". . .

Unlike the rest of government the military enjoyed a remarkably steady climb in popularity throughout the 1980s and early 1990s. And indeed it had earned the admiration of the public. Debilitated by the Vietnam War, the US military set about reinventing itself. As early as 1988 *U.S. News & World Report* heralded the result: "In contrast to the dispirited, drug-ravaged, do-your-own-thing armed services of the '70s and early '80s, the US military has been transformed into a fighting force of gung-ho attitude, spit-shined discipline, and ten-hut morale." After the US military dealt Iraq a crushing defeat in the First Gulf War, the ignominy of Vietnam evaporated. . . .

While polls showed that the public invariably gave Congress low marks, a February 1991 *Washington Post* survey disclosed that "public confidence in the military soar[ed] to 85 percent, far surpassing every other institution in our society." The armed forces had become America's most—and perhaps only—trusted arm of government. . . .

In the 1980s, Congress initiated the use of "national defense" as a rationale to boost military participation in an activity historically the exclusive domain of civilian government: law enforcement. Congress concluded that the "rising tide of drugs being smuggled into the United States . . . present[ed] a grave threat to all Americans." Finding the performance of civilian law enforcement agencies in counteracting that threat unsatisfactory, Congress passed the Military Cooperation with Civilian Law Enforcement Agencies Act of 1981. In doing so Congress specifically intended to force reluctant military commanders to actively collaborate in police work.

This was a historic change of policy. . . .

Rampant Crime

It wasn't too long before 21st-century legislators were calling for more military involvement in police work. Crime seemed out of control. Most disturbing, the incidence of violent crime continued to climb. Americans were horrified and desperate: a third even believed vigilantism could be justified. Rising lawlessness was seen as but another example of the civilian political leadership's inability to fulfill government's most basic duty to ensure public safety. People once again wanted the military to help. . . .

Concern about crime was a major reason why General Brutus's actions were approved in the Referendum. Although voter participation by the general public was low, older Americans voted at a much higher rate. Furthermore, with the aging of the baby boom generation, the block of American voters over 45 grew to almost 53 percent of the voters by 2010. This wealthy, older electorate welcomed an organization which could ensure their physical security. When it counted, they backed Brutus in the Referendum—probably the last votes they'll ever cast. . . .

Even the youngest citizens were co-opted. During the 1990s the public became aware that military officers had the math and science backgrounds desperately needed to revitalize US education. In fact, programs involving military personnel were already under way while we were at the War College. We now have an entire generation of young people who have grown up comfortable with the sight of military personnel patrolling their streets and teaching in their classrooms. . . .

By the year 2000 the armed forces had penetrated many vital aspects of American society. More and more military officers sought the kind of autonomy in these civilian affairs that they would expect from their military superiors in the execution of traditional combat operations. Thus began the inevitable politicization of the military. With so much responsibility for virtually everything government was expected to do, the military increasingly demanded a larger role in policymaking. But in a democracy policymaking is a task best left to those accountable to the electorate. Nonetheless, well-intentioned military officers, accustomed to the ordered, hierarchical structure of military society, became impatient with the delays and inefficiencies inherent in the democratic process. Consequently, they increasingly sought to avoid it. They convinced themselves that they could more productively serve the nation in carrying out their new assignments if they accrued to themselves unfettered power to implement their programs. They forgot Lord Acton's warning that "all power corrupts, and absolute power corrupts absolutely."

Military Plenipotentiary Act of 2005

Congress became their unwitting ally. Because of the popularity of the new military programs—and the growing dependence upon them—Congress passed the Military Plenipotentiary Act of 2005. . . .

In passing this legislation Congress added greater authority to the military's top leadership position. Lulled by favorable experiences with Chairmen like General Colin Powell, Congress saw little danger in converting the office of the Chairman of the Joint Chiefs of Staff into the even more powerful Military Plenipotentiary. No longer merely an advisor, the Military Plenipotentiary became a true commander of all US services, purportedly because that status could better ameliorate the effects of perceived interservice squabbling. Despite warnings found in the legislative history of Goldwater-Nichols and elsewhere, enormous power was concentrated in the hands of a single, unelected official. Unfortunately, Congress presumed that principled people would always occupy the office. No one expected a General Brutus would arise.

The Military Plenipotentiary was not Congress's only structural change in military governance. By 2007 the services were combined to form the Unified Armed Forces. . . . But unification ended the creative tension between the services. Besides rejecting the operational logic of separate services, no one seemed to recognize the checks-and-balances function that service separatism provided a democracy obliged to maintain a large, professional military establishment. . . .

Ever since large peacetime military establishments became permanent features after World War II, the great leveler of the officer corps was the constant influx of officers from the Reserve Officers Training Corps program. The product of diverse colleges and universities throughout the United States, these officers were a vital source of liberalism in the military services.

By the late 1980s and early 1990s, however, that was changing. Force reductions decreased the number of ROTC graduates the services accepted. Although General Powell called ROTC "vital to democracy," 62 ROTC programs were closed in 1991 and another 350 were considered for closure. The numbers of officers produced by the service academies also fell, but at a significantly slower pace. Consequently, the *proportion* of academy graduates in the officer corps climbed. Academy graduates, along with graduates of such military schools as the Citadel, Virginia Military Institute, and Norwich University, tended to feel a greater homogeneity of outlook than, say, the pool of ROTC graduates at large, with the result that as the proportion of such graduates grew, diversity of outlook overall diminished to some degree. . . .

The Second Gulf War

What made this all the more disheartening was the wretched performance of our forces in the Second Gulf War. Consumed with ancillary and nontraditional missions, the military neglected its fundamental raison d'etre. As the Supreme Court succinctly put it more than a half century ago, the "primary business of armies and navies [is] to fight or be ready to fight wars should the occasion arise." When Iranian armies started pouring into the lower Gulf states in 2010, the US armed forces were ready to do anything but fight.

Preoccupation with humanitarian duties, narcotics interdiction, and all the rest of the peripheral missions left the military unfit to engage an authentic military opponent. Performing the new missions sapped resources from what most experts agree was one of the vital ingredients to victory in the First Gulf War: training. Training is, quite literally, a zero-sum game. Each moment spent performing a nontraditional mission is one unavailable for orthodox military exercises. We should have recognized the grave risk. . . .

Drug Interdiction

The military's anti-drug activities were a big part of the problem. Oh sure, I remember the facile claims of exponents of the military's counternarcotics involvement as to what "valuable" training it provided. Did anyone really think that crew members of an AWACS—an aircraft designed to track high-performance military aircraft in combat—significantly improved their skills by hours of tracking slow-moving light planes? Did they seriously imagine that troops enhanced combat skills by looking for marijuana under car seats? Did they truly believe that crews of the Navy's sophisticated anti-air and anti-submarine ships received meaningful training by following lumbering trawlers around the Caribbean? Tragically, they did. . . .

The result? People in the military no longer considered themselves warriors. Instead, they perceived themselves as policemen, relief workers, educators, builders, health care providers, politicians—everything but warfighters. When these philanthropists met the Iranian 10th Armored Corps near Daharan during the Second Gulf War, they were brutally slaughtered by a military which had not forgotten what militaries were supposed to do or what war is really all about. . . .

Some Advice

We must remember that America's position at the end of the Cold War had no historical precedent. For the first time the nation—in peacetime—found itself with a still-sizable, professional military establishment that was not preoccupied with an overarching external threat. Yet the uncertainties in the aftermath of the Cold War limited the extent to which those forces could be safely downsized. When the military was then obliged to engage in a bewildering array of nontraditional duties to further justify its existence, it is little wonder that its traditional apolitical professionalism eventually eroded.

Clearly, the curious tapestry of military authoritarianism and combat ineffectiveness that we see today was not yet woven in 1992. But the threads were there. Knowing what I know now, here's the advice I would have given the War College Class of 1992 had I been their graduation speaker:

• *Demand that the armed forces focus exclusively on indisputably military duties.* We must not diffuse our energies away from our fundamental responsibility for warfighting. To send ill-trained troops into combat makes us accomplices to murder.

• *Acknowledge that national security does have economic, social, educational, and environmental dimensions but insist that this doesn't necessarily mean the problems in those areas are the responsibility of the military to correct.* Stylishly designating efforts to solve national ills as "wars" doesn't convert them into something appropriate for the employment of military forces.

• *Readily cede budgetary resources to those agencies whose business it is to address the non-military issues the armed forces are presently asked to fix.* We are not the DEA [Drug Enforcement Administration], EPA [Environmental Protection Agency], Peace Corps, Department of Education, or Red Cross—nor should we be. . . .

- *Divest the defense budget of perception-skewing expenses.* Narcotics interdiction, environmental cleanup, humanitarian relief, and other costs tangential to actual combat capability should be assigned to the budgets of DEA, EPA, State [Department], and so forth. . . .
- *Continue to press for the elimination of superfluous, resource-draining Guard and Reserve units.* Increase the training tempo, responsibilities, and compensation of those that remain.
- *Educate the public to the sophisticated training requirements occasioned by the complexities of modern warfare.* . . .
- *Resist unification of the services not only on operational grounds, but also because unification would be inimical to the checks and balances that underpin democratic government.* . . .
- *Assure that officer accessions from the service academies correspond with overall force reductions (but maintain separate service academies) and keep ROTC [Reserve Officers' Training Corps] on a wide diversity of campuses.* If necessary, resort to litigation to maintain ROTC campus diversity.
- *Orient recruiting resources and campaigns toward ensuring that all echelons of society are represented in the military, without compromising standards.* Accept that this kind of recruiting may increase costs. It's worth it.
- *Work to moderate the base-as-an-island syndrome by providing improved incentives for military members and families to assimilate into civilian communities.* . . .

Finally, I would tell our classmates that democracy is a fragile institution that must be continuously nurtured and scrupulously protected. I would also tell them that they must speak out when they see the institution threatened; indeed, it is their duty to do so. . . .

The catastrophe that occurred on our watch took place because we failed to speak out against policies we knew were wrong. It's too late for me to do any more. But it's not for you.

Best regards,
Prisoner 222305759

Periodical Bibliography

The following articles have been selected to supplement the diverse views presented in this chapter.

Bill Clinton   "We Must Secure Peace," *Vital Speeches of the Day*, October 15, 1994.

David Halberstein   "Coming in from the Cold War," *The Washington Monthly*, January/February 1992.

J. Bryan Hehir   "The Future of Foreign Policy," *Commonweal*, December 2, 1994.

Richard H. Kohn   "Out of Control: The Crisis in Civil-Military Relations," *The National Interest*, Spring 1994. Available from 1112 16th St. NW, Suite 540, Washington, DC 20036.

Richard D. Lamm   "Future View: Indicators of Decline," *The Futurist*, July/August 1993.

Kevin Phillips   "Fat City," *Time*, September 26, 1994.

Thomas E. Ricks   "Colonel Dunlap's Coup," *The Atlantic Monthly*, January 1993.

Linda Rothstein   "Hail to the Military Plenipotentiary," *The Bulletin of the Atomic Scientists*, March 1993.

Benjamin C. Schwarz   "The Arcana of Empire and the Dilemma of American National Security," *Salmagundi*, Winter/Spring 1994. Available from Skidmore College, Saratoga Springs, NY 12866.

Benjamin C. Schwarz   "Is Capitalism Doomed?" *The New York Times*, May 23, 1994.

Stephen Slavin   "Terminal Decline of a Nation," *USA Today*, March 1994.

James H. Snider   "Democracy On-Line: Tomorrow's Electronic Electorate," *The Futurist*, September/October 1994.

Lester Thurow   "Who Owns the Twenty-first Century?" *Sloan Management Review*, Spring 1992. Available from 292 Main St., Rm. E38-120, Cambridge, MA 02139.

Michael Wines   "Washington Really Is in Touch. We're the Problem," *The New York Times*, October 16, 1994.

Glossary

AFDC   Aid to Families with Dependent Children; a federal government program that provides monthly payments to poor families.

biomass   Natural products such as charcoal, wood, and agricultural and animal wastes burned for energy in much of the world.

CFCs   Chlorofluorocarbons; synthetic compounds composed of chlorine, fluorine, and carbon atoms; CFCs have been used commercially as coolants and in other products and are potentially damaging to the earth's ozone layer.

Cold War   Roughly the period from 1945 to 1990, when a "war" of opposing ideologies polarized Western democracies and Communist nations.

cyberspace   The dimensions where various types of computer communications take place.

deflation   A contraction in the volume of available money or credit that results in a general decline in prices.

entitlements   Federal benefits, such as Social Security and **Medicare/Medicaid**, that are provided mostly to poor and senior citizens.

European Community (EC)   An economic and political union of twelve European nations that has alleviated travel and trade restrictions among them, created a common currency, and devised common technical standards, among other measures.

GATT   General Agreement on Tariffs and Trade; a compact among 126 nations to ease world trade rules. The United States signed the agreement in 1994. That same year, GATT created the World Trade Organization to administer GATT directives and standards.

GDP   Gross domestic product; the value of the goods and services produced within a country in a given period, regardless of who owns the production facilities.

GNP   Gross national product; the value of the goods and services produced by a country during a given period, even if production facilities are located in another country.

greenhouse gases   Atmospheric gases such as carbon dioxide, chlorofluorocarbons, methane, and water vapor that hold in and reflect back infrared energy from the earth's surface, thus heating the atmosphere.

hyperinflation   A runaway rate of **inflation** in the double-digit range.

inflation   An increase in the volume of money and credit relative to available goods and services, resulting in a continuing rise in the general price level.

IT   Information technology; communications and computer technology.

laissez-faire   A French term meaning "let (people) do (as they choose)," often used to describe capitalism or economic affairs without government interference.

Medicaid   A federal program in every state, which provides medical care for many people who cannot afford it.

Medicare   A federal health insurance program available to nearly all Americans aged sixty-five or older and to many disabled people.

NAFTA   North American Free Trade Agreement; the 1993 agreement among

America, Canada, and Mexico to create a free-trade zone.

New World Order   The evolving interrelation and hierarchy of nations following the end of the **Cold War**.

Pacific Rim   Nations in Asia and the Americas that border the Pacific Ocean and that are frequent trading partners.

S&Ls   Savings and Loan associations; institutions similar to banks in that they accept savings deposits and offer loans but that are more limited in their activities and subject to different regulations than banks. In the late 1980s, thousands of S&Ls failed, leaving the government and, ultimately, the taxpayers to cover the customers' losses.

SDI   Strategic Defense Initiative; a defunct 1980s Pentagon program that would have deployed space-based weapons to intercept missiles aimed at the United States. The Pentagon continues to study similar defense systems.

Smoot Hawley Tariff   Signed into law by President Herbert Hoover in 1930, the tariff's high rates aggravated the global economic depression.

Third World   The whole of the world's poor and developing nations.

For Further Discussion

Chapter 1

1. Christopher J. Check is an associate director of an institute that promotes family unity. How is his affiliation reflected in his argument? How do you believe Claudia Wallis would respond to Check's assertions? Contrast Check's and Wallis's different visions of families of the future. Which do you think is most likely? Why?

2. David Pesanelli envisions electronic schools of the future revolutionizing learning. George H. Jacobson argues that America's substandard education system could deteriorate further and weaken the nation. Which view of the future is most convincing? Why? Do you believe that computerized classrooms would significantly improve education? Why or why not?

3. Peter Francese believes that immigration will strengthen America by increasing the pool of skilled workers for the workforce. Joseph F. Coates's view is that immigrants—primarily Hispanics—are not embracing American culture. Do you believe that increased immigration will benefit or harm America? Explain. Make your own forecast of immigrants' role in the nation and Americans' attitudes toward them.

4. Walter A. Hahn believes that increases in life expectancy and the number of elderly Americans will likely have major impacts on the social fabric of the nation. His four scenarios are designed to create an impression of what life could be like between 1999 and 2040 from the viewpoint of subsequent elder generations. Which of Hahn's scenarios do you believe will most likely occur? Why?

5. Rushworth M. Kidder believes that the ethical standards of the twentieth century are inadequate to allow America to thrive in the next century. How does your concern for ethics compare to Kidder's? Do any of the author's examples of lapses in ethical behavior apply to you or someone you know? Explain.

Chapter 2

1. Andrew Pollack and his *New York Times* colleagues identify emerging technologies in the coming years but do not make ethical judgments on their social impact. Chellis Glendinning cautions that technology could become "out of control" and that society must consider whether a new technology is beneficial to humanity. Do you believe that new technologies

should be allowed to develop on a "come-what-may" basis? Why or why not?

2. William E. Halal writes that the information technology age means revolutionary changes—new dangers as well as new benefits. Tom Forester asserts that information technologies are evolutionary—with few sudden and powerful impacts. Do you believe that information technology is proving to be evolutionary or revolutionary as it affects your life? Explain.

3. Alvin Toffler and Heidi Toffler believe there are "technology societies" emerging that will do the "world's economically relevant knowledge work." Nicholas Wade argues that technological change impacts society less, and occurs much more slowly, than is commonly thought. Do you see information-age knowledge technologies proving significant in your everyday life? Explain.

Chapter 3

1. Shawna Tracy and Roberta Stauffer believe that alternative fuels will replace gasoline over the long term, resulting in energy sustainability and slower global warming. Len Frank and Dan McCosh offer findings that they say show that reformulated gasoline is superior to alternative fuels. After reading both viewpoints, whose argument do you find more reliable? Why? Which of the viewpoints comes closer to what you believed before reading them?

2. Harold W. Bernard Jr. uses a future history scenario based on greenhouse effect research to forecast the impact of a major drought in "America's Breadbasket" during the late 1990s. Robert C. Balling Jr., on the other hand, presents research to argue that there is little, if any, evidence that greenhouse warming is occurring. How could you go about further investigation to determine which viewpoint is more valid?

Chapter 4

1. Daniel Patrick Moynihan argues that entitlement programs such as Social Security are the most solvent part of the federal budget and will be sustainable well into the twenty-first century. The Bipartisan Commission, concerned about increasing numbers of older Americans, is pessimistic about the future viability of these entitlement programs. Which viewpoint do you find more convincing? Why? How does this issue relate to Walter A. Hahn's scenarios on the aging of America in Chapter 1?

2. Alfred L. Malabre Jr. uses scenarios to depict possible future outcomes regarding the debt America is accumulating from "living far beyond our means." His three scenarios concern hyperinflation, deflation, and increased government regulation. Which scenario do you believe is most likely to occur? Why? Can you think of a different scenario than these? Explain.

Chapter 5

1. Robert L. Bartley is optimistic about the future of America; he argues that the future will be one of increasing opportunity and prosperity. Edward N. Luttwak is pessimistic; he believes that conditions in America could soon resemble those of a Third World nation. Can you identify examples, if any, of exaggerated or inflammatory language in these viewpoints? Explain.

2. Charles J. Dunlap Jr. presents a future narrative from the year 2012 to illustrate how a military coup could place a dictator in power. Do you find this scenario plausible? Why or why not?

Organizations to Contact

The editors have compiled the following list of organizations concerned with the issues debated in this book. The descriptions are derived from materials provided by the organizations. All have publications or information available for interested readers. The list was compiled on the date of publication of the present volume; names, addresses, and phone numbers may change. Be aware that many organizations take several weeks or longer to respond to inquiries, so allow as much time as possible.

Brookings Institution
1775 Massachusetts Ave. NW
Washington, DC 20036
(202) 797-6000
fax: (202) 797-6004

Brookings is a nonprofit public policy research foundation that sponsors conferences, seminars, roundtables, and other educational activities. It has numerous publications available, including books, papers, and the quarterly magazine *Brookings Review*.

Congressional Clearinghouse on the Future
Ford House Annex 2, #555
Washington, DC 20515
(202) 226-3434
fax: (202) 225-0972

The clearinghouse helps members of Congress explore the policy implications of emerging demographic, technological, and economic trends. It develops extensive projects on issues pertinent to each session of Congress. The clearinghouse provides a variety of publications and briefings, including *What's Next?* a quarterly newsletter offering information about new technologies and policy-related forecasts, and *Emerging Issues* briefs, a monthly series of concise one-page briefing papers for members of Congress.

Future Problem Solving Program (FPSP)
315 W. Huron, Suite 140 B
Ann Arbor, MI 48103-4203
(313) 998-7377
fax: (313) 998-7663

The program is composed of students and teacher-coaches whose purpose is to motivate and assist students in developing and improving creative thinking, information gathering, and other skills in communication, problem solving, research, and teamwork. It seeks to increase students' interest in the future and encourages them to exercise creative, critical, and analytical thought. FPSP organizes teams of students in grades four through twelve, who compete against each other. Teams cover issues such as nuclear waste, nuclear war, computers, ocean communities, and robotics. Judges score the teams in scenario-writing and community problem-solving competitions. The program publishes a quarterly newsletter and the quarterly *Creative Express* and provides the video *Preparing Today's Students for Tomorrow's Problems*.

Institute for Alternative Futures (IAF)
100 N. Pitt St., Suite 235
Alexandria, VA 22314
(703) 684-5880
fax: (703) 684-0640

The institute consults with, and provides speakers to, various organizations concerned with health futures, information futures, and business and community futures. Books published by IAF include *Mending the Earth: A World for Our Grandchildren* (1990), *Regulating Change: The Regulation of Foods, Drugs, Medical Devices, and Cosmetics in the 1990s* (1990), and *20-20 Visions: Health Care Information, Standards, and Technologies* (1993).

Institute for the Future (IFTF)
2744 Sand Hill Rd.
Menlo Park, CA 94025-7020
(415) 854-6322
fax: (415) 854-7859

IFTF is a research and consulting firm that evaluates long-term trends and their implications in fields such as information technology and health care. It helps public and private organizations plan their futures and recommends specific opportunities presented by market trends and new technologies. Its publications include the quarterly *IFTF Perspectives* and several books, including *Leading Business Teams: How Teams Can Use Technology and Group Process Tools to Enhance Performance* (1991).

Institute for Futures Research
Studies of the Future Program
2700 Bay Area Blvd.
Houston, TX 77058-1090
(713) 283-3320

This academic program offered by the University of Houston at Clear Lake is the only one in America to offer a master's degree in futures studies. The curriculum covers a detailed review of the techniques used to understand and plan the long-term future. Depending upon career objectives, students tailor their degree to specific methodologies or topics, such as business, government, information technology, environmental issues, or space commercialization. The program sponsors workshops with industry and government regarding futures-related activity. Its research reports have been published in *The Futurist* and *Fu-*

tures. Books it has published include *Information and the Future* (1988) and *Changing Images of Man* (1988).

Office of Technology Assessment (OTA)
U.S. Congress
600 Pennsylvania Ave. SE
Washington, DC 20510
(202) 224-8996

The OTA's objective is to provide early indications of probable beneficial and adverse impacts of new applications of technology and to gather related information that may assist Congress in policymaking. It has numerous books and research reports available; contact the OTA for a complete list.

Resources for the Future (RFF)
1616 P St. NW
Washington, DC 20036
(202) 328-5000
fax: (202) 939-3460

RFF is concerned with the conservation, management, and development of natural resources. Areas of interest include forestry economics, land use and planning, surface and groundwater resources, energy, and environmental quality. It publishes the periodicals *Resources* and *Research Digest* and the books *Public Policies for Environmental Protection* (1990) and *Mineral Wealth and Economic Development* (1992).

Stanford Research International
333 Ravenswood Ave.
Menlo Park, CA 94025
(415) 326-6200
fax: (415) 326-5512

The organization is a nonprofit research and consulting firm whose objectives are to assist public and private organizations with research and consulting services and to be a source of future perspectives for business and government. It publishes the books *American Social Trends* (1989), *The Power of Strategic Vision* (1991), *Visioning (and Preparing for) the Future* (1991), and *Rewriting the Corporate Social Charter* (1992).

Strategic Studies Institute
U.S. Army War College
Carlisle Barracks, Room A203
Carlisle, PA 17013-5050
(717) 245-3234
fax: (717) 245-3606

The institute conducts independent research and analysis of national security and other defense issues for the purpose of policy recommendation to national decision makers. Some books and reports are available to the public, including *A World 2010: A New Order of Nations* (1992) and *Challenges to Eastern European Security in the Nineties* (1992).

The Urban Institute
2100 M St. NW
Washington, DC 20037
(202) 833-7200
fax: (202) 223-3043

The institute is a nonprofit public policy research foundation. It investigates social and economic problems confronting the nation and assesses government policies and public and private programs designed to alleviate such problems. Its publications include the periodicals *Policy and Research Report*, *Policy Bites*, and *Update*.

U.S. Environmental Protection Agency (EPA)
Futures Studies Group
Washington, DC 20460
(202) 260-6523
fax: (202) 260-4903

This EPA group collects, analyzes, and disseminates information on emerging environmental trends, issues, and events. It seeks to use futures research in strategic planning and coordinates forecasting and futures activities throughout the EPA. It publishes the quarterly *Futures*, the reports *Agricultural Futures Project* (1992, by the National Center for Food and Agricultural Policy) and *The Future of Residential Water Use and the Environment* (1992), and the books *A Review of Possible Environmental Impacts from the Development of Selected New Technologies* (1992) and *Implications of Advanced Computing and Networks for Environmental Protection* (1993).

World Future Society
7910 Woodmont Ave., Suite 450
Bethesda, MD 20814
(301) 656-8274
fax: (301) 951-0394

The society serves as a national clearinghouse for ideas and information about the future, including forecasts, recommendations, and alternative scenarios. These ideas help people anticipate what may happen in the next five, ten, or more years and to distinguish between possible, probable, and desired futures. The society publishes the periodicals *The Futurist* and *Futures Research Quarterly* and the books *Futures Research Directory: Organizations and Periodicals* (annually) and *The 1990s and Beyond* (1990).

World Resources Institute (WRI)
1709 New York Ave. NW
Washington, DC 20006
(202) 638-6300
fax: (202) 638-0036

WRI is a nonprofit research foundation. Its policy research is aimed at global resources, environmental conditions, emerging issues, and public understanding of these issues. WRI publishes books, reports, and papers; holds briefings, seminars, and conferences; and provides the print and broadcast media with new perspectives and background materials on environmental issues. The institute publishes the periodicals *NGO Networker* and *The Information Please Environmental Almanac.*

Bibliography of Books

Steve Aukstakalnis   *Silicon Mirage: The Art and Science of Virtual*
and David Blatner   *Reality.* Berkeley, CA: Peachpit Press, 1992.

Ravi Batra   *Downfall of Capitalism and Communism.* Dallas:
                     Venus Books, 1990.

Richard Carlson and *Fast Forward: Where Technology, Demographics,*
Bruce Goldman   *and History Will Take America and the World in*
                     the Next Thirty Years. New York: Harper Busi-
                     ness, 1994.

Marvin Cetron and   *Educational Renaissance: Our Schools at the Turn*
Margaret Gayle   *of the Twenty-First Century.* New York: St. Mar-
                     tin's Press, 1991.

William H. Davidow   *The Virtual Corporation: Structuring and Revitaliz-*
and Michael S. Malone *ing the Corporation for the Twenty-First Century.*
                     New York: Harper Business, 1992.

Harry S. Dent   *The Great Boom Ahead: Your Comprehensive*
                     Guide to Personal and Business Profit in the Era of
                     Prosperity. New York: Hyperion, 1993.

Eric Drexler and   *Unbounding the Future: The Nanotechnology Revo-*
Chris Peterson   *lution.* New York: Quill, 1991.

Harry E. Figgie   *Bankruptcy 1995: The Coming Collapse of Amer-*
                     ica and How to Stop It. Boston: Gerald J. Swan-
                     son, 1992.

Jeffrey A. Fisher   *Our Medical Future: Breakthroughs in Health,*
                     Medicine, and Longevity by the Year 2000 and
                     Beyond. New York: Pocket Books, 1992.

Al Gore   *Earth in the Balance: Ecology and the Human*
                     Spirit. Boston: Houghton Mifflin, 1992.

John Harris   *Wonderwoman and Superman: The Ethics of Human*
                     Biotechnology. Oxford: Oxford University Press,
                     1992.

George Heaton,   *Transforming Technology: An Agenda for Environ-*
Robert Repetto,   *mentally Sustainable Growth in the Twenty-First*
and Rodney Sobin   *Century.* Washington: World Resources Institute,
                     1991.

Robert K. Heldman   *Future Telecommunications: Information Applica-*
                     tions, Services, and Infrastructure. New York:
                     McGraw-Hill, 1993.

Hazel Henderson   *Paradigms in Progress: Life Beyond Economics.*
                     Indianapolis: Knowledge Systems, 1991.

Seymour W. Itzkoff — *The Decline of Intelligence in America: A Strategy for National Renewal.* New York: Praeger, 1994.

Paul Kennedy — *Preparing for the Twenty-First Century.* New York: Random House, 1993.

Laurence J. Kotlikoff — *Generational Accounting: Knowing Who Pays, and When, for What We Spend.* New York: Free Press, 1992.

Keith Kozloff and Roger Dower — *A New Power Base: Renewable Energy Policies for the Nineties and Beyond.* Washington: World Resources Institute, 1993.

James McKenzie — *Electric and Hydrogen Vehicles: Transportation Technologies for the Twenty-First Century.* Washington: World Resources Institute, 1994.

Donella H. Meadows, Dennis L. Meadows, and Jorgen Randers — *Beyond the Limits: Confronting Global Collapse, Envisioning a Sustainable Future.* Post Mills, VT: Chelsea Green, 1992.

Ian Morrow and Greg Schmid — *Future Tense: The Business Realities of the Next Ten Years.* New York: William Morrow, 1994.

Brent A. Nelson — *America Balkanized.* Monterey, VA: American Immigration Control Foundation, 1994.

Jon Ogden and Robert Williams — *Solar Hydrogen: Moving Beyond Fossil Fuels.* Washington: World Resources Institute, 1989.

Lewis J. Perelman — *School's Out: Hyperlearning, the New Technology, and the End of Education.* New York: Avon, 1992.

Research Alert — *Future Vision: The 189 Most Important Trends of the 1990s.* Naperville, IL: Sourcebooks, 1991.

Howard Rheingold — *The Virtual Community: Homesteading on the Electronic Frontier.* Menlo Park, CA: Addison-Wesley, 1993.

John Roper, Masashi Nishihara, Olara A. Otunnu, and Enid C.B. Schoettle — *Keeping the Peace in the Post–Cold War Era: Strengthening Multilateral Peacekeeping.* New York: Trilateral Commission, 1993.

Cheryl Russell — *The Master Trend: How the Baby Boom Generation Is Remaking America.* New York: Plenum, 1993.

Howard P. Segal — *Future Imperfect: The Mixed Blessings of Technology in America.* Boston: University of Massachusetts Press, 1994.

Peter Singer — *Practical Ethics.* New York: Cambridge University Press, 1993.

Bruce Smart, ed.   *Beyond Compliance: A New Industry View of the Environment.* Washington: World Resources Institute, 1992.

Jim Snider and   *Future Shop: How New Technologies Will Change*
Terra Ziporyn   *the Way We Shop and What We Buy.* New York: St. Martin's Press, 1992.

Don Tapscott and   *Paradigm Shift: The New Promise of Information*
Art Caston   *Technology.* New York: McGraw-Hill, 1993.

Alvin Toffler   *Powershift: Knowledge, Wealth, and Violence: At the Edge of the Twenty-First Century.* New York: Bantam, 1990.

Alvin Toffler and   *War and Anti-War: Survival at the Dawn of the*
Heidi Toffler   *Twenty-First Century.* Boston: Little, Brown, 1993.

United Way   *What Lies Ahead: A Decade of Decision.* Alexan-
of America   dria, VA: United Way, 1992.

U.S. Department   *Projections of Education Statistics to 2004.* Wash-
of Education   ington: U.S. Government Printing Office, 1993.

Joseph Vranich   *Supertrains: Solutions to America's Transportation Gridlock.* New York: St. Martin's Press, 1991.

World Future Society   *Issues of the Nineties.* Bethesda, MD: World Future Society, 1990.

Index

Luddites, neo-, 83-88, 254
Ludwig, Donald, 197
Luntz, Frank, 180
Luttwak, Edward N., 240, 243, 250

Malabre, Alfred L., Jr., 170
Malaysia, 139
Malone, Thomas, 149
Malthus, Thomas, 253
Manage, Syukuro, 224
Mander, Jerry, 84, 85, 86
Mark, Margaret, 29
Markoff, John, 73
Matthews, Downs, 213
McCosh, Dan, 211
Mead, Margaret, 27
Mearns, Linda, 231
media, is changing society, 108, 109
Medicaid, 156, 158-59
Medicare, 46-48, 60
  changes must be made in, 156,
    158-59
  Hospital Insurance (HI), 159
  Supplementary Medical Insurance
    (SMI), 159
  surplus in, 154
melting pot, 50, 64
men
  changing roles of, 29-30
  and home-based work, 22
Metzger, Robert, 39
Mexico, 50-53
micromachines, 75-76
Microsoft, 138, 139
microwave ovens, 115
Middle East, 185
Military Cooperation with Civilian
  Law Enforcement Agencies Act, 284
Minkin, Barry, 185
Moore, Richter H., Jr., 125
Moore, Stephen, 183, 184
Morita, Akio, 166
motor vehicles
  alternative fuels for, 204-10, 211-17
  Impact (electric car), 205, 207
  manufacturers, 205, 208, 208
  pollution by, 204, 206, 216
Moynihan, Daniel Patrick, 151
Mumford, Lewis, 84
Murphy, Austin, 23
Muslims, 26, 54

Nader, Ralph, 276
Nagel, David, 91
National Aerospace Plane, 80
National Climatic Data Center, 228
National Science Foundation, 75-76
natural resources

exploitation of, 198-201
  fish, 199-201
  forests, 199, 200
  management of, 201-202
  water, 193
    for irrigation, 201, 223, 224
    as source of hydrogen fuel, 209,
      216
neo-Luddites, 83-88, 254
North American Free Trade Agreement (NAFTA), 142, 143, 276, 279
nuclear material
  Chernobyl accident, 66
  smuggling, 130-31
  technology, 85, 86
Nyerere, Julius, 192

optical disks, 90-91

Pacific salmon, 199, 200-201
Pacific sardine, 200
parents
  child support, 29
  working at home, 20, 22, 29, 94-95
Peace Corps, 258
Pearcey, Nancy R., 20
Peddling Prosperity (Krugman), 145
Peruvian anchoveta, 200
Pesanelli, David, 31
pesticides, 86
Peters, Tom, 137
Peterson, George, 185, 186
Petrella, Riccardo, 108-109
Piccoli, Sean, 277
police, 118, 124
politics
  America as a third world country,
    246
  antimilitarism in, 283
  based on "second wave," 276
  dissatisfaction with, 276, 283
  and exploitation of resources,
    198-99, 202
  and family values, 26
  and home-based businesses, 23
  immigrants' use of, 51-54
  and minorities, 258
  power structure changing, 95
  technology is, 84-87, 117
  "third wave" will affect, 276-79
Pollack, Andrew, 73
pollution, 83, 85
  acid rain, 83
  California laws on, 206, 212-13
  changes climate, 204, 208, 210
    cold weather, 221-22, 226
    effect on animals, 225
    hotter weather, 219-22, 225

precipitation, 222-23
Clean Air Act, 184, 204, 206
cleanup costs, 179
and electric batteries, 207
motor vehicle, 204, 206
taxes on, 162
water, 193
population
growth must decline, 192, 202
growth rates, 44, 96, 181, 192, 263
poverty
children in, 45
elderly in, 63
Powell, Colin, 285
Prestowitz, Clyde, 163
Prewo, Karl, 80
Prodigy, 93, 114
publishing
electronic, 93
glut of information, 104-105

Ravitch, Diane, 41
Reagan, Ronald, 175, 176-77, 251
Reddell, Donald, 224
Reich, Charles A., 153
Reserve Officers Training Corps
(ROTC), 286
Revel, Jean-François, 248
revolutions, history of, 253-55, 276
Ricks, Thomas E., 283
Robinson, John, 200
robotics
domestic, 102, 258
and education, 33-35
industrial, 99-100, 118, 120-21, 258,
262
in Japan, 75
Rudman, Warren, 183

salmon, Pacific, 199, 200-201
Saraswat, Krishna C., 79
sardine, California, 199
savings and loan crisis, 60, 66, 162
Sawhill, Isabel, 186
Schnaars, Steven, 101-102
Scholastic Aptitude Test (SAT), 37, 40
schools
and businesses, 32-34, 37, 41, 261
cable-access classes, 32, 33
changes in, 29, 32-35
and computers, 32-35, 261
dropout rate, 37, 41, 243
home-based, 19, 22
in shopping malls, 34
spending for, 40
test scores decline, 37-38
violence in, 37, 41
and workplace learning, 32, 33

see also education
Schreiber, William F., 78
Schumpeter, Joseph, 114
scientists, infotech will change work
of, 119-20, 124
Scully, John, 90
Sears, 93, 114
"second wave" society, 110, 276-79
Sematech, 79
semiconductors, 74, 78, 262
Shanker, Albert, 37, 42
Shaw, Peter, 120
Shell, Adam, 40
silicon circuits, 78
Singapore, as technical society, 108,
110, 139
Sipchen, Bob, 85
Smith, Adam, 162
Smyser, W.R., 272
Snyder, David Pearce, 30
Snyder, Julian, 174
Social Security
and baby boomers, 46, 61, 262
funding for, 46-48, 58, 60
not an entitlement program, 152-53
policy changes must be made in,
156, 159
solvency of, 154, 159-60
surplus in, 153-54
society
agrarian, 108, 109, 110, 276
cashless, 126-27
"first wave," 110, 276
industrial, 108, 109, 110
information-based, 90, 91, 276
and information technology
glut is damaging, 104-105
will change, 93-96
knowledge-based order in, 96-97,
252, 257
and leisure time, 99, 264
and media, 85, 86, 108, 109, 139
new structures in, 108-109
"second wave," 110, 276-79
technology's effect on, 83-88, 107-11
"third wave," 110, 276-79
values trends, 264-65
virtual community, 95-96
Software Engineering Institute, 81
Sony, 166
Soviet Union, 108
breakup of, 131, 248
civil war in, 184, 270
military competition with U.S., 248
weapons, 130
Sowell, Thomas, 40
Stauffer, Roberta, 203
Stein, Herbert, 182

and sustainable development, 194
technology trends in, 258-60
trade
    deficit, 250-51
    global, 145, 146, 249
    with Japan, 268-69
transportation technology, 258
universities in, 143, 245-46, 249,
    261
values trends in, 264-65
wealthy in, 244-45, 249, 257
weather trends in, 229-32, 235-36
world influence of, 248, 255
US West, 139

values
    changing, 51
    family, 26
    trends, 264-65
Viacom, 108
videocassette recorder (VCR), 101,
    114, 115
Vinovskis, Maris, 26
virtual reality systems, 118, 121, 122
Volker, Paul, 257
Volunteers in Service to America
    (VISTA), 258
Von Glinow, Mary Ann, 39

Wade, Nicholas, 112
Wallis, Claudia, 25
Walters, Carl, 197
war and technology, 85, 86, 104, 106,
    110
Watt, James, 252, 253
weapons
    space, 84
    technological, 85, 86, 104, 111
        used for crime, 129, 130
    United Nations proposal for, 164
Weber, Jonathan, 103
Wells, H.G.
    The Future in America, 50
Wildlife Conservation Society, 200
Williamson, John, 181
Wilson, Edward, 191
Wilson, Karen, 29
Winner, Langdon
    Autonomous Technology, 87
Wolf, Charles, 252
Wolfe, Leslie, 26

women
    are changing workforce, 29, 262,
        263
    life expectancy of, 57
    mothers telecommuting, 19, 263
    and politics, 265
    and prostitution, 130
    relationships are changing, 26, 28
    roles are changing, 29-30, 263
workforce
    changes in types of, 18, 20
    competency of U.S., 39
    creating jobs, 141, 162
    decline in, 263
    eliminating jobs, 141-42
    in farming, 169
    and foreign competition, 39-40, 45
    and guest workers, 54
    health care coverage for, 183
    in health care field, 45
    home-based, 17-24, 29, 94-95, 101
        benefits of, 18
        statistics on, 18
    hours increasing, 243
    immigrants would help, 45, 46, 47,
        181
    in information positions, 96
    information technology will change,
        116-24
    Japanese, 169
    job mobility, 258, 263
    knowledge work, 60, 61, 108
    retirement funds, 183, 263
    service jobs, 96, 140, 147, 278
    shortages in, 45, 46
    specialization of, 262
    statistics on, 181
    and sustainable development, 199
    technology affects jobs, 109
    time spent working, 99, 261
    unions declining, 262-63
    unqualified, 38
    vacations, 264
    wages decreasing, 243-44
    and women, 29, 262, 263
World Commission on Environment
    and Development, 202
Wrigley Company, 145

Ziegenfuss, James T., Jr., 259
Zinsmeister, Karl, 165, 168

312